"David W. Fagerberg combines an integral view of the reality of Plato's Christian heirs, the intellectual inquisitiveness and insight of G. K. Chesterton and the literary imagination of C. S. Lewis. Fagerberg, having lectured on theology at the University of Notre Dame for many years, can be described as a 'school' theologian, one might say a 'professional' one. But he is also a theologian in life. His theological way of life is also a liturgical style in which the measure of everything is the glorification of God. Even though from a formal point of view his theological discipline is liturgy, I would never call him a stereotypical liturgist, who focuses on the details of liturgical celebration. He is a theological *leitourgos* who worships God with his theology and a liturgical theologian who transforms the liturgy into fundamental theology, not in the sense of an apology for faith but for whom worship is a paradigm of doing theology. His cosmic theology covers the universe and its history but also the microcosm of the life of every Christian. Those will benefit the most from his book who seek to be motivated for living for God, but also those who seek their way to God or are only at its beginning."

Fr. Boguslaw Migut
The John Paul II Catholic University of Lublin, Poland

"David Fagerberg has dedicated his life's work to deepening and 'thickening' our understanding of what the liturgy is and does in the life of the Church. *The Liturgical Cosmos* beautifully illustrates how liturgy is a point of synthesis at the very heart of Christian life, an intricate web woven around strands of asceticism, mysticism, eschatology, and the entire cosmos. In broadening the scope of liturgical theology through these fresh, inspiring essays, Fagerberg offers a welcome antidote to the superficial, ideological, and acerbic conversations that too often surround the question of the liturgy today. The ultimate goal of liturgical renewal is to move us closer to the mystery of divine love, and Fagerberg here presents himself as an experienced mystagogue to guide our journey."

Kevin D. Magas
University of St. Mary of the Lake, Mundelein Seminary

"David Fagerberg draws an impressive range of theological voices into a profound conversation that elucidates how the Church's divine worship prepares us beyond all human limitation to share in the communion of love that is the Blessed Trinity. The masterful essays collected in this volume explore different aspects of how the mystery celebrated in the liturgy overflows into the whole of human life and orders it towards its supernatural end. I warmly recommend this book to all who want to deepen their appreciation of how the liturgy expresses the Christian faith's understanding of God, the world, and ourselves."

Fr. Uwe Michael Lang
St. Mary's University, Twickenham, London

"Is the liturgy an imaginary flight from the world or a revelation of its very heart? In *The Liturgical Cosmos*, David Fagerberg makes the case for the latter with a cheerful confidence that invites and persuades rather than argues or disputes. Fagerberg shows how the liturgy illuminates and clarifies the purpose of the interior life, of the ascetic impulse, of the Church, and of the cosmos as a whole. Nobody makes the case for such an expansive view of the liturgy as well as Fagerberg, who invariably challenges us to think anew of the Christian mysteries and to open ourselves to their transforming power."

Jonathan Martin Ciraulo
Saint Meinrad Seminary

"Fifty years ago, the Church embarked on a renewal of the liturgy in obedience to the call of the Constitution on the Sacred Liturgy. These decades have witnessed a prodigious composition of new ritual editions and much scholarly activity in the new discipline of liturgical theology. Yet many have realized that this is not enough, and that renewing rituals and theology is vanity if it is not accompanied by the renewal of the hearts and lives of the Christian faithful. Throughout his career David Fagerberg has labored to bridge the gap between scholarship and the real-life practice of Christianity itself, publishing extensively on liturgy as the original theology (*theologia prima*) and the need to accompany it with a lived and genuine liturgical asceticism. In addition to his many books, Fagerberg has written many articles over the years. This new publication is a very welcome selection of his articles. These allow us to approach the subject of liturgical theology from a new perspective. They will help readers of many persuasions to appreciate liturgy as the practice of authentic theology and will offer an opportunity to meet the living Christ who is eternally present in the celebration of the liturgical mysteries."

Fr. Neil Xavier O'Donoghue
St. Patrick's Pontifical University Maynooth, Ireland

"From *Theologia Prima* to *Liturgical Asceticism* to *Consecrating the World* to *Liturgical Mysticism* to *Liturgical Dogmatics,* Dr. David Fagerberg has continued to unfold, with unparalleled clarity and depth, the liturgical theology school of Fathers Schmemann and Kavanaugh, drawing us ever more deeply into the critical, life-giving connection of *leitourgia, theologia,* and *askesis.* Having intensely mined the riches of the thought of these two scholars, Dr. Fagerberg imparts a view that is uniquely additive given his own breadth of vision, yet consonant with and ever vivifying the other two. And just when one thinks there is no more to be said, Dr. Fagerberg brings us *The Liturgical Cosmos: The World through the Lens of the Liturgy,* a brilliant exposé of the insights permeating his previous works. We are reminded by Dr. Fagerberg once again of the limitless depths of the riches of Christ and of his Church, the source of all true liturgical theology."

Norbertine Canonesses
of the Bethlehem Priory of St. Joseph, Tehachapi, California

"David Fagerberg is a paradox. A practical mystic, he has a contemplative mind that is ranging, fertile, synthetic, creative—and he uses it to fashion a liturgical worldview that is classic, patristic, and deeply scriptural. He leads us not just back to the sources but into them, both Eastern and Western, and we see them as if for the first time. More than that, we see the world itself as if for the first time, and as if it's created anew—because it is. These essays, each and all, are works of a singular yet humble genius."

Scott W. Hahn
Franciscan University of Steubenville

The
LITURGICAL
COSMOS

The
LITURGICAL COSMOS

THE WORLD THROUGH THE LENS OF THE LITURGY

DAVID W. FAGERBERG

EMMAUS
ACADEMIC
Steubenville, Ohio
www.emmausacademic.com

EMMAUS
ACADEMIC

Steubenville, Ohio
www.emmausacademic.com
A Division of The St. Paul Center for Biblical Theology
Editor-in-Chief: Scott Hahn
1468 Parkview Circle
Steubenville, Ohio 43952

© 2023 David W. Fagerberg
All rights reserved. Published 2023.
Printed in the United States of America

Library of Congress Cataloging-in-Publication Data applied for.

ISBN: 978-1-64585-280-3 Hardcover | 978-1-64585-281-0 Paperback | 978-1-64585-282-7 Ebook

Unless otherwise noted, Scripture quotations are taken from The Revised Standard Version Second Catholic Edition (Ignatius Edition) Copyright © 2006 by the Division of Christian Education of the National Council of the Churches of Christ in the United States of America. Used by permission. All rights reserved.

Excerpts from the Catechism of the Catholic Church, second edition, copyright © 2000, Libreria Editrice Vaticana—United States Conference of Catholic Bishops, Washington, D.C. Noted as "CCC" in the text.

Cover design and layout by Emma Nagle
Cover image: *Divine Liturgy* by Michael Damaskinos, 16th century.

Nihil Obstat: Msgr. Michael Heintz
Censor Librorum
January 7, 2022

Imprimatur: Kevin C. Rhoades
Bishop of Fort Wayne-South Bend
October 12, 2022

The *nihil obstat* and *imprimatur* are declarations that work is considered to be free from doctrinal or moral error. It is not implied that those who have granted the same agree with the content, opinions, or statements expressed.

Table of Contents

Introduction xi

Liturgy and Asceticism

Desert Asceticism
"Prayer as Theology" 1

Beauty and Asceticism
"The Beauty of God as Ground for
Obedience in the Ascetical-Contemplative Tradition" 21

Liturgical Fasting
"On Liturgical Fasting" 37

Liturgy and Theology

Schmemann's Cost
"The Cost of Understanding Schmemann in the West" 59

Schmemann's Anchor
"The Anchor of Schmemann's Liturgical Theology" 85

Liturgy and Its Celebration

Scripture
"*Theologia Prima*: The Liturgical
Mystery and the Mystery of God" 111

Sacrifice
"Divine Liturgy, Divine Love: Toward a New
Understanding of Sacrifice in Christian Worship" 127

Sacrament
"The Sacraments as Actions of the Mystical Body" 147

Liturgy and the Cosmos

Liturgical Cosmology
  "Doing the World Liturgically:
  Stewardship of Creation and Care for the Poor" 163

Liturgical Morality
  "On Liturgical Morality" 181

Liturgical and Pastoral Theology
  "The Church as Pastoral Icon
  of the Mercy of the Good Shepherd" 203

Liturgical Persons

Icon as Image of the Deified Person
  "Icon as Image of Asceticism and Deification" 225

Mary
  "Mary as Liturgical Person" 245

Conclusion 261

Introduction

When liturgy entered the academy, which was not so very long ago, the scholars put on all their glasses to look at it. Liturgics had been keeping residence mainly in seminaries, where rubrics were employed for training celebrants, and canon law might be employed for questions of validity concerning the sacraments celebrated within it. But academia put on all its spectacles when it turned its gaze upon liturgy. History came first, with a specialization in comparative structural units. This was followed rapidly by ritual studies, utilizing interpretive anthropology. All sorts of disciplines soon found liturgy a fruitful place where they could study their particular topic, such as musicology, architecture, art, allegory, sacred texts, pilgrimage, etc. And then all sorts of methodologies found liturgy a congenial subject on which to exercise their procedures, such as ethnography, symbology, philology, semantics, hermeneutics, inculturation, cultural studies, etc. It is also worth remembering that most of this was done within the context of liturgical reform and renewal, which had given its own impetus to liturgical studies. Many examined liturgy out of a concern for fostering full, conscious, and active participation in it.

We learned a lot when the academy began to look at liturgy, and I do not deny its value. It is important to study a history of liturgical development because otherwise the theologian's ideas of sacrament and sacrifice and doxology and worship come out of his own head and not from the practice of the Church. It is important to study the ritual structure and practices of liturgy because it creates and forms communities. It is rewarding for the academy to discover the fascination liturgy could hold for its many subjects and methodologies, each of which can unfold another facet of liturgy for our consideration. Nevertheless, I equally insist that liturgiology is at service of another purpose. There is a rough parallel to scriptural studies here. As one cannot do biblical theology without first doing biblical criticism, so one cannot do liturgical theology without first doing liturgiology, but the Sabbath was made for man, and biblical criticism was made for biblical theology, and liturgiology was made for liturgical theology. There is a risk to an academic investigation that looks exclusively at liturgy. The risk is that liturgy will be studied in isolation from the Christian life, from the fullness of doctrine, from its spiritual consequences, from the cosmic and eschatological economy that God is discharging. All theology is Eucharistic, but the Eucharist is not the only thing theology talks about. We will see much by putting liturgy under the academic microscopes, but might we also be missing much?

A person can look *at* a window to notice its glass, its framing, and its glazing, but a person can also look *through* a window to see what is happening outside. This collection of essays does not plan to look at the liturgy, it will attempt to look through liturgy at theological topics. What does liturgy show us? Where does liturgy take us? What relevance does it have outside the temple? What resonance does it have for us after the ritual has ended? The liturgical microcosm includes temple, priesthood, sacrament, and icon; the liturgical macrocosm includes time and cosmos, asceticism and deification, icons and beauty, sacrifice and social renewal, death and resurrection, Scripture and spirituality. The liturgy that arises from the Church-in-motion invites us to look through itself at the whole cosmos. Liturgical theology is found at the Church's regular encounter with Christ the priest at the altar of the Lord, but this altar is where heaven and earth meet, and Christ is High Priest not only of the sacramental liturgy; he is also High Priest of the cosmic liturgy. As much as the liturgical history and ritual deserves studious examination, it is only the tip of an iceberg, the part of the *leitourgia* that we can see. It is connected to a massive work of God called the economy of salvation, and liturgical theology wants to explore the connection between what is above and below the waterline: cult and cosmos, sacred and profane, Church and world, religion and spirituality, ritual liturgy and lived liturgy. Christ did not come so that we could have rubrics, and have them abundantly. He came to offer us his own life, life eternal, a different kind of life than the world can offer, a life communicated sacramentally and celebrated cultically, but a life lived daily as the Holy Spirit conforms us to Christ, the image of the Father. Therefore, liturgical theology is also concerned with the massive reality that undergirds our ceremonies and services, which turns out to be the same reality that beckons us to deification and refreshes our world. This reality is ultimately beyond our rational comprehension and requires an experiential knowledge that is characteristic of liturgical theology.

Splendor means "to shine," and the splendor of liturgy shines from the altar into the nave, crosses the liminal narthex, and shines upon the cosmos so that we can see it correctly. The effect of original sin has been cataracts upon our eyes, dimming and distorting our sight, and baptism is

Introduction

necessary in order to restore a vision that can observe the three essential topics of theology: God, humanity, and the world. Liturgical theology sees by means of the light of Mount Tabor splendoring from liturgy. At the Divine Liturgy we stand aright in the presence of God the Father, reconciled to him by the High Priest who has penetrated heaven and who has sent the Holy Spirit to make us into temples for the indwelling of the Trinity. This is liturgical triadology. In the Eucharist, matter is spiritualized and utilized for its original purpose of sacramental descent and sacrificial ascent. This is liturgical cosmology. Adam and Eve were created to be the tongue of mute creation, adding the praise of irrational creatures to the angelic choirs. This is liturgical anthropology. The Fall was the forfeiture of our liturgical career. This is liturgical hamartiology. Then a second Adam, a new Adam, the last Adam came and restored mankind to the work it had neglected, placing in our human hands the liturgy he effected in his divine-human nature. This is liturgical soteriology. Christ's work is to glorify God and sanctify man, which he accomplished through a liturgical life of oblation that culminated in the Cross and Resurrection. This is liturgical Christology. All the baptized are liturgical apprentices to Christ the High Priest, to cooperate in his *leitourgia* on behalf of the world. This is liturgical ecclesiology. Such is a sampling of topics in this collection. All this is going on in the cultic and sacramental liturgy, but all this is also continuing in the mystical and spiritual liturgy of our lives. It is not left behind when we leave the temple, it is not finished when we end the ritual. The liturgy is eternal, even if our temporal liturgies start and stop.

The Church herself is a sacrament. A sacrament is an efficacious sign that causes what it signifies. Question: What does the Church signify, and so cause? Answer: The irruption of the Kingdom of God into history and into lives. The Church is the sacrament of creation's transfiguration and humanity's deification, already begun and awaiting eschatological completion. This significant activity of the Church is her *leitourgia*, her work, and she does it in obedience to Christ and by the power of Christ. The Church joins Christ's liturgy. "The word 'liturgy' originally meant a 'public work' or a 'service in the name of/on behalf of the people.' In Christian tradition it means the participation of the People of God in 'the work of God.' Through the liturgy Christ, our redeemer and high priest, continues the work of our redemption in, with, and through his Church."[1] Liturgy is the activity of the *totus Christus*, the head with his body, the body with its head. The Church was born from the side of Christ on the Cross, and by

---

[1] *Catechism of the Catholic Church*, §1069.

entering into the flood of liturgy opened by the soldier's spear, a believer can swim upstream into the very heart of Christ. By the water and blood that issued, a believer can imbibe Christ's life and, by being thus made alive himself, can join Christ's cosmic liturgy. Just as there are many facets to the mysteries of Christ, so are there many origins of liturgy. It begins at his Incarnation, during his life, upon the Cross, at the Resurrection, and by Pentecost, not to mention the preincarnate activity of the Logos recognized by Christian typological reading of Scripture. Liturgy creates the Church by springing from the Paschal mystery, which is the mystery that the Church proclaims and celebrates so that the faithful may live from it and bear witness to it in the world. And there is a cost to this witness. It requires the mortification of our passions, which is why asceticism is required as a capacitation to perform liturgy. The liturgy of the Church must be connected to asceticism, even as liturgy is connected to theology. Liturgical theology is the reunification of liturgy-theology-asceticism, and a sufficient liturgical theology cannot be had if one of these is missing. This collection of essays seeks to understand this connection and its fructifying consequences.

Preparing such a collection involves reminiscence because it entails retrospection. Putting the essays together required me to look backward—over the shoulder, so to speak—which stirred a curiosity about providence. From God's point of view, providence looks forward at the effects he plans to bring about; from the human point of view, providence is always more perspicuously seen by looking backward at a string of effects coming from causes unknown at the time. When C. S. Lewis wrote an account of his conversion in *The Pilgrim's Regress*, he spoke not only to himself but to all of us when he has the Guide say to John: "You may be sure the Landlord has brought you the shortest way: though I confess it would look an odd journey on a map."[2] Everyone's life would look like an odd journey if it were mapped out. Providence is deliberate, but not always direct. I have not organized my essays chronologically, yet when selecting them, they revealed some surprises I underwent in my intellectual journey. I was detoured from my plan to perform a systematician's dissection upon liturgy when I collided with Aidan Kavanagh in person, and with Alexander Schmemann in his books. I was redirected by the desire to understand what the former meant when he said liturgy is theology being born, and what the latter meant when he said liturgy is the ontological condition for

---

[2] C. S. Lewis, *The Pilgrim's Regress: Wade Annotated Edition* (Grand Rapids, MI: William B. Eerdmans, 2014), 177.

theology. These two seemed to think that the liturgy itself was a theological act, and I wondered how that could be. So I gave my dissertation a simple and forthright title—"What Is Liturgical Theology?"—in order to start my investigation, and I have been adding to my definition of it ever since.

These essays want to *use* liturgical theology, however, which is different from *defining* it. Except for a couple of initial essays to lay the groundwork, I will not here continue the act of definition I have done elsewhere. Still, it might help the reader to keep five things in mind about liturgical theology as it will be employed in the articles that follow. These were five discoveries I made during the course of my career, so I will tell about them somewhat autobiographically—or I could say "autobibliographically."

First, it supposes a thicker concept of liturgy than is commonly encountered.[3] The word is frequently used to mean the Church's complex of official services, the rites, ceremonies, sacraments, and prayers, and while this is a true definition, it is too small a definition. Schmemann frequently used the Greek word *leitourgia* in order to signal that he meant something bigger than the liturgy that celebrates it. Liturgy's inside is bigger than its outside. Perhaps we can jostle ourselves into understanding what he means by creating a neologism. *Leitourgia* is the action being carried out when the Church "cults." By "culting," the Church exercises her *leitourgia*, becomes her true self, enjoys her substantial mystery. The Church does not do cult, she uses cult to do *leitourgia*, and the *leitourgia* performed in her liturgy transforms her because it is God's activity and not ours. Therefore, I have thickened my definition of liturgy by beginning with the Trinity: *Liturgy is the perichoresis of the Trinity kenotically extended to invite our synergistic ascent into deification.* This suggests that liturgy comes from a place where we don't normally look for it. We normally look for the origin of liturgy in ancient history, in religious purity rituals, in human need, in communal fellowship, but I am proposing that we do not begin the liturgy, the Trinity does. The bulb from which the liturgical tulip grows is not a human decision, it is a divine one. The liturgy is not the invention of the Jesus club when it gets together, it is rather a response to God's own self-disclosure and redemptive action. The Trinity's circulation of love turns inside out, ecstatically, and in humility the Son and Spirit work the Father's good pleasure for all creation, which is to invite our ascent to

---

[3] See David W. Fagerberg, *Theologia Prima: What Is Liturgical Theology?* (Chicago: Hillenbrand Books, 2004).

participate in the very life of God; this cannot be forced, it must be done with our cooperation.

Liturgy has traditionally been said to have two purposes: the glorification of God and the sanctification of man. Luckily for us, the former happens when the latter is accomplished. Both are the work (*leitourgia*) of Christ, and therefore everything must pass through the hypostatic union before it is of any use to liturgy, because liturgy is the saving activity of Christ being continued. "For the liturgy, 'through which the work of our redemption is accomplished,' most of all in the divine sacrifice of the Eucharist, is the outstanding means whereby the faithful may express in their lives, and manifest to others, the mystery of Christ and the real nature of the true Church."[4] Although elements of liturgy look the same as other religious activities, such things as liturgical sacrifice, priesthood, sabbath, art, temple, etc., are different when they have come out of Christ's hypostatic union. Liturgy is the work of God and the activity of man. Insofar as liturgy involves human activity, we may speak about temporal development, cultural instantiation, and ritual systems, but insofar as liturgy is the *opus Dei*, it is permanent, persistent, and perpetual. Without this thickened sense of liturgy, the idea of *lex orandi* establishing *lex credendi* would sound blasphemous because it would imply that we should base our belief upon our own activity. Liturgy is not one of Adam's religions, it is the cult of the New Adam perpetuated by and in the members of his mystical body.

Second, this understanding of liturgical theology supposes a thicker definition of theology, and I found the Eastern Orthodox treatment of asceticism immensely helpful for this task.[5] Liturgy is participation by the body of Christ in the perichoresis of the Trinity; asceticism is the capacitation of a soul to participate in that perichoresis; the result is theology as union with God. Evagrius of Pontus describes three stages in the way of the soul. He calls the first stage *praktike*, because it is the very practical art of combating the passions, acquired through practice and action. He calls the second stage *physike*, because once we are freed in some measure from the passions, we can see the physical creation around us as God's handiwork. And in the third stage we come into union with God, no longer contemplating the creature but rather the Creator himself. Evagrius calls this third stage *theologia*. This kind of theology does not begin in the card catalogue; instead it begins with prayer, fasting, and almsgiving. It comes

---

[4] Second Vatican Council, Constitution on the Sacred Liturgy *Sacrosanctum Concilium* (1963), §2.

[5] See David W. Fagerberg, *On Liturgical Asceticism* (Washington, D.C.: The Catholic University of America Press, 2013).

at the cost of an ascetical denial of self and mortification of the passions. This theology belongs to saints, not scholars, and even though theology has found its useful place as the Queen of the Sciences in the academy, we ought not to forget this earlier, traditional definition of theology as union with God because it means that all the baptized are called to be theologians, since they are all called to be ascetics. I repeat again that liturgical theology is the restored connection of liturgy-theology-asceticism. Asceticism would not be required if the *liturgy* under consideration were merely Church services; asceticism would not be required if the *theology* under consideration were merely study in the library; but asceticism is, in fact, required if *leitourgia* is heaven on earth and *theologia* is union with God. Liturgy produces theologians, and the patristic understanding treats theology as an experimental knowledge. The knowledge of God that takes form in a person through prayerful liturgy is theology and is available to every person of prayer who is formed by the grammar of liturgy, even if they have not been to university to learn the academic jargon. Such liturgical theology is written with incense and icon and temple and feast and sacrament and relic. Such liturgical theology is as much a practice as it is a cognition, as much a vision as it is a study. Becoming a theologian consists of receiving the eye of the dove by liturgical asceticism.

Third, the extent or range of liturgical theology is larger than we think.[6] Thickening our understanding of liturgy and of theology by the application of asceticism has the end result of extending the range and magnitude of liturgical theology. Becoming a theologian requires the cataracts of sin be removed by grace under the discipline of asceticism so that by the light of Mount Tabor the healed eye can see the cosmos bathed in liturgical light. And at what does liturgical theology look? Everything! To what does liturgy have relevance? Everything! Liturgical theology takes a view of cosmos and time, earth's matter and heaven's empyrean, man and woman as cosmic priests, the eschatological telos toward which we journey, the route of the Cross by which we journey, death being trampled down by death, the new Jerusalem, history's fulfillment, and humanity's deification. The children of Adam and Eve are restored to their cosmic priesthood by becoming apprentices to Christ, the High Liturgist, and they can perform their liturgical ministry of consecrating the world. The sacramental liturgy is a condensed expression of the cosmic liturgy, and the cosmic liturgy is a diffused celebration of the sacramental mysteries.

---

[6] See David W. Fagerberg, *Consecrating the World: On Mundane Liturgical Theology* (Kettering, OH: Angelico Press, 2016).

We rehearse the reality that the divine playwright is inscribing in our lives on the stage of ritual liturgy; therefore, liturgical theology does not look only at the ritual, it looks through liturgy to the reality in and behind the ritual, the reality caused by the ritual, the reality we celebrate ritually and live regularly.

Fourth, all this resonates with liturgical mysticism.[7] We can make the question "What happens in liturgy?" more precise by asking, "What happens *to us* in liturgy?" Liturgical theology is translated into liturgical mysticism. The river of liturgy flows from the heavenly throne and pools up in the Church on earth, but then that sacramental reservoir overflows its ecclesiastical lip to flood our personal lives. Liturgical mysticism is the normal crowning of the baptized Christian life. A person who has been initiated into Christ's mystical body is by definition a mystical person by his inclusion, and commences a spiritual life in which the theological virtues of faith, hope, and charity are quickened. Baptismal grace initiates us into spiritual warfare (asceticism) and enlightens our understanding (theology), making us neophytes (newly planted) in Christ's liturgical work of glorifying his Father and sanctifying his brothers and sisters. Liturgical mysticism is the Trinitarian mystery mediated by sacramental liturgy and hypostasized as personal liturgy. It anchors the substance of our lives. In every Eucharist there are two liturgies, one external and visible, the other internal and mystical. Baptism drops the Spirit of the Holy One into our veins, but there is no fire where there is no matter to burn; asceticism must make us combustible to that mystical fire. We should be prepared to put our hands through the liturgy and touch the fire of a bush burning without being consumed. Moses would have missed the point if, instead of taking off his shoes to stand on the holy ground, he scraped a sample of dirt to take back for study. And so would we.

Fifth, the absolute difference between Creator and creature is addressed without being denied.[8] There is an ontological gulf between God and ourselves that translates as an epistemological gulf. God is incomprehensible, inscrutable, and unfathomable. He is indescribable: literally "not-able-to-be-written-down." But the one who cannot be known can be loved. Despite this absolute difference, we find a movement from one side to the other, and back again. What knowledge cannot fasten together, love can unite, and this is expressed in liturgical dogmatics. The

---

[7] See David W. Fagerberg, *Liturgical Mysticism* (Steubenville, OH: Emmaus Academic Press, 2019).

[8] See David W. Fagerberg, *Liturgical Dogmatics: How Catholic Beliefs Flow from Liturgical Prayer* (San Francisco: Ignatius Press, 2021).

union of apophatic with cataphatic happens in a liturgical circulation. We stammer to say cataphatically what has been apophatically encountered in the Mysteries of Christ experienced liturgically. Cataphatic dogma arises from apophatic liturgy: *credendi* arises from *orandi*. Liturgical dogmatics can speak of a relationship between the liturgy and God's economy of salvation in such a way that what God does in his macrocosmic actions in the world can be detected in his microcosmic activity in our soul's experience of asceticism and deification. Then dogma can be examined in the light of liturgy. A dogma is a consequence of divine revelation, but what is the purpose of revelation? It is not for footnotes, not to fill library shelves, not for academics to play with at recess. The purpose of God's revelation is so that creatures can be received into his glory, which will be finalized in heaven but can be begun on earth because liturgy spans the abyss between heaven and earth.

These five thickened dimensions will enter into play when we attempt to use liturgical theology in the essays ahead. To recapitulate, *leitourgia* has a miraculous consequence that is often overlooked by a simplistic understanding of liturgy; *theologia* is union with God, not an erudition, and depends upon the ascetical capacitation of a person; liturgical theology raises its eyes to an expanded horizon because it is cosmic in scope and eschatological in ambition; the liturgical person is a mystic, and his liturgical life is a mysticism begun; and the legacy of dogma in the Church grows because we still taste and see. G. K. Chesterton said the Church is "the trysting-place of all the truths in the world,"[9] and that seems about right. A tryst is an agreement, as between lovers, to meet at a certain time and place. Liturgy is the trysting place of God with the human race. Here is where God has promised to come to his people with transfiguring power to graft them into his own divine life, and it is the vocation of every liturgist (I mean every baptized Christian) to grapple with what that means. These essays offer what little help they can with that.

I have already mentioned that I am not organizing these essays chronologically, so let me go directly on to describing the thematic organization I have chosen.

I will make two admissions. First, I admit the repetition of certain quotations. I excuse myself from this embarrassment with a quotation (ironically enough) from Bartolomeo de Dominici's description of the reading style of Catherine of Siena. "She was not concerned about reading

---

[9] G. K. Chesterton, *The Thing: Why I Am a Catholic*, in *The Collected Works of G. K. Chesterton* (San Francisco: Ignatius Press, 1990), 3:132.

a lot or saying many prayers. Rather she would chew on every single word, and when she found one she especially liked, she would stop for as long as her mind found pleasure grazing there."[10] Apparently, certain passages have given me a cud I continued to chew in more than one context. The stone they provided fit into more than one arch. Second, I admit to ignoring the academy when it advises with a hoarse whisper, "Specialize! Stay in your field! Narrow your reading list!" I admit to a range of topics, which means I cannot claim expertise in each subject. But maybe this strategy of specialization treats theology under the wrong paradigm. Maybe it is using a paradigm from the empirical sciences, where what counts as progress is only when new information is discovered or added. In the sciences, one does not research in order to repeat. No one praises the graduate student who announces that every action has an equal and opposite reaction: the student studies Newton in order to surpass him. But can we apply this methodology to theology? If theological progress only happens when absolutely new information is added to a cumulative pile, then innovation and novelty must be the order of the day. A "new thought" must mean a novel thought, a different thought, a thought never thought before. (And how are we to know if a thought is truly original? I guess that's what doctoral examination boards are for.)

In the academy it is called plagiarism when one uses another person's words (unquoted), but I actually find this to be the most satisfying experience in reading theology. Sometimes it is my thought appearing in the author's words; sometimes it is the author's thoughts appearing in my words. The delight is in the meeting of minds. Louis Bouyer writes:

> No idea was more foreign to the ancients than the modern idea that the multiplication of definitions constitutes progress. This proliferation corresponds (in their view) to scars on the Body of Truth, inflicted by the errors over which it triumphs.
>
> The only genuine progress in the knowledge of God, beyond what has been transmitted from the beginning by Christ and the apostles, results from the transition from faith to vision on the Last Day. The only anticipation we can have of it is not in

---

[10] Bartolomeo de Dominici's testimony, cited in Suzanne Noffke's introduction to Catherine of Siena, *The Dialogue* (New York: Paulist Press, 1980), 22.

doctrinal development ... but in what they call the "science of the saints": gnosis, or mystical theology.

The accumulation of new formulas has no positive value but an indirect one, insofar as it corresponds to successive penetration of different cultures by the Gospel and, more directly, to attraction to and fuller saturation with the different possibilities of human experience by the Spirit of Christ. Outside this gradually universalized accession of everything human to the reign of Christ, logical development of the propositions in the primitive kerygma is absolutely sterile. If it does not veer from orthodoxy, it is merely tautological.[11]

I would be pleased if the ideas in these essays were found to be repetitive and tautological, because then they would not be veering from a trajectory set by liturgical theology, which is the teacher.

---

[11] Louis Bouyer, *The Church of God: Body of Christ and Temple of the Spirit* (Chicago: Franciscan Herald Press, 1982), 356. Thirty years ago, I situated the publication of my dissertation between two quotations that make the same point. From Josef Pieper: "In this realm, originality of thought and diction is of small importance—should, in fact, be distrusted" (Preface to *The Four Cardinal Virtues* [New York: Harcourt, Brace & World, Inc., 1965], xii). And in class Paul Holmer would frequently say: "You cannot peddle truth or happiness. What a thought cost in the first instance, it will also cost in the second."

Liturgy and Asceticism

Desert Asceticism
Prayer as Theology*

There is an old joke about a man who went into a meditation class puffing on a lit pipe. The instructor said, "Excuse me, sir, but you can't smoke your pipe while you meditate," to which the man replied, "Do you mind, then, if I meditate while I smoke my pipe?"

It might be tempting to apply this framework also to the relationship of prayer and theology, as if they are two independent actions which might sometimes coincide, but not always. On the one hand, we could imagine a person praying while thinking theological thoughts—to that theologian's credit in circles which find theology to be dry and erudite, and to that theologian's discredit in circles which eschew mixing piety with objective thought. On the other hand, we could imagine a person theologizing while engaged in prayer—to that doxologist's credit in circles which emphasize meaning over performance, and to the doxologist's discredit in circles which fear an over-intellectualization of prayer. In this framework, it would not seem difficult to imagine someone theologizing while meditating, or meditating while theologizing, rather like the pipe smoker. Two discrete activities could be combined, with emphasis placed sometimes upon the one and sometimes upon the other.

The desert tradition invites us to deepen our concept of prayer by declining this compromise. The understanding of prayer and theology in the Desert Fathers[1] is different from ours, and we are tripped up by the very bluntness of Evagrius of Pontus: "If you are a theologian you truly

---

* David W. Fagerberg, "Prayer as Theology," in *A History of Prayer: The First to the Fifteenth Century*, ed. Roy Hammerling (Leiden: Brill, 2008), 117–36.

[1] I shall use both the word "monk" and the title "Desert Fathers" to refer to both men and women, both Abbas and Ammas, because both sexes may achieve virility in their asceticism, and because women ascetics also implant the seed of wisdom. *The Sayings of the Desert Fathers* records this story: "Two monks came from Pelusium to see Sarah. On the way they said to each other, 'Let us humiliate this amma.' So they said to her, 'Take care that your soul be not puffed up, and that you do not say, "Look, some hermits have come to consult me, a woman!"' Sarah said to them, 'I am a woman in sex, but not in spirit'" (Benedicta Ward, trans., *The Desert Fathers: Sayings of the Early Christian Monks* [London: Penguin Books, 2003], 10).

pray. If you truly pray you are a theologian."[2] Prayer and theology are very nearly convertible as terms. If the theological act is the fruit of prayer, then one cannot be said to import theology as an accompaniment to prayer nor seek ways to adjoin prayer to the theological act. According to the lesson learned in the desert school, the ascetical path to prayer results in a theologian, and a theologian may be defined as someone capacitated to pray. These are not two activities to be coordinated (like meditating and smoking); they have an inherent connection (like music and the stroke of a bow across violin strings).

This point of view is not Evagrius's invention, though he was among its earliest and most systematic recorders. Evagrius lived in the theological orbit of the Cappadocians:

> He was of the Pontic race, of the city of Ibora, son of a chor-bishop, and he was ordained lector by Saint Basil, bishop of the church at Caesarea. Then after the death of Saint Basil, the bishop Gregory of Nazianzus, a man most wise, most serene, and brilliant in learning, took note of his fitness and ordained him deacon. Then in the great synod at Constantinople he left him to the blessed bishop Nectarius as one most skillful in confuting all the heresies. He flourished in the great city, confuting every heresy with youthful exuberance.[3]

He left for Jerusalem in 382 after an amorous affair with the wife of a nobleman. Evagrius had a dream or vision in which an angel cast him into prison and then promised him deliverance if he would depart from the city. He swore he would. "And when Evagrius woke up from his sleep, he thought within himself and said, 'Although the words of the oaths have been uttered in a dream, it is right that I should fulfill that which I have promised'; so he put his things in a ship and departed to Jerusalem"[4] where he first dwelled at the monastic communities of Rufinus and Melania on the Mount of Olives, but from there he was pointed toward the deeper Egyptian deserts where he lived the remaining sixteen years of his life until

---

[2] Evagrius, *The Praktikos and Chapters on Prayer*, trans. John Bamberger (Collegeville, MN: Cistercian Publications, 1981), 65.
[3] Palladius, *The Lausiac History* (Westminster, MD: Newman Press, 1965), 110–14.
[4] E. A. Wallis Budge, trans., *The Paradise of the Holy Fathers* (London, Chatto & Windus, 1907), 1:222–24. The wording in *The Lausiac History* is: "As the oath was finished he came back out of his ecstasy. He got up and decided that 'even if this oath was made in my vision, nevertheless I did swear it.' Putting everything aboard ship, he went onto Jerusalem" (112).

his death in 399. "While in Egypt he had as his spiritual father the priest of Kellia, St. Makarios of Alexandria, and it is probable that he also knew St. Makarios the Egyptian, the priest and spiritual father of Sketis. In the person of these two saints he came into contact with the first generation of the Desert Fathers and with their spirituality in its purest form."[5] He was thus contemporary with Pachomius (+346), who wrote the first Eastern cenobitic rule; Basil (+379), whose *Longer Rules* expressed the community of love; Antony (+356), the "first monk" whose life Athanasius immortalized as a primordial model; Paul (+348), who had fled to the desert the year before Antony was born; and John Cassian (+435), Evagrius's own pupil, who carried the institutes of Egyptian monasticism to the West where it influenced the ascetical tradition as well as future reflection on the vices and virtues. "There can be no doubt that Evagrius stands at the fountainhead of Christian commentary on the ascetical life for both East and West, for Moscow and Constantinople as well as for Monte Cassino and Rome."[6]

Two Sayings make it quite clear that in these matters Evagrius is a student, not an innovator:

> Some time ago Abba Evagrius went to Scete to a certain father and said to him, "Speak some word whereby I may be able to save myself." The old man saith unto him, "If thou wishest to be saved, when thou goest unto any man speak not before he asketh thee a question." Now Evagrius was sorry about this sentence, and shewed regret because he had asked the question, saying, "Verily I have read many books and I cannot accept instruction of this kind"; and having profited greatly he went forth from him.[7]
>
> On one occasion there was a congregation in the Cells concerning a certain matter, and Abba Evagrius spoke. And a certain elder said unto him, "We know, Abba, that hadst thou been in thine own country where thou art a bishop and the governor of many, [thou wouldst have been right in speaking]; but in this place thou sittest [as] a stranger." Now Evagrius was sorry, but he was not offended, and he shook his head, and bent his gaze downwards, and he wrote with his finger and said unto them,

---

[5] Introductory note to Evagrius's writings in *The Philokalia*, ed. G. E. H. Palmer, Philip Sherrard, and Kallistos Ware (Boston: Faber and Faber, 1979), 1:29.
[6] Aidan Kavanagh, "Eastern Influences on the Rule of Saint Benedict," *Monasticism and the Arts*, ed. Timothy Verdon (Syracuse, NY: Syracuse University Press, 1984), 57.
[7] Budge, *The Paradise*, 1:15.

"Verily, it is even as thou sayest, O my fathers; I have spoken once, but I will not do it a second time."[8]

So Evagrius listened. And he learned. And he recorded what he learned. And what he recorded influenced later spiritual authors, so although we use Evagrius's name most, this prayer tradition should not be thought of as idiosyncratically his. His ascetical work was adopted and modified by a stream of theologians who nuanced the doctrine of dispassion, including Diadochus, Maximus the Confessor, John Climacus, Hesychius, Nicetas, Symeon the New Theologian, and culminating in Gregory Palamas.[9]

Evagrius proposes three stages on which the struggle to learn prayer occurs, summarized briefly here and detailed more completely below, and the desert's definition of theology may be found by noting their very sequence. These three stages stand under two major divisions: "*Praktike*, where the concern is purifying the passionate part of the soul; and knowledge [*theoria*], where the rational part of the soul devotes itself to contemplation and knowledge."[10] Think of it as 1, 2a, and 2b. The first stage, that of *praktike*, is, as we might expect, highly practical in dealing with methods to overcome the passions. Upon this stage[11] one does battle with "the eight evil thoughts," which are the ground of the passions (*pathe*). To put the passions away is to attain a state of freedom—*apatheia*, or dispassion—which "marks a decisive turning point in the spiritual itinerary of the Christian. It is the door to contemplation, or more exactly, its vestibule. For charity, the finest fruit of *apatheia*, is the door to contemplation."[12] The fundamental division, therefore, is between discipline and contemplation (*praktike* and *theoria*), but the two types of contemplative knowledge are further distinguishable by their mutual objects, i.e., according to whether one is contemplating created natures or God. Evagrius calls the second stage *physike* because it is the act of contemplating the cosmos in the light of revelation. This can be called spiritual, for one sees beyond appearances to know the Creator in the signs of his creatures. The third stage

---

[8] Ward, *The Desert Fathers*, 64.
[9] For an easy overview of these hesychastic authors, see John Meyendorff, *St. Gregory Palamas and Orthodox Spirituality*, trans. Adele Fiske (Crestwood, NY: St. Vladimir's Seminary Press, 1974).
[10] Jeremy Driscoll, O.S.B., *The "Ad Monachos" of Evagrius Ponticus: Its Structure and a Select Commentary* (Rome: Pontificio Ateneo S. Anselmo, 1991), 11.
[11] It seems better to say "upon this stage" than "in this stage," because the stages are not really phases one passes through to leave behind. The same observation about human nature is made by Kierkegaard when he speaks of stages. That said, it must be acknowledged that Evagrius is more confident than the later tradition in talking about *apatheia* as being an achievement.
[12] Evagrius, *The Praktikos and Chapters on Prayer*, lxxxvii.

contemplates God himself, and thus knows the mystery of the Trinity experientially. "It amounts to the experiential knowledge of God through the highest form of prayer."[13] This third stage, this summit Evagrius calls *theologia*. Participation in the life of the Trinity is the ultimate goal of ascetical prayer. This is not knowledge about God, it is experiential knowledge of the Trinity made possible by the Son's revelation of the Father and made available by the Holy Spirit's indwelling in us as God's temple. "Prayer lifts man above his very nature, to set him on a level with the angels. 'By true prayer a monk becomes the equal of an angel.' By his contemplation he also becomes a temple of God. Finally, it elevates him to the knowledge of the very Trinity itself."[14] "The sense of the word *theology* [*theologia*] is reserved by Evagrius to refer to the Trinity."[15]

Evagrius summarizes the sequence of *praktike-physike-theologia* several times in *The Praktikos*, the clearest case being in the first entry of the hundred chapters that make up this book. "Christianity is the dogma of Christ our Savior. It is composed of *praktike*, of the contemplation of the physical world, and of the contemplation of God."[16] A second summary is to be found in the book's introductory letter to Anatolius, where Evagrius records the words spoken to a new monk when he receives the habit:

> The fear of God strengthens faith, my son, and continence in turn strengthens this fear. Patience and hope make this latter virtue solid beyond all shaking, and they also give birth to *apatheia*. Now this *apatheia* has a child called *agape* who keeps the door to deep knowledge of the created universe. Finally, to this knowledge succeed theology and the supreme beatitude.[17]

A third summary is found in chapter 84, where Evagrius describes the originating point of the ascetical stage, and the originating point of the contemplative stages. Since the demons also know these originating points, this is where they attack:

> The goal of the ascetic life is charity; the goal of contemplative knowledge is theology. The beginnings of each are faith and

---

[13] Evagrius, *The Praktikos and Chapters on Prayer*, lxxxiin231.
[14] Evagrius, *The Praktikos and Chapters on Prayer*, 48
[15] Driscoll, *The "Ad Monachos" of Evagrius Ponticus*, 17.
[16] Evagrius, *The Praktikos and Chapters on Prayer*, chap. 1.
[17] Evagrius, *The Praktikos and Chapters on Prayer*, 14. See the "Introductory Letter to Anatolius," which accompanies the *The Praktikos*.

contemplation of nature respectively. Such of the demons as fall upon the affective part of the soul are said to be the opponents of the ascetic life. Those again who disturb the rational part are the enemies of all truth and the adversaries of contemplation.

It would seem, then, by this organization, that theology is what awaits a person at the top of an arduous ascetical climb called *praktike*. The whole aim of asceticism is to capacitate a person for prayer, and the highest experience of prayer is *theologia*.

The root of the word "asceticism" implies a training designed to produce a specific character or pattern of behavior. Used of an athlete, it referred to the training one underwent in order to accomplish a goal:

> The word "asceticism" derives from the Greek term for physical exercise, such as athletic practice. The idea of training the soul to virtue by disciplining the body is fundamental to monastic theory. Here, Christian monasticism provided a distinct and original anthropology. In many Greco-Roman theories the purpose of "philosophic" asceticism was to purify the soul of the body's influence.... In its purest form the Christian concept of *ascesis* seeks not the liberation of the soul from the body but the integration of the person, spiritually and materially. *Ascesis* was thus a manner of disciplining the body and training the mind by prayers, vigils and fasting, until the whole person was attuned to his or her best ability to hear and obey the voice of God.[18]

Asceticism is not an end in itself, as Abba Moses explains in *The Conferences* recorded by John Cassian. Abba Moses notes that every human task is engaged toward an end, or goal: the farmer suffers heat and blisters to bring in a good crop, the merchant risks storms at sea to ship cargo, and soldiers suffer present hardships and wars to obtain honor. Abba Moses asks Cassian what his goal was in becoming an ascetic. Cassian answers simplistically that it was for the sake of the kingdom of heaven. This prompts Abba Moses to distinguish two kinds of ends or goals, which he calls *scopos* (short-term) and *telos* (ultimate). The farmer's ultimate goal is to have plenty and live free from care, but to reach that *telos* he has the more immediate *scopos* of keeping his field clear from all brambles and

---

[18] John McGuckin, "Monasticism," in *The Blackwell Dictionary of Eastern Christianity*, ed. Ken Parry, David J. Melling, Dimitri Brady, and Sidney H. Griffin (Oxford: Wiley-Blackwell, 1999), 321.

weeds. The businessman chooses carefully the most economical path to wealth, and the ones seeking honor make up their minds to what duties and conditions they must devote themselves. Similarly, there is a *telos* and *scopos* for the monastic ascetic. "The end of our profession indeed, as we have said, is the kingdom of God or the kingdom of heaven: but the goal or scopos is purity of heart, without which it is impossible for anyone to reach that end."[19] Purity of heart is how John Cassian translates his master's word, *apatheia*, in order to make it more acceptable to Western readers. *Praktike* is a discipline that strives for dispassion, and the finest fruit of *apatheia* is charity, which is the door to contemplation. Blessed are the pure in heart, for they shall see God.

Praktike

To consider each of these three stages in greater detail we must begin with an understanding of what this tradition means by a "passion." In modern English, the word can be used either positively or negatively, that is, for either a positive or negative emotion. The word roughly means feeling something deeply, a sort of ardor or zeal, and so we use the word to speak of both a "passion for art" and killing someone "in a state of passion." The word itself is neutral and only indicates the heightened state in which an end is pursued with fervor, be that end admirable or condemnable. The Western Fathers of the Church generally used the word "passion" in this way, too, which led Jerome and Augustine to complain about the condemnation of passions by some. But the word played in a different language game in the ascetical jargon of the Eastern Desert Fathers. For them the word "passion" generally had a negative meaning because it referred to a disoriented and discordant and diseased heart, a condition called *pathe*. "For the Eastern Fathers, the passions could be neither good nor indifferent. The soul is by nature the image of God. As the result of sin, it has been cloaked with various passions. The aim of *praxis* is to strip the soul of these *pathe*."[20] When the desert tradition speaks of the passions, it means those thoughts and states which separate a person from God because they dampen *agape*. In this sense, they name the spiritual rebellion that distorts an otherwise good creation—in somewhat the same manner that the New Testament speaks of overcoming the world, even though "world" could

---

[19] John Cassian, *The Conferences*, trans. Boniface Ramsey, O.P. (Mahwah, NJ: Paulist Press, 1997), 43.
[20] Tomáš Špidlík, *The Spirituality of the Christian East*, trans. Anthony P. Gythiel (Collegeville, MN: Cistercian Publications, 1986), 268.

also name God's good and innocent creation. In fact, St. Isaac the Syrian says that when we say "the world," we simply mean the passions in total. "By contemplative examination, the world is also called the aggregate of the collective noun which is applied to the separate passions. When we wish to give a collective name to the passions, we call them *world*. And when we wish to designate them specifically according to their names, we call them *passions*."[21]

From the instruction Evagrius received at the feet of his spiritual directors, he discerned "eight evil thoughts" (*logismoi*) which, if left unchecked, can become passions:

> There are eight general and basic categories of thoughts in which are included every thought. First is that of gluttony, then impurity, avarice, sadness, anger, *acedia*,[22] vainglory, and last of all, pride. It is not in our power to determine whether we are disturbed by these thoughts, but it is up to us to decide if they are to linger within us or not and whether or not they are to stir up our passions.[23]

Following the Greek assessment of the soul, Evagrius sees three faculties in a human being: the concupiscible, the irascible, and the rational. If not distorted by the passions, these three faculties could be moved properly, as Maximus the Confessor notes: "The soul is moved reasonably when its concupiscible element is qualified by self-mastery, its irascible element cleaves to love and turns away from hate, and the rational element lives with God through prayer and spiritual contemplation."[24] The first three passions in Evagrius's list are distortions of our concupiscible faculty (gluttony, lust, avarice), the second three are distortions of our irascible faculty (sadness, anger, acedia), and the last two afflict our right reason (vainglory,

---

[21] Homily 2, in *The Ascetical Homilies of Saint Isaac the Syrian*, trans. Dana Miller (Brookline, MA: Holy Transfiguration Monastery Publications, 1984), 14.

[22] This roughly means "slothfulness in religious duty," although it is more complicated than our current use of the word "sloth." For the evolution of this term into what it means today, see Siegfried Wenzel, *The Sin of Sloth: Acedia in Medieval Thought and Literature* (Chapel Hill, NC: University of North Carolina Press, 1967).

[23] This is chapter six of *The Praktikos*, and then he turns to each of the eight evil thoughts individually in chapters seven through fourteen.

[24] Maximus the Confessor, *The Four Hundred Chapters on Love*, in *Maximus Confessor: Selected Writings*, trans. George Berthold (Mahwah, NJ: Paulist Press, 1985), 77.

pride). We should note in passing that this list influenced the West via John Cassian and Pope Gregory the Great, as Kallistos Ware explains:

> Evagrius' disciple, St. John Cassian, transmitted this list of the eight "thoughts" to the West, but made one change in the sequence: to make more evident the connection between dejection and despondency, he moved anger up to the fourth place, after avarice. Further changes were made by St. Gregory the Great, Pope of Rome (590–604), known in the East as "Gregory the Dialogist." He set pride in a class on its own, as the source and mother of all other vices, and omitted dejection, regarding this as the same as despondency, while adding envy to the list. In this way he produced the catalogue of the "seven deadly sins," familiar to the Western Middle Ages.[25]

Evagrius bespeaks a long-standing psychological intuition of the ascetical tradition when he observes that it is not in our power to determine whether we are disturbed by these thoughts. A distinction is made between the first tickle of a temptation and what is finally a fully developed and ensnaring passion. Keeping constant watch enables one to see the beginning of the temptation and to cut off the head of the serpent before the whole body gets into the tent. The *logismoi* are first whispered by demons in obedience to the will of the Satan (the Tempter), whose envy of and hatred for human beings knows no bounds. These thoughts "are the seeds of the 'passions,' those suggestions or impulses that emerge from the subconscious and soon become obsessive. In the ascetic sense, remember, the 'passions' are blockages, usurpations, deviations that destroy the human being's basic desire. They are forms of idolatry, of that 'self-idolatry' that deflects towards nothingness our capacity for transcendence."[26] Thoughts are used by the demons to trouble an ascetic; sometimes each thought is said to correspond to a demon; the demons set the *logismoi* in motion. But these thoughts are, so to speak, just the seeds of temptation, and a person is not culpable for suffering them. Even Jesus suffered the *logismoi*, as his temptation in the desert reveals (thus he is like us in all things, sympathizing with our condition, yet can be said to be without sin). The thought only becomes a sin if a person couples with it, then wrestles against it but

---

[25] Fr. Kallistos Ware, introduction to John Climacus, *The Ladder of Divine Ascent*, trans. Colm Luibheild and Norman Russell (Mahwah, NJ: Paulist Press, 1982), 63.

[26] Olivier Clément, *The Roots of Christian Mysticism*, trans. Theodore Berkeley, O.C.S.O., and Jeremy Hummerstone (New York: New City Press, 1996), 167.

fails, and finally assents to it willingly. Then the passion takes the sinner captive.[27] The demons' goal is to prevent the person from reaching passionlessness, so they attack that part of the soul where the passions reside in such a way as to set them in motion. Evagrius describes this with a language typically precise. "*Demons* inspire *thoughts*, and these, when they are allowed to linger, unleash the *passions* in us. The remedy against this system of demonic attacks is a constant vigilance over thoughts, never allowing them to linger. *Praktike* is learning this art."[28]

Were our focus on asceticism, rather than upon prayer as the fruit of asceticism, we would tarry to consider each passion in more detail, and how it afflicts the human psyche. Instead, suffice us to summarize that the road to prayer leads through this art, practiced under the tutelage of a spiritual guide, requiring the powers of fasting, temperance, poverty, joyful hope, meekness, ready obedience, humility, and charity. These are, so to speak, antidotes to the poison, and the spiritual guide mixes up the medicament in the exact dosage each sinner requires. It was for the sake of researching these medicaments that Christian monks headed into the desert in the fourth century. They wanted to see what it would take to order a life to God, and to ascertain this knowledge they resolved to conduct an experiment upon their own human hearts.[29] Now, every science student knows that an experiment requires that one must remove external factors that might affect the experiment: this is called a controlled environment. The Desert Fathers also sought a controlled environment for their experiment, but they removed the external factors by *removing themselves* from the world. They left city, family, wealth, and property, not because they thought these things were bad (they weren't dualists), and not to do something which didn't concern all the faithful, but to search for the tranquility required to notice the movements of the heart, much like a person would shut down other causes of noise in order to listen more

---

[27] John of Damascus summarizes it thus: "It does not lie within our power to decide whether or not these eight thoughts are going to arise and disturb us. But to dwell on them or not to dwell on them, to excite the passions or not to excite them, does lie within our power. In this connection, we should distinguish between seven different terms: provocation, coupling, wrestling, passion, assent [which comes very close to performance], actualization and captivity" (*On the Virtues and the Vices*, in *The Philokalia*, ed. G. E. H. Palmer, Philip Sherrard, and Kallistos Ware [Boston: Faber and Faber, 1981], 2:337–38). They are also dealt with by Peter of Damascus in *A Treasury of Divine Knowledge*, in *The Philokalia*, ed. G. E. H. Palmer, Philip Sherrard, and Kallistos Ware (Boston: Faber and Faber, 1986), 3:207.

[28] Driscoll, *The "Ad Monachos" of Evagrius Ponticus*, 14.

[29] This was the metaphor under which I conceived flight into the desert in "Time in the Desert Fathers," *The American Benedictine Review* 50, no. 2 (June 1999): 180–202.

attentively to a muffled sound. Tranquility "gives the soul the opportunity to look at the impressions previously stamped on the mind, and to struggle against each one and eliminate it."[30] *Apatheia* is water without ripples so the mind can reflect—and reflect upon—images of truth. When two men came to ask their friend what progress he had made as a monk, he was silent for a little, then poured some water into a cup.

> And he said: "Look at the water." And it was cloudy. And after a little he said again: "Now look, see how clear the water has become." And when they leant over the water, they saw their faces as in a glass. And then he said to them: "So it is with the man who lives among men. He does not see his own sins because of the turmoil. But when he is at rest, especially in the desert, then he sees his sins."[31]

Physike

Not until the passions are under control (*apatheia*) is it possible to do cosmology or, as Evagrius calls it in the second stage, *physike*. Neither Evagrius nor the larger tradition ever lost sight of the reason for asceticism. It is certainly not born of dualism or self-disgust. Maximus defines passion as "a movement of the soul contrary to nature. . . . Vice is the mistaken use of ideas from which follows the abuse of things. . . . As with everything, misuse is sin."[32] And so Peter of Damaskos identifies the problem in the spirit, not in the object. "For it is not food, but gluttony, that is bad; not money, but attachment to it; not speech, but idle talk; . . . not authority that is bad, but the love of authority; not glory, but the love of glory and—what is worse—vainglory. . . . It is not the thing itself, but its misuse that is evil."[33] This is thoroughly Christian and quite different from a Manichean loathing for materiality. The ascetic life is the spiritual method for cleansing the soul, Evagrius says, in order that the soul can see clearly, for how could we see the world as it really is if our lenses were blurred by the passions? We might see food gluttonously, our neighbor resentfully, the goods of the earth avariciously and not sacramentally. The battleground is the human heart, where the passions reside, and this will

---

[30] St. Neilos the Ascetic, *Ascetic Discourse*, in *The Philokalia*, 1:232.
[31] *Sayings of the Desert Fathers*, in *Western Asceticism*, ed. Owen Chadwick (Philadelphia: Westminster Press, 1958), 43.
[32] Berthold, trans., *Selected Writings*, 48.
[33] St. Peter of Damaskos, *A Treasury of Divine Knowledge*, in *The Philokalia*, 3:156.

not be cured by eliminating external material stimuli.[34] "For Evagrius passions in the concupiscible and irascible parts have to be defeated for virtue to be established in the rational part."[35] The rational part of the soul cannot turn to *gnosis* (knowing) unless the concupiscible and irascible are apathetic. The ascetical tradition finds a connection between purity of heart and clarity of mind. Dionysius also says that the struggle for the virtues concludes with *apatheia* and *agape*, as Alexander Golitzin explains:

> This may be defined as the harmonious and measured working of our present [mode of being] under the guiding sovereignty of our reason. . . . *Apatheia* does not, perhaps, mean the cessation of passionate thoughts here below, but it clearly does insist that the intellect ceases to be ruled by these forces. It is thus the pre-condition for all further spiritual development, the requisite ordering and directing of the soul's movement toward further knowledge.[36]

The passions in the concupiscible and irascible faculties must be defeated for virtue to be established in the rational faculty. This is a truth that Plato partially saw when he noted that the body upsets the soul. But since for the Christian the soul is not in the body, like wine is in a bottle, or a sailor is in a ship, or a prisoner is in a dungeon, the cure is different from the one envisioned by Platonic Gnostics. The purpose of asceticism is not to free the soul from the body, but to free both the soul and body from the passions. ("An athlete exercises his body; an ascetic, his flesh."[37]) To that end, and to Plato's surprise, we can even use the body to cure the soul,

---

[34] This point is driven home in a story that also comments on the need for community. "A brother was restless in his community and he was often irritated. So he said, 'I will go and live somewhere by myself. I will not be able to talk or listen to anyone and so I shall be at peace, and my passionate anger will cease.' He went out and lived alone in a cave. But one day he filled his jug with water and put it on the ground. Suddenly it happened to fall over. He filled it again, and again it fell. This happened a third time. In a rage he snatched up the jug and smashed it. Coming to his senses, he knew that the demon of anger had mocked him, and he said, 'Here I am by myself, and he has beaten me. I will return to the community. Wherever you live, you need effort and patience and above all God's help.' So he got up, and went back" (Ward, *The Desert Fathers*, 71).

[35] Driscoll, *The "Ad Monachos" of Evagrius Ponticus*, 131.

[36] Fr. Alexander Golitzin, *Et Introibo Ad Altare Dei: The Mystagogy of Dionysius Areopagita, with Special Reference to Its Predecessors in the Eastern Christian Tradition* (Thessaloniki, GR: Patriarchikon Idrima Paterikon Meleton, 1994), 331.

[37] Paul Evdokimov, *The Struggle with God* (Mahwah, NJ: Paulist Press, 1966), 60. Reprinted as *Ages of the Spiritual Life* (Crestwood, NY: St. Vladimir's Seminary Press, 1998).

and that is precisely how *praktike* operates in the first stage. Although the Fall took place on a spiritual level, it affected matter, which is why this asceticism must also be done to the body, through the body, by the body, for the body. "By what rule or manner can I bind this body of mine?" asks John Climacus. "He is my helper and my enemy, my assistant and my opponent, a protector and a traitor. ... If I strike him down I have nothing left by which to acquire virtues."[38]

Symeon the New Theologian reminds us that because we are both matter and spirit, we were made to see both materially and spiritually:

> Know then that you are double
> and that you possess two eyes,
> the sensible and the spiritual.
> Since there are also two suns
> there is also a double light,
> sensible and spiritual,
> and if you see them, you will be the man
> as you were created in the beginning to be.
> If you see the sensible sun
> and not the spiritual sun,
> you are really half dead.[39]

There is nothing wrong with the world, but the sinner wrongs the world when he sees it passionately. Matter is not corrupt, but the one looking at matter has been corrupted and so sees the world corruptly. It would seem, then, that between being an ascetic and a theologian, one must become a physician. Not the medical kind, and not the scientific kind, either. Evagrius's physics transcends our splintered definitions because his is the kind of physics which heals (like the former) by means of knowing (like the latter). A true physician knows the world to be a temple. He knows what matter is for, and therefore knows the cure for what is the matter with the world.[40] "Contemplation in this view, then, is not a mere luxury

---

[38] John Climacus, *The Ladder of Divine Ascent*, 185–56.
[39] Symeon the New Theologian, *Hymns of Divine Love*, trans. George A. Maloney (Denville, NJ: Dimension Books, 1976), 123.
[40] For these thoughts, see David Fagerberg, "On Liturgical Asceticism," *Diakonia* 31, no. 1 (1998): 31–60.

for a few specially favored souls. It is the indispensable activity of every Christian who would become perfect."[41]

Theoria physike is a contemplation of nature, of beings, of the created. "That God can be known from his works was proclaimed by all the Fathers.... For the friends of God the universe therefore becomes an open book, a school for souls."[42] But it is more than nature walks in the woods. This second stage, the first phase of the contemplative life,

> includes penetration into the meaning of Scripture. Also included is the structured order of the universe, the varieties of natural phenomena and the natural symbols that fill our world—all these provide material for the pure of heart to grow in understanding of the ways of God with men, and so reveal something further about the nature of God himself.[43]

Physike involves seeing the right order of things with an upright mind, an order which was written by the Word of God. If the second person of the Trinity was called *Logos* for being word, reason, rational, order, intelligible, and if through him all things were made, therefore creation is reasonable, rational, ordered, and can be spoken about intelligently. Medieval theologians used to speak of two books in which God had written his revelation: the book of nature, and the book of Scripture. Created things each possess their *logoi* (plural of Logos), and a heart that knows how to judge things correctly can see God behind the reason of things. Because Adam practiced *physike*, he could call the animals by their right names. But for us there is a requisite moral dimension to this contemplation of nature because it is accessible only to the pure of heart, who know how to draw knowledge about the attributes of God from creation.

Natural contemplation also concerns itself with the providence of God that makes up the fabric of this creation. Louis Bouyer describes the interlocked connection between visible and invisible creation in this way:

> The tradition of the Fathers has never admitted the existence of a material world apart from a larger creation, from a spiritual universe. To speak more precisely, for them the world, a whole and a unity, is inseparably matter and spirit.... Across this continuous

---

[41] Evagrius, *The Praktikos and Chapters on Prayer*, lxxxvii.
[42] Špidlík, *The Spirituality of the Christian East*, 336–67.
[43] Evagrius, *The Praktikos and Chapters on Prayer*, lxxxix.

chain of creation, in which the triune fellowship of the divine persons has, as it were, extended and propagated itself, moves the ebb and flow of the creating *Agape* and of the created *eucharistia*. Descending further and further towards the final limits of the abyss of nothingness, the creating love of God reveals its full power in the response it evokes, in the joy of gratitude in which, from the very dawn of their existence creatures freely return to him who has given them all. Thus this immense choir of which we have spoken, basing ourselves on the Fathers, finally seems like an infinitely generous heart, beating with an unceasing diastole and systole, first diffusing the divine glory in paternal love, then continually gathering it up again to its immutable source in filial love.[44]

Dionysius will be the one to influentially envision creation in the light of God's full economy, finding signs of God's providential goodness in the world offered for our contemplation. Dionysius's famous hierarchies are the golden chain that binds the Creator and creation together. Alexander Golitzin's study on the Areopagite explains the novelty of a "downward ecstasy." The Greeks were accustomed to saying that if the created mind encountered the divinity in darkness, it was no longer a creature *qua* creature, because to have any contact with the Creator, the creature must go outside of himself (*ekstasis*—the very definition of religious ecstasy). What was unthinkable is that God could go outside of himself!

If the creature may only encounter God as the latter is in his transcendence through "passing out" of its proper being, then conversely God may enter into relationship, including the act of creation, only through a kind of "self-transcendence." Moved to create . . . God "leaves" in a sense that state of being, or "super-being," proper to him. He goes "outside" his hidden essence. It is this divine "out-passing" that is the foundation or subject of the *Divine Names* and, in so far as they are the mirrors of God, of the Celestial and Ecclesiastical Hierarchies as well. God as he is known in his names and in his creation is God "outside," as it were, of his essence.[45]

---

[44] Louis Bouyer, *The Meaning of the Monastic Life* (London: Burns & Oates, 1955), 28–29.
[45] Golitzin, *Et Introibo Ad Altare Dei*, 48–49.

To the one who has clear sight, the order and beauty of creation will be read as images of God because they are God outside himself. God is beside himself with love. The energies of God are his version of our ecstasy, although the essence of God will forever be unknowable.[46] God exceeds himself in creation, and from the moment of God's first act of creation, the economy was under way that would lead to the moment when God would appear in the midst of his ecstatic product. Jesus is the reason for the hierarchies; creation and redemption cooperate.

Theologia

If *praktike* makes *theoria* possible, contemplation of the world is still not the ultimate goal. It is a marvel to see a mediated God in the thousand mirrors of a thousand creatures, but it is penultimate to the third and final stage, the one Evagrius calls *theologia*. George Berthold summarizes Maximus's view of theology by describing it as "direct communion with God in pure prayer, and 'to theologize' is to pray in spirit and in truth."[47] Maximus writes:

> The mind that has succeeded in the active life advances in prudence; the one in the contemplative life, in knowledge. For to the former it pertains to bring the one who struggles to a discernment of virtue and vice, while to the latter, to lead the sharer to the principles of incorporeal and corporeal things. Then at length it is deemed worthy of the grace of theology when on the wings of love it has passed beyond all the preceding realities, and being in God it will consider the essence of himself through the Spirit, insofar as it is possible to the human mind.[48]

Theologia is not just knowing; it is better understood as a kind of participation. Yves Congar writes a history of the use of the word "theology" that is enormously helpful in realizing that for Christians the word originally

---

[46] Eastern Christianity has regularly critiqued the Western idea of the beatific vision because, I've come to suspect, of a confusion in language games. For the East, beatific vision is a theological category and they refuse it because they say the essence of God will never be known by any creature—neither a human being in the grip of mysticism, nor the highest angel, nor the beatified human being in paradise. For the West, beatific vision is an anthropological and epistemological category, and refers to the transition from faith to sight, which is the perfection of man as an intelligent being.

[47] George Berthold's description, in Berthold, trans., *Selected Writings*, 92.

[48] Berthold, trans., *Selected Writings*, 50.

meant something considerably more than our words about our concept of God. For the Fathers, "theology" is the science of the true God, known through Christ, who reveals the Trinity. That is why Athanasius uses the term *theologia* to refer to the *sacra doctrina de Trinitate*, and Basil uses it to signify the divinity common to the three Persons, and Gregory Nazianzen simply names the persons of the Trinity "theologians," without further distinction.

> The word *theologia* takes on a special meaning with the monks and mystical writers. For them it means a knowledge of God which is either the highest form of the gnosis or of that illumination of the soul by the Holy Spirit which is more than an effect since it is the very substance of its divinization or godlike transformation. For Evagrius Pontikus, followed by Maximus Confessor and others, *theologia* is the third and the most elevated of the degrees of life. In short, it is that perfect knowledge of God which is identified with the summit of prayer.[49]

The one who reaches the summit of prayer is called a theologian not for having a reasoned understanding of the divine but for knowing God experientially.

To grasp this completely, it is important to return to the root understanding of *theoria*, contemplation. "For Clement of Alexandria, *gnosis* is 'that light which is kindled in the soul as the result of obedience to the commandments.'"[50] Add to this the Hebrew intuition for a kind of knowing that assumes an existential relationship ("Abraham knew Sarah"), and one can realize that one "knows" God only by entering into his covenant and attaining intimacy with him. In this tradition, theology is God's knowledge of himself placed in the human heart, which is why *theologia* is fundamentally knowledge of the Trinity. Alexander Schmemann has defined faith as Christ's memory realized in us through our memory of

---

[49] Yves Congar, *A History of Theology* (New York: Doubleday, 1968), 31. Congar goes on to note that the term has a different history in the West: "Among the Latin Fathers up to and including St. Augustine, the term *theologia* did not attain its own ecclesiastical meaning. Several Fathers apparently do not even know the term; ... Augustine, however, borrowing the term from the pagans, examined its etymological sense and stressed the fact that a *true* theology would lead them to Christianity. But this *true* theology for him is still only a philosophy. . . . Indeed, it seems we must wait for Abelard before the term *theologia* receives the meaning it has for us" (32). Thomas only uses the term three times in the *Summa*, usually preferring *sacra doctrina* or *haec doctrina*, which occur about eighty times.

[50] Špidlík, *The Spirituality of the Christian East*, 328, quoting Clement's *Stromata* 3.5.44.

Christ.[51] And a more recent and Western thinker, Columba Marmion, has defined faith as "a participation in the knowledge that God has of himself";[52] faith is "the light that reveals the Divine thoughts to us and makes us penetrate into God's designs";[53] "What in fact is faith? It is a mysterious participation in the knowledge that God has of Himself. God knows Himself as Father, Son, and Holy Spirit."[54] We ought to take care that when we do our theology, we do not forget the *Theou Logos*. Tomáš Špidlík urges us to find the splendor of words now shopworn after long use. "The ancient Christian East understood the practice of theology only as a personal communion with *Theos*, the Father, through the *Logos*, Christ, in the Holy Spirit—an experience lived in a state of prayer."[55] Theology is as much a practice as it is a cognition.

Faith is participatory knowledge. This participation in the circulation of love (*perichoresis*) that flows between Father, Son, and Holy Spirit is the apex of prayer which was sought by the ascetic. There is no true knowledge without love, which is why Evagrius says *praktike* attains to *apatheia*, and *apatheia* has a child called *agape* who keeps the door to deep knowledge. Sometimes a mischief-maker likes to suggest that Evagrius is more Greek and philosophical because he places *gnosis* at the summit, while Maximus is more Christian and biblical because he places *agape* at the summit, but Jeremy Driscoll thinks this overlooks how knowledge and love intertwine. Posing the question as "love or knowledge" is to pose the question in the wrong way. It is not a question of one or the other for Evagrius because the two are dynamically united, explains Driscoll. "Knowledge of God is knowledge of a God who is love. And love is not merely a passageway; it must remain a permanent part of one who has entered into knowledge.... Love remains a permanent part of knowledge for a necessary reason: because knowledge means knowledge of a God who is love."[56] One realizes again why the path to *gnosis* must lead through a

---

[51] Alexander Schmemann, *The Eucharist: Sacrament of the Kingdom*, trans. Paul Kachur (Crestwood, NY: St. Vladimir's Seminary Press, 1987), 128.

[52] Columba Marmion, *Christ in His Mysteries* (St. Louis, MO: B. Herder Book Co., 1931), 180. For a summary of Marmion's thought, see David Fagerberg, "*Theosis* in a Roman Key: The Conferences of Columba Marmion," *Antiphon* 7, no. 1 (2002): 30–39.

[53] Columba Marmion, *Christ, the Ideal of the Monk* (St. Louis, MO: B. Herder Book Co., 1922), 291–92.

[54] Marmion, *Christ in His Mysteries*, 237.

[55] Špidlík, *The Spirituality of the Christian East*, 1.

[56] Driscoll, *The "Ad Monachos" of Evagrius Ponticus*, 168.

pass surrounded by the high walls of *praktike* where our capacity for love is ordered (*ordo amoris*).

To attain knowledge of God (to learn about God) is not the same as to possess the knowledge *of* God (the knowledge God has). By *physike* we know something about the Creator, but there is an invitation to take one more step up and to share the knowledge of Christ:

> Evagrius distinguishes between an heir of Christ and a coheir of Christ. He says, "The 'heir' of Christ is the one who knows the reasons for all created things subsequent to the first judgment." Then he says, "The 'coheir of Christ' is the one who arrives in the Unity and who enjoys contemplation with Christ." Thus, a coheir of Christ is someone who enjoys the same contemplation, the same knowledge of the Unity, as Christ. But one must first receive the lesser knowledge of created things. This is being an heir. . . . Being separated from this knowledge is what characterizes the present human condition, and it is re-acquiring this knowledge which constitutes salvation.[57]

We are speaking here of deification (*theosis*): participation in the life of God, which is *agape*.

Bamberger distinguishes *physike* from *theologia* on several fronts: the former remains in the state of multiplicity, while the latter attains complete simplicity of thought; the former is marked by effort and struggle and sometimes a degree of frustration, while the latter is marked by great peace and calm and tranquility of possession; the former does not imply unusual mystical graces, while the latter is dependent upon an elevated contemplation by the Spirit and requires complete nudity of the intellect. "This kind of penetration into the Divinity is an exalted state and as such is beyond the mere capacity of man. Man can only pray for it and humbly and gratefully receive it as a gift. . . . In this mysticism at its highest point it is the Blessed Trinity that is the object of vision. . . . Pure prayer brings the soul to a glorious experience of interior light."[58] This is the summit of prayer. It is already participating in eternal life on earth. It is the life which Christ came to give to his kin, the deified sons and daughters of God, and it is the life that awaits them at the end of the stony path of ascetically exorcising from their hearts anything that would hinder this

---

[57] Driscoll, *The "Ad Monachos" of Evagrius Ponticus*, 76.
[58] Evagrius, *The Praktikos and Chapters on Prayer*, xc-xci.

circulation of love. In the final step of *The Ladder of Divine Ascent* John Climacus writes, "It is risky to swim in one's clothes. A slave of passion should not dabble in theology."[59]

The path to prayer is memory repair: *anthropos* was created to remember God (*mnesis*), but has forgotten (*amnesia*), so men and women must be re-capacitated if they are to make *anamnesis*. This ascetical path does not simply improve our faith, hope, and love. At the summit the faith the Son has in the Father is made ours, the hope the Son has in the Father is made ours, the love the Son has for the Father is made ours, all by Holy Spirit. Prayer is the Trinity's *perichoresis* kenotically extended to invite our ascension. Thus does prayer appear in various definitions in Evagrius's *Chapters on Prayer*:

3. Prayer is a continual intercourse of the spirit with God.
35. Prayer is an ascent to the spirit of God.
52. The state of prayer can be aptly described as a habitual state of imperturbable calm [*apatheia*]. It snatches to the heights of intelligible reality the spirit which loves wisdom and which is truly spiritualized by the most intense love.
60. If you are a theologian you truly pray. If you truly pray you are a theologian.

Paul Evdokimov describes the kingdom of God in this way: "It is in the offering of the heart to God that the Spirit manifests itself and introduces the human being into the eternal circulation of love between the Father and the Son, and this is the 'Kingdom.'"[60] The person of prayer lives in this circulation of love; even more, the person of prayer becomes this love. Ask any Desert Father how to reach prayer and you would be directed to a methodical *scopus*, but they would never lose sight of the *telos*. "Abba Lot went to see Abba Joseph and said: 'Abba, as far as I can, I keep a moderate rule, with a little fasting, and prayer, and meditation, and quiet: and as far as I can I try to cleanse my heart of evil thoughts. What else should I do?' Then the old man rose, and spread out his hands to heaven, and his fingers shone like ten candles: and he said: 'If you will, you could become a living flame.'"[61]

---

[59] John Climacus, *The Ladder of Divine Ascent*, 262.
[60] Paul Evdokimov, "Saint Seraphim of Sarov," *The Ecumenical Review* 15, no. 3 (April 1963): 273.
[61] Chadwick, *Western Asceticism*, 142.

Beauty and Asceticism
The Beauty of God as Ground for Obedience in the Ascetical-Contemplative Tradition[*]

I am probably violating the rules of rhetoric by putting my conclusion at the beginning of my paper. Rhetoric would urge a writer to bring his readers through the maze first, give them a tour of the issues, and set up questions before revealing his prepared answer. I am probably also violating the rules of the academy by expressing my conclusion with a scene from a book of children's fantasy. The academy would urge a writer to dissect the matter into fine points, complex of five questions so that he appears to be doing serious work, and then lead his readers through a labyrinth of grandiloquent authors to support himself. Instead, I am going to begin with my conclusion, and I am going to take it from the fictional Chronicles of Narnia by C. S. Lewis.

In *The Horse and His Boy*, Lewis describes the several encounters that two children and two horses have with lions during their attempted escape from captivity to the freedom of Narnia. At the end, it turns out there has been only one lion, who has been taking various shapes. It is Aslan, King of Narnia, Son of the Emperor beyond the Sea. When Aslan finally reveals himself, he appears "bigger and more beautiful and more alarming than any lion they had ever seen." He approaches silently, and after startling one of the horses who thought him only a myth, there was a moment of intense silence. Then the mare named Hwin, "though shaking all over, gave a strange little neigh, and trotted across to the Lion. 'Please,' she said, 'you're so beautiful. You may eat me if you like. I'd sooner be eaten by you than fed by anyone else.'"[1] You're so beautiful, she says. And what was her reaction to his beauty? *Latria*, obedience, compliance, submission, sacrifice, loyalty, allegiance.

There are three words in the title of this third journal volume, and one of them does not seem like the other two. "Law" and "legalism" belong together, but including the word "delight" with them seems out of place.

---

[*] David W. Fagerberg, "The Beauty of God as Ground for Obedience in the Ascetical-Contemplative Tradition," *Sacrum Testamentum* 3 (forthcoming 2023).
[1] C. S. Lewis, *The Horse and His Boy* (New York: HarperCollins, 2001), 299.

It seems like serving a piece of cake on a plate of broccoli and cabbage. What right does delight have to associate with matters of law, to mingle with jurisprudence, to enter the land of Torah? The answer we are proposing in this article is beauty. God is so beautiful that obedience becomes our heartfelt desire when we see him. God is so beautiful that conversion happens, and the current of desire is reversed within us. Instead of eating from creation, we would sooner be eaten by the Creator; instead of desiring God only for the benefits he can give to us, we would sooner obey God out of a desire to please and glorify him; instead of avoiding God, we would sooner draw closer to God by following that path to proximity that was paved by the law. Augustine defined sacrifice as "every action done so as to cling to God in communion of holiness, and thus achieve blessedness."[2] This is precisely what the law wants for us, namely, communion, holiness, blessedness. This is precisely what the law is designed to accomplish in us, and what it will achieve for us if we will only give ourselves over to God. This surrender to God—its practice and its purpose—is asceticism that equips for contemplation. Hwin has identified the ground of asceticism, and it turns out to be a combination of law and ecstasy (as strange a juxtaposition as legalism and the delight of the law).

Instead of amassing temporal goods, we would sooner sell them all and buy the field with the pearl of great value in it, which is what the monastic ascetics do exteriorly and what secular ascetics do interiorly. All Christians are commanded by the law to be ascetics; the monk does not do a different thing, he only does the thing differently. Therefore Paul Evdokimov calls the asceticism practiced by laypeople in the world *interiorized monasticism*. "Monasticism will surely keep its unique testimony to the end of the world. However, the baptized world is sufficiently Christian to hear the monastic message and to assimilate it in its own way.... The testimony of the Christian faith in the framework of the modern world necessitates the universal vocation of interiorized monasticism."[3] Asceticism was perfected in the sands of the desert, but it was born in the waters of the baptismal font. This ascetical life is sacrificial: clinging to God, offering ourselves to be eaten by God, recovering our identity as cosmic priests, finding delight in the Torah. That is why Evdokimov observes how near priesthood and asceticism are to each other. "Offering the totality of one's life, serving the Lord in every deed and word, in other words, referring the entire content

---

[2] Augustine, *The City of God* 10.6.
[3] Paul Evdokimov, *Ages of the Spiritual Life* (Crestwood, NY: St. Vladimir's Seminary Press, 1998), 135.

of one's life to God—we see how closely the royal priesthood in its pure form approximates the monastic state."[4]

Alexander Schmemann also finds connection between asceticism and humanity's cosmic priesthood. He says the difference between the state of original justice and original sin can be understood as the difference between living as a priest or living as a consumer. "The first consumer was Adam himself. He chose not to be priest but to approach the world as consumer: to 'eat' of it, to use and to dominate it for himself, to benefit from it but not to offer, not to sacrifice, not to have it for God and in God."[5] We have abandoned our post as priest, and the Fall is the forfeiture of our liturgical career. Original Sin is the loss of our desire to be priest and the failure to give God the highest good we possess, namely ourselves. We have inverted our appetites and would now rather eat the world than be consumed by the divine. Thus Schmemann concludes:

> In the mythology of creation, man is created a hungry being; that is why God made the world as his food. Man is dependent.... The priest is first and foremost the sacrificer.... And so he is the man who can freely transform that dependence: he is the man who can say *thank you*. For the moment when the slave whom God has created can thank Him for his life and for his food, he is liberated; sacrifice, the thank-offering is liberating. I've always understood the fall (or what is called "Original Sin") as the loss of man's desire to be a priest; or perhaps you might say the desire he has *not* to be a priest but a consumer.[6]

Asceticism simply consists of getting our appetites right. "Control your appetites before they control you," counsels John Climacus.[7] When we do, then we can live in the world right side up instead of in our current upside-down posture. Asceticism simply consists of restoring our sense of taste, and when we do, we will taste grace under every nature, the

---

[4] Paul Evdokimov, *Woman and the Salvation of the World* (Crestwood, NY: St. Vladimir's Seminary Press, 1994), 106.

[5] Alexander Schmemann, *Of Water and the Spirit: A Liturgical Study of Baptism* (Crestwood, NY: St. Vladimir's Seminary Press, 1974), 96

[6] Alexander Schmemann, "Sacrifice and Worship," in *Liturgy and Tradition: Theological Reflections of Alexander Schmemann*, ed. Thomas Fisch (Crestwood, NY: St. Vladimir's Seminary Press, 1990), 132.

[7] John Climacus, *The Ladder of Divine Ascent*, trans. Colm Luibheild and Norman Russell (Mahwah, NJ: Paulist Press, 1982), 167.

supernatural sweetness infused in every natural good. This is what the law is designed to do for us. The beauty of God is the ground for our obedience. The Torah becomes a delight because we see how beautiful is the One who gave it to us, as well as the beatitude he intends for us by it.

This truth was not lost on either the ascetics in the East or scholastics in the West. We will look at both, and turn our eyes eastward first.

In the eighteenth century two Greek Orthodox scholars, named Nicodemus of the Holy Mountain and Macarius of Corinth, compiled a collection of writings they found in the libraries of monasteries on Mount Athos. They selected from among texts composed between the fourth and fifteenth centuries and written for the guidance and instruction of monks living the contemplative life. They titled their collection *The Philokalia*. Even rudimentary Greek recognizes the first half of the word: *philia* is one of the Greek words for love, alongside *eros* and *agape*. The second half of the word may be less familiar. *Kallos* basically means beauty, so they were calling this collection *The Love of Beauty*, yet these five volumes take an approach that modern sensibilities would not expect. This is no lyrical vision about idyllic nature, no pop psychology about loving your interior beauty, no philosophical discourse about beauty in art, nature, and the human form. Instead the tone of *The Philokalia* can be gotten from the first sentence of the first book of the first volume, which reads, "There is among the passions an anger of the intellect, and this anger is in accordance with nature. Without anger a man cannot attain purity: he has to feel angry with all that is sown in him by the enemy."[8] These volumes will deal with the devil and the passions, with asceticism and purity, with the virtues that derive from obedience to the commandments of God and the vices that derive from *philautia* (self-love).

Obeying the commandments is a theme sounded repeatedly by authors in *The Philokalia*. Theodoros the Great Ascetic says that "since by God's grace we have renounced Satan and his works, and have sworn allegiance to Christ, both at our baptism and now again through our profession as monks, let us keep His commandments."[9] Peter of Damascus urges us to hate the passions and "show our love for Christ through the keeping of His commandments. And how shall we keep His commandments unless we relinquish our own will and thought—the will and thought, that is to

---

[8] St. Isaiah the Solitary, *Unguarded Intellect*, in *The Philokalia*, ed. G. E. H. Palmer, Philip Sherrard, and Kallistos Ware (London: Faber and Faber, 1979), 1:23.
[9] Theodoros the Great Ascetic, *A Century of Spiritual Texts*, in *The Philokalia*, ed. G. E. H. Palmer, Philip Sherrard, and Kallistos Ware (London: Faber and Faber, 1981), 2:14.

say, which are opposed to the commandments of God?"[10] The obedience we vowed at baptism has similarities to a nuptial vow, says Simeon the New Theologian. "It is as if the contract were written through the practice of the commandments and then signed and sealed by the virtues. Only then does Christ, the bridegroom, give His ring—the pledge of the Holy Spirit—to the soul that is his bride-to-be."[11] The angel given to a person in divine baptism is "to guard the soul of every believer," according to Peter of Damascus, and "to act as his conscience and to remind him of the divine commandments of Christ. If the baptized person keeps these commandments, the grace of the Holy Spirit is preserved in him."[12]

We can see, then, that this is not an ordinary book on ordinary beauty. It is a spiritual book on spiritual beauty, attained by spiritual obedience to the spiritual law. Mark the Ascetic offers two hundred texts on the spiritual law; Hesychios the priest speaks of watchfulness and holiness; John Cassian writes about eight vices; and Maximus the Confessor, who takes up the most space in the five volumes, begins by saying, "Dispassion engenders love, hope in God engenders dispassion, and patience and forbearance engender hope in God; these are the product of complete self-control, which itself springs from fear of God. Fear of God is the result of faith in God."[13] We are startled that Macarius and Nicodemus call their five volumes concerning fasting, vigils, self-discipline, constant prayer, and internal struggle, "a love of *kallos*," so perhaps that Greek word has a thicker meaning than our simplistic understanding of beauty.

A Greek concordance reveals additional dimensions of the word. *Kallos* can be defined as beautiful to look at, yes, but it also means shapely and magnificent; good and excellent in nature; morally good; well-adapted to its ends; pure, praiseworthy, and honorable; noble, valuable, and virtuous. *Philo-kalia* is a love of these goods, these goods are beautiful, it is a love of these beautiful goods. We can sense the mixture of "good" and "beauty" by sampling some verses of Scripture where *kallos* appears. Which word would you use to translate the following? Matthew 3:10: "that [which] does not bear *kalon* fruit is cut down." Matthew 5:16: "that they may see your *kala* works and give glory to your Father." Mark 9:5: "Master,

---

[10] Peter of Damascus, *A Treasury of Divine Knowledge*, in *The Philokalia*, ed. G. E. H. Palmer, Philip Sherrard, and Kallistos Ware (London: Faber and Faber, 1986), 3:82.

[11] Symeon the New Theologian, *Practical and Theological Texts*, in *The Philokalia*, ed. G. E. H. Palmer, Philip Sherrard, and Kallistos Ware (London: Faber and Faber, 1999), 4:4.

[12] Peter of Damascus, *A Treasury of Divine Knowledge*, in *The Philokalia*, 3:76.

[13] Maximus the Confessor, *400 Texts on Love: First Century*, in *The Philokalia*, ed. G. E. H. Palmer, Philip Sherrard, and Kallistos Ware (Boston: Faber and Faber, 1981), 2:53.

it is *kalon* that we are here." John 10:11: "I am the *kalos* shepherd." Beauty, goodness, morality, nobility, honor, and virtue are reflected in each other, and asceticism is the crucible where they can be compounded. Why would that be? Perhaps a more favorable definition of asceticism is required.

Understanding the word poses a challenge to modern ears. Asceticism conjures up pictures of a bad-tempered Puritan, or holier-than-thou arrogance, or overzealous piety that cripples one from enjoying even innocent pleasures. We do not speak wistfully and wantingly of becoming an ascetic. But we can understand the word better if we look at its root. *Askein* has to do with training, or discipline, and was first used especially of athletes, who disciplined their bodies, and later of philosophers, who disciplined their mind and character. Asceticism involves self-denial, but not for reasons of masochism. Rather, the discipline of one's appetites, one's regimen, one's body, even one's mind is in order to attain a certain end. It is a relevant question to ask what end the asceticism is targeting. The athletic ascetic trains in order to play the game better, the moral ascetic trains in order to live the good life, the stoical ascetic trains in order to be unaffected by pain or pleasure. But such examples only raise the question as to why the Christian ascetic trains. Toward what end? The answer is holiness. Deification. Sin is a sickness unto death, and Christian *askesis* is in the service of overcoming sickness, preventing death, and restoring life. *Askesis* refreshes the *imago Dei*, according to Olivier Clément. "Ascesis then is an awakening from the sleep-walking of daily life. It enables the Word to clear the silt away in the depth of the soul, freeing the spring of living waters. The Word can restore to its original brightness the tarnished image of God in us, the silver coin that has rolled in the dust but remains stamped with the king's likeness (Luke 15:8–10). It is the Word who acts, but we have to co-operate with him, not so much by exertion of will-power as by loving attentiveness."[14]

Askesis appears negative when we restrict our attention to the initial steps, when our clenched hands are being pried open. That's the part of the therapy that hurts. The death of the Old Adam is usually a strenuous process, after all. But ultimately *askesis* liberates—like a statue is liberated from the stone, like a butterfly is liberated from the cocoon, like an eagle is liberated from the eggshell. Resurrection is flight, but first comes the ascetical task of pecking through the shell. When the commandments are first obeyed, they seem restrictive, like memorizing the alphabet and

---

[14] Olivier Clément, *The Roots of Christian Mysticism*, trans. Theodore Berkeley, O.C.S.O., and Jeremy Hummerstone (New York: New City Press, 1996), 130–31.

rules of grammar seem limitative, but the commandments actually lead to freedom and more freedom.

Asceticism is both liturgical and personal. We cannot progress without the sacramental power bestowed in liturgy, but the liturgy cannot produce this ascetical beauty without our permission and cooperative work. Of what that work exactly consists was studied by the first monks in the desert, which is why Makarios and Nicodemus turned to them, as Christians have ever since. The Desert Fathers observed the human heart in order to see what was required for conforming it to Christ, the Beautiful One. The lessons they learned spread from the deserts of Egypt and Palestine into both the East and West, a point vividly summarized by Aidan Kavanagh when he says that Evagrius "stands at the fountainhead of Christian commentary on the ascetical life for . . . Moscow and Constantinople as well as for Monte Cassino and Rome."[15] In his opinion and experience, "Ascetics blaze the trail all must follow, but they do not walk it alone."[16] And, "This is a life expected of every one of the baptized, whose ultimate end is the same supreme beatitude. It is a life all the baptized share, a life within which the professed ascetic is nothing more or less than a virtuoso who serves the whole community as an exemplar of its own life. The ascetic is simply a stunningly normal person who stands in constant witness to the normality of Christian *orthodoxia* in a world flawed into abnormality by human choice."[17]

The volumes of *The Philokalia* are about beauty, but they discuss asceticism. We might call it an *ascetic aesthetic*! And Thomas Aquinas can help us understand that paradox (and attempted linguistic pun) so let us now turn westward.

Chesterton provides us with an anecdote that can start us off. It comes from his days at the Slade School of Fine Art where he met people who wanted to be avant-garde by pushing the boundaries of both aesthetics and morality. Chesterton thinks they mistook unorthodoxy for courageousness. Chesterton records a conversation with one such person, a conversation that turned out to be his own escape hatch from nihilism. Chesterton began the discussion: "I hate modern doubt because it is dangerous." His interlocutor, whom Chesterton simply calls "the Diabolist," rejoined: "You

---

[15] Aidan Kavanagh, "Eastern Influences on the Rule of Saint Benedict," in *Monasticism and the Arts*, ed. Timothy Verdon (Syracuse, NY: Syracuse University Press, 1984), 57.
[16] Kavanagh, "Eastern Influences," 57.
[17] Aidan Kavanagh, *On Liturgical Theology* (Collegeville, MN: Pueblo, 1984), 161.

mean dangerous to morality. I expect you are right. But why do you care about morality?" And Chesterton gave his now-famous answer:

> "That is all that I ask you to admit," said I. "Give me those few red specks and I will deduce Christian morality. Once I thought like you, that one's pleasure in a flying spark was a thing that could come and go with that spark. Once I thought that the delight was as free as the fire. Once I thought that red star we see was alone in space. But now I know that *the red star is only on the apex of an invisible pyramid of virtues. That red fire is only the flower on a stalk of living habits*, which you cannot see.... That flame flowered out of virtues, and it will fade with virtues. Seduce a woman, and that spark will be less bright. Shed blood, and that spark will be less red."[18]

Here is the application I want to make. *Beauty* is the apex of an invisible pyramid of virtues. Beauty is at the summit of obedience. Beauty is grounded in obedience to natural and divine law. Beauty is a flower on a stock of living habits, habits which cannot be seen but which are necessary for beauty to exist. Beauty is not as free as the fire; it comes from obedience to limits laid down by God. And beauty can be more permanent than the flying spark of pleasure, soon to extinguish. Something is beautiful when it is true and good: untruth can never be beautiful, and wickedness can never be beautiful. And the thinker to help us reconnect truth, beauty, and goodness is Thomas Aquinas.

This triad, he says, corresponds to a triad of human activities. We *know* truth, we *love* the good, and we *delight* in beauty. These transcendentals yield knowledge, morality, and art. Beauty is connected to reality as much as—and in the same way, and for the same reason—that truth and goodness are connected to reality. Such an assertion is met with skepticism these days, I know. One has trouble arguing that there is a real truth, because that denies me my own private truth; one has trouble arguing there is a morality rooted in truth, because that denies me my subjective moral judgment; and most troublesome of all, one has trouble arguing that there is a real beauty, which denies that beauty is in the eye of the beholder. We prefer our subjective anarchy over objective orders of truth. (By "orders" in that sentence I mean both "commands" and "structures.")

---

[18] G. K. Chesterton, *Tremendous Trifles* (New York: Dodd, Mead and Company, 1909), chap. 34, https://www.gutenberg.org/ebooks/8092, italics added.

But, as usual, Thomas thinks his way through the puzzle and provides some help in understanding the relationship of objectivity and subjectivity. Here is a rough and ready way to distinguish them: ask whether something is beautiful because it gives pleasure, or whether something gives pleasure because it is beautiful. The former is a subjective conclusion, and the latter an objective one. The thought is not original to me, or Thomas; the question comes from Augustine. Our day tends toward the subjectivist pole and concludes that something is beautiful because it gives me pleasure (beauty is in the eye of the beholder). The ancient and medieval eras tended toward the objectivist pole and concluded that something gives pleasure because it is beautiful (beauty has objective traits independent of our perspective and opinion).

There seems to be an element of truth in both. Let us first offer some support for the objectivists, the realists. The point can be made by asking the same question of the other two terms in the triad of transcendentals. Is something *good* because it is desired, or is it desired because it is good? And is something *true* because it gives knowledge, or does it give knowledge because it is true? Doing so gives some additional force to the objectivist's position. Since childhood we have been learning that just because we want something does not make it good, and that some things we think are true turn out to be false. Conclusion: If something might be bad even if we mistake it for good, and something might be false even if we mistake it for truth, then might not something be ugly even if our underdeveloped taste mistakes it for beautiful? Beauty dwells in the heart of things, in the heart of reality—the same reality that is desired by our willing and targeted by our knowing.

After this defense of realism, it might come as a surprise to hear Thomas Aquinas's definition of beauty: things are called beautiful because they "please upon being seen."[19] He defines beauty as *Id quod visum placet*— that which gives pleasure on sight. Did Thomas think beauty is in the eye of the beholder, as the subjectivists say? In a certain sense he did, but not in the way they mean it. Most philosophers up to that point (even including his own teacher, Albert the Great) thought of beauty primarily as a perfection belonging to being. They distinguished three constituents of beauty, namely *proportion*, *integrity*, and a kind of brightness they called *claritas*, which is hard to translate. It means more than just being "lit up." *Claritas* is the communicability of the essence of the thing; it is a kind of

---

[19] Thomas Aquinas, *Summa Theologica*, trans. Fathers of the English Dominican Province (Westminster, MD: Christian Classics, 1981), I, q. 5, a. 4, obj. 1, resp.

splendor; it is a brightness that shines forth. The philosophers had defined beauty as something possessing proportion, integrity, and *claritas*, and Thomas agreed with this tradition, but being the great synthesizer that he was, he went on to consider not only the objective qualities of beauty but also our experience of beauty. New attention was being paid to the perceiver, which was a rather fresh step.

Is beauty in the eye of the beholder? Yes. Beauty is that which pleases upon being seen. But the eye must be clear. For the eye to perceive proportion, integrity, and *claritas*, it must be healthy. Only then is there a "matching up" of knowing, loving, and delighting with truth, goodness, and beauty. A pleasure can be found in all three: *truth* is pleasing to our intellect, *goodness* is attractive to our desire, and *beauty* is delightful to our perception. The truth, goodness, and beauty of reality are there to be seen, but only if the eye of the beholder is healthy, clear, unclouded, chaste, pure.

And now there is an additional fact. Not only can a human being see beauty if his eye is healthy; the human being can become beautiful if his life is healthy, clear, unclouded, chaste, pure. The beauty of a life also stands as the apex of an invisible pyramid of virtues. A beautiful life is also the flower on a stalk of living habits. A beautiful life is ascetically attained. A beautiful life is an ascetical accomplishment. Beauty is dependent upon obedience to God's law. All this returns us to Hwin's preference for being eaten by Aslan instead of being fed by anyone else. Aslan's beauty is the ground for our obedience to his laws. Beauty is the perfection resulting from the fusion of proportion, integrity, and *claritas*, and it is congruent with a perfection of obedience that is actually a perfection of love. Karl Rahner defines Christian perfection as consisting "simply and solely in the perfection of the love which is given us in Christ by the Spirit of God."[20] Is such perfection possible? Yes, he answers; that is why God has called us to this beatitude. However, we presently stand on the far side of a canyon caused by the earthquake of original sin that split paradise, and for us to cross over that gorge a perfect love will have to be laid down as a bridge for us to walk over. It has been. It is the Cross. Every baptized Christian spends his or her life walking across the lowered drawbridge of the Cross toward eschatological glory. This involves a renunciation, says Rahner, an obedience that is radical. This obedience is demanded of

---

[20] Karl Rahner, "Reflections on the Theology of Renunciation," in *Theological Investigations*, vol. 3, *The Theology of the Spiritual Life* (New York: Crossroad, 1982), 47.

both the Christian in the world and the Christian who has left the world, although they do it differently.

One day someone asked Jesus, "Teacher, what good deed must I do, to have eternal life?" and Jesus replied, "If you would enter life, keep the commandments." When the man asked which ones he meant, Jesus summarized the law from Sinai. These commandments are the ones he should keep. The young man protested that he had done so, and still felt he was lacking something. So Jesus told him, "If you would be perfect, go, sell what you possess and give to the poor, and you will have treasure in heaven; and come, follow me" (see Matt 19:16–21). That is the very gospel that Anthony of Egypt heard being read one day in church, so he did what the words of Jesus told him to do and became the "first monk." Poverty is one of the evangelical counsels, along with chastity and obedience.

This situation sets up a series of questions. *Must all Christians obey the counsels?* No, says Rahner: "There is a Christian perfection in this world distinct from the practice of the Evangelical Counsels of poverty, celibacy, obedience. The Christian in the world does not have the 'spirit' of the Evangelical Counsels, and moreover should not have it."[21] *But does this let us off the hook?* No, says Rahner: they are describing renunciations expected of every Christian. Renunciation means that one sacrifices a lower good for a higher good, and we do it all the time in the realm of nature. We renounce that second piece of pie for the higher good of fitness; we renounce that night of television to take our children to the park. But the peculiarity of Christian renunciation is that the higher good for which we renounce the world is a good that cannot be experienced yet. We renounce even the highest natural goods for a supernatural good, and, for now, this supernatural good can only be known by faith and in hope. *Must everyone make such a renunciation?* Yes, eventually, says Rahner: "In death, man is really asked in the most fundamental manner whether he will allow himself to be disposed beyond himself into what is hidden, and thereby renounce himself."[22] The Church is a visible sign of the eschatological presence of God's salvation, and she is called to manifest this eschatological love visibly. Therefore every Christian, including those in the world, will make this renunciation apparent eventually, and in the meantime,

---

[21] Rahner, "Reflections on the Theology of Renunciation," 50.
[22] Rahner, "Reflections on the Theology of Renunciation," 54.

every day since our baptism, we are commanded to practice dying. Every day includes an obedient death to self-love, and self-will, and self-esteem.

The beauty of God is the ground for our obedience, and the Church must cause to appear what she lives interiorly. The evangelical counsels of poverty, chastity, and obedience are the law expressed in its most strenuous form, and Francis de Sales recognizes that "the counsels are all given for the perfection of the Christian people, but not for that of each Christian in particular."[23] And yet everyone is obliged to love them because they are all very good. "Will you throw a ring into the dirt because it fits not your finger? We shall sufficiently testify our love for all the counsels, when we devoutly observe such as are suitable to our calling."[24] In the *Catechism of the Catholic Church* these three counsels are defined in ways that can be lived even by Christians not in religious orders. Every Christian should live with poverty ("In the Beatitudes 'poverty' is the virtue of sharing: it calls us to communicate and share both material and spiritual goods, not by coercion but out of love, so that the abundance of some may remedy the needs of others"[25]), chastity ("Chastity means the successful integration of sexuality within the person and thus the inner unity of man in his bodily and spiritual being"[26]), and obedience ("The duty of obedience requires all to give due honor to authority and to treat those who are charged to exercise it with respect, and, insofar as it is deserved, with gratitude and good-will"[27]). Obedience to the fullness of the law is required for beauty. Prudence does not enter by deciding which laws to obey, it enters by deciding how to obey the law in our particular form of life. Therefore the *Catechism* judges that "Christ proposes the evangelical counsels, in their great variety, to every disciple."[28]

The Church obeys her Lord's command when she puts love on display. She does so in hidden sacramental signs, she does so in the construction of virtuous lives, she does so in the visible manifestation of religious orders. The presence of the Church in a sacramental, ascetical, and vowed life is a beautiful thing to behold, according to St. Ambrose. When he reads the Song of Songs, he hears the bridegroom speaking to one newly baptized. "Christ, beholding His Church . . . seeing, that is, a soul pure and washed in the laver of regeneration, says: 'Behold, you are beautiful, My

---

[23] Francis de Sales, *Treatise on the Love of God* (Blacksburg, VA: Wilder Publications, 2011), 272.
[24] De Sales, *Treatise on the Love of God*, 278.
[25] *Catechism of the Catholic Church*, §2833.
[26] *CCC*, §2337.
[27] *CCC*, §1900.
[28] *CCC*, §915.

love, behold you are fair, your eyes are like a dove's."[29] The baptized are beautiful for having the Holy Spirit now living in them, looking out from their eyes, so to speak; they are beautiful for being transparent to the light of the indwelling Spirit. Therefore, Ambrose concludes, "the Church is beautiful in them."[30] If Thomas is correct, and things are beautiful because they please upon being seen, then we can think of a saint as a beautiful person who pleases upon being seen. He pleases God when he sees them, he pleases other people when they see them. This "witness by beauty" that arises from conversion and obedience is the *martyria* (witness) commanded by baptism and constructed across a life of asceticism. Our beauty comes from participating in the liturgical mysteries. The Mystical Body glorifies the Father in the light of the Holy Spirit that shines forth from Christ upon his disciples. The Transfiguration atop Mount Tabor continues. But, as we have been saying, this requires the obedience that kills the Old Adam so that the New Adam, Christ, can reside within us. Our personhood is wounded, which is why our humanity must be healed and find its completion in recovery of goodness. Then beauty will be revealed.

Plato defined beauty as the splendor of truth, from *splendere*, which means "to shine." When truth shines, there is beauty. Beauty is truth splendoring. The brilliance of truth and goodness is beautiful when it comes up to our admiring gaze from the depths of reality. God makes statements of truth: they are two statements about what makes for righteousness and upright lives. He makes statements of moral truth in the form of commandments because he is not giving a theoretical definition to admire, he is instead giving an injunctive invitation to enter into the moral truth and become beautiful. To accomplish this, he had to bring the human race further than commandments alone can bring them. The beauty that will inspire our obedience must become personal—must become personal to us, and must come from a person. Paul Evdokimov says the sort of splendor Plato is talking about "does not exist in the abstract. In its fullness, truth requires a personalization and seeks to be enhypostazied, that is, rooted and grounded in a person."[31] Truth will be fully splendored only when it is manifested at the highest created level, which is personhood. Jesus is the beautiful one whom we obey. And when we are conformed to him (deified), then the highest truth, the fullest beauty, the greatest good will begin to shine also from us as an *imago Dei*. Our obedience will make us

---

[29] Song 1:15.
[30] Ambrose, *On the Mysteries*, 7:37.
[31] Paul Evdokimov, *The Art of the Icon: A Theology of Beauty* (Redondo Beach, CA: Oakwood Publications, 1990), 24.

an icon of the icon of the Father. Something is called good, says Thomas, when it has the perfection proper to it. Sharp vision is the good of the eye, cutting easily is the good of the knife, but what is a good person? What is the perfection proper to a human being? It is deification. The perfection proper to a human being is to be deified by growing from the image of God into the likeness of God. This growth in goodness requires an ascetical process in which the personalized truth (Jesus) results in a true person (a saint). Ascetic aesthetics is the splendor of truth in a person who obeys God's designs.

If liturgy means sharing the life of Christ (being washed in his Resurrection, eating his body), and if *askesis* means discipline (in the sense of forming), then liturgical asceticism is the discipline required to become an icon of Christ and make his image visible in our faces.[32] The twin purposes of liturgy are the sanctification of man and the glorification of God, and the latter happens when the former happens. When God sanctifies us, he receives glory. We are drawn toward God—even to the point of letting him eat us!—when we love *kallos*, when we love beauty and goodness. We are drawn toward God's commandments because they expose God's glory, and his glory pleases upon being seen (if our eyes are healthy and our souls are whole). Liturgy is beautiful because it tells the world the eschatological truth about itself, i.e., how it should be done, for what reason it exists, what is a perfect human being. The beautiful goodness of an obedient, ascetical life tells the truth. It shines. It splendors. It glorifies God. Then the Church glistens, and the cosmos sparkles with sacramental potential, and man and woman become anointed priests and crowned royalty. And such beauty is worth the sacrifice of obedience, which brings us back to Hwin.

There is only one God whom we must obey. We might give many other objects or persons a sort of allegiance and reverence, but only the one, true God receives our worship. The Greeks made this clear by distinguishing two words: *latria* and *dulia*. Distinguished personages can receive *dulia* (the archangel Gabriel, clerics, or monks), and even places (the grotto on my campus at the University of Notre Dame), but God, and only God, because he is God, gets *latria*. When analyzing this fact, Paul Holmer concludes that whether we give *latria* or *dulia* to something does not therefore depend upon how we feel about the thing; it depends upon the objectivity involved. "Dulia does not differ from latria by degree

---

[32] David W. Fagerberg, *On Liturgical Asceticism* (Washington, D.C.: The Catholic University of America Press, 2013), 12.

but in kind. The difference is determined by the objectivities involved, by one being a creature, though a mighty emperor, the other being God. The object, not the subject, calls forth the proper kind of worship."[33] If Hwin had approached in some other way, with some other attitude, it would have meant that she mistook Aslan for an ordinary lion. In fact, it is Aslan, not Hwin, who determines what should be her proper behavior. If I am not to commit idolatry, I must give God *latria*. For, Holmer says, "It is only for a God like that, whose grace is our boundary and whose pleasure is a life of glory for us that a liturgy makes sense. No wonder, thusly, that only that God, not just any god, can mend our broken lives, pardon our sins, and, finally, redeem our careers. We cannot beg forgiveness for our sins from anyone else; we cannot pray for mercy to just anyone who happens by. The thorough and total humbling that true worship becomes is also our surest way to know the true God."[34]

The fact that the commandments come from the true God means that they are true commandments, and our obedience to the law has an element of worship about it. This is liturgical obedience (as an act of *latria*) to a liturgical beauty, made possible by a liturgical asceticism coming from an act of liturgical theology. "Because God is who he is," concludes Holmer, "there are some standard relations to his creatures."[35] That God is who he is determines our worship (which must be done in truth, beauty, and goodness) and our obedience (which also must be done in truth, beauty, and goodness). Because God is so beautiful, there is a paradigmatic obedience demanded of us. And we are happy to give it, because there is more beatitude in being eaten by God than by being fed by anyone else.

---

[33] Paul Holmer, "About Liturgy and Its Logic," *Worship* 50, no. 1 (January 1976): 10.
[34] Holmer, "About Liturgy and Its Logic," 21–22.
[35] Holmer, "About Liturgy and Its Logic," 23.

Liturgical Fasting
On Liturgical Fasting[*]

You've heard an old saying that "those who can, do; those who can't, teach." This strikes me as particularly apt in today's situation. I'd like to speak about fasting, but I'm no particular expert in practice. Nobody has to worry they'll feel guilty as a result of my personal story. Rather, I'd like to go to the liturgical tradition and discover what theological truths lie there. My hypothesis is quite simple: there can be many reasons for fasting, but only one reason for the liturgical fast, and of that reason we are informed by Scripture: "Man shall not live by bread alone." The liturgical fast inducts us into that scriptural wisdom about the relationship of God, man, and matter.

I say there are many other reasons to fast, and with a little reflection you can think of as many as I can. People fast for health reasons (like when your cholesterol is too high), for medical reasons (like before a blood test), for reasons of vanity (like the magazines encourage), for athletic purposes (like the coach insists), for moral reasons (in protest of animal husbandry practices), for religious reasons (all religions use fasting as a tool), and there is even restraint from food that comes from mood swings (like depression or the sad illness of anorexia). But just as the fast of the hospital patient is different from the fast of the supermodel by reason of motive and end, so too the liturgical fast is different from all other fasts by its purpose and telos. And its reason for being is biblically explained: "Man shall not live by bread alone."

I pause to note that this is a fine example of Jesus confirming the Word of God. We sometimes see only points of contrast between the two testaments, but here is a lived point of congruence between the Old Testament and the New Testament. This wisdom appears in Deuteronomy 8 and is quoted by Jesus in Matthew 4. More than quoted, it is lived by Jesus. Jesus is the confirmation of every truth revealed in Scripture, including this one. He is the New Adam and shows in his person the anthropological truth

---

[*] David W. Fagerberg, "On Liturgical Fasting," *Logos: A Journal of Eastern Christian Studies* 48, nos. 1–2 (2007): 83–104.

bespoken in Deuteronomy: he did not live by bread alone, but by every word which came from his Father's mouth.

To explore my hypothesis, I shall try to do three things: (1) describe what I mean by the phrase "liturgical asceticism," of which fasting is a concrete expression; (2) describe repentant fasting as a therapeutic struggle with sin; and (3) describe fasting as liturgical act.

Liturgical Asceticism

To understand what I mean by the term "liturgical asceticism," a twofold correction is required, one to the term "liturgical" and the other to the term "asceticism." It is common to define liturgy as the fifty-five minutes on a Sunday morning, as rubrics and Ordos, as incense and vestments. And it is common to define asceticism as paucity, starkness, and painful severity. If we were to leave the definitions at that, then the phrase "liturgical asceticism" would seem to mean austere church decor, or frugally performed rites, or the pain of putting up with badly done ritual. I should instead like to dilate both terms in order to deepen the meaning of the conjoined phrase.

First, I want to expand the word "liturgy." The public and corporate liturgy is the Church's faith in motion, as Aidan Kavanagh used to say. But the ritual is just the tip of the liturgical iceberg. Robert Taft writes, "The purpose of all Christian liturgy is to express in a ritual moment that which should be the basic stance of every moment of our lives."[1] I suggest that liturgy is participation in the circulation of love between the divine persons of the Trinity. That communion of interpenetrating life which revolves between the three persons was called *perichoresis* by the Greeks and *circumincessio* by the Latins, and man and woman were created toward the end of participating in the Trinity's perichoresis. We are liturgical beings designed for deification, opened up to mankind by the hypostatic union of the human and divine natures in Jesus of Nazareth. Liturgy is the ongoing saving work of God's only begotten Son. Liturgy is cosmic in scope and eschatological in ambition. This fallen world has become subject to various powers and principalities, world rulers and evil spirits (Eph 6), but into it has come a new power, a new principle, a new *arche*. There is a new priest, a supreme *iereus*, practicing a ministry of reconciliation in heaven. It was prepared for through the service rendered by the house of

---

[1] Robert Taft, "Sunday in the Byzantine Tradition," in *Beyond East and West: Problems in Liturgical Understanding*, 2nd ed. (Rome: Pontifical Oriental Institute, 1997), 52.

Israel, and this *arche* irrupted into history with Christ's ministry, and it is continued in his body the Church.[2] His ministry is an *iereus arche*, and into his hierarchy Christ initiates his disciples.

Christ initiates his people into his work. The term "liturgy" comes from *leitourgia*, which meant a work (*ergeia*) done by a few on behalf of a people (*laos*). Christ did a work for the reconciliation of mankind, and that work is now shared by his liturgical apprentices. The work done at liturgy by Christ's holy people is the perpetuation of Christ's own sacrificial priesthood. His life in the Father is shared with his people, and spiritually active by the power of the third person of the Trinity. This is a people called out—which is the meaning of the Greek word for Church, *ekklesia*—we are called out by Christ, for Christ, through Christ, around Christ, under Christ, or, best of all, "with Christ." Taft writes:

> To express this spiritual identity, Paul uses several compound verbs that begin with the preposition *syn* (with): I suffer with Christ, am crucified with Christ, die with Christ, am buried with Christ, am raised and live with Christ, am carried off to heaven and sit at the right hand of the Father with Christ.... This seems to be what Christian liturgy is for St. Paul. Never once does he use cultic nomenclature (liturgy, sacrifice, priest, offering) for anything but a life of self-giving, lived after the pattern of Christ. When he does speak of what we call liturgy ... he makes it clear that its purpose is to contribute to this "liturgy of life," literally to edify, to build up the Body of Christ into that new temple and liturgy and priesthood in which sanctuary and offerer and offered are one.[3]

Notice that I have made my definition of *leitourgia* in conjunction with *hierarchy* and *ekklesia*. To be a Christian means to participate in Christ's liturgical posture toward his Father as Son, and in his liturgical posture toward the world as suffering servant. The basic stance of every moment of a Christian life is Christ's posture. It is his posture that is expressed ritually in the liturgical rhythm of the Church, including the Liturgy of the Hours, and especially in the Mass, which is Eucharistic thanksgiving, anamnetic memorial, epicletic supplication, intercessory prayer, mystical

---

[2] On priesthood as ministry of reconciliation, see Avery Dulles, *The Priestly Office: A Theological Reflection* (Mahwah, NJ: Paulist Press, 1997).

[3] Robert Taft, "Toward a Theology of the Christian Feast," in *Beyond East and West*, 21.

communion, and propitiatory sacrifice. Liturgy therefore encompasses both the evangelical personal life and the public ceremonialized cult. Indeed, the pious reality of the heart and the ritual reality of the cult are but two movements of the same liturgy. They are, in the words of Jean Corbon, liturgy lived and liturgy celebrated:

> The liturgy is not reducible to the content of our celebrations of it. Christ, in the Holy Spirit and together with "the assembly of the first-born," is at every moment celebrating the liturgy before the Father.... Our celebrations are moments in which "all who want it may have the water of life, and have it free" (Rev 22:17).... A celebration can now be seen as a "moment" in which the Lord comes with power and his coming becomes the sole concern of those who answer to his call.... This moment is ecclesial or it does not exist at all.[4]
>
> The liturgy, which is celebrated at certain moments but lived at every moment, is the one mystery of the Christ who gives life to human beings. When it is celebrated, it does not offer us a model that is then to be imitated in the rest of life; if this were the case, we would be back in the separation of sacred ritual from moral conduct. The Christ whom we celebrate is the identical Christ by whom we live; his mystery permeates both celebration and life.[5]

"To swim" is a verb, "swimmer" is the noun; "liturgy" is a verb, "Christian" is the noun.

Second, I want to expand the word "asceticism." *Askesis* was the word meaning "a discipline or practice." It was used of athletes. As John McGuckin explains:

> The word "asceticism" derives from the Greek term for physical exercise, such as athletic practice. The idea of training the soul to virtue by disciplining the body is fundamental to monastic theory. Here, Christian monasticism provided a distinct and original anthropology. In many Greco-Roman theories the purpose of "philosophic" asceticism was to purify the soul of the body's influence.... In its purest form the Christian concept of ascesis seeks

---

[4] Jean Corbon, *The Wellspring of Worship*, trans. Matthew J. O'Connell (San Francisco: Ignatius Press, 1988), 78–79.

[5] Corbon, *The Wellspring of Worship*, 141.

not the liberation of the soul from the body but the integration of the person, spiritually and materially. Ascesis was thus a manner of disciplining the body and training the mind by prayers, vigils and fasting, until the whole person was attuned to his or her best ability to hear and obey the voice of God.[6]

So asceticism is not masochism, as it is commonly taken to mean in ordinary English. Neither is it only for monks, nor just a matter of celibacy, nor a pinched and puckered view of life, nor beating one's head against a Lenten wall because it feels good to stop at Easter. Asceticism is the discipline which trains us for the Kingdom of God. *Askesis* capacitates us for beatific vision.

In his foreword to *Unseen Warfare*, Nicodemus of the Holy Mountain describes the book's ascetical subject matter in this way: "It teaches not the art of visible and sensory warfare, and speaks not about visible, bodily foes but about the unseen and inner struggle, which every Christian undertakes from the moment of his baptism, when he makes a vow to God to fight for Him, to the glory of His divine name, even unto death."[7] If we remember that the word *sacramentum* once meant the vow taken by a soldier upon enlistment in the army (something Tertullian remembered when he first enlisted the word in his writing), then we could understand liturgical asceticism as the fulfillment of every Christian's baptismal *sacramentum*. Asceticism is keeping our baptism. Liturgical *askesis* is the perfection of baptism.

Liturgical asceticism (as opposed to asceticism that is not liturgical), is an *askesis* that is baptismal in origin because there the Christian was grafted into Christ. If you'll permit me a shortcut of quoting some definitions I attempted in an earlier article:

- Asceticism that is liturgical is asceticism that has liturgy as its ontological condition.
- Christian asceticism is substantially a liturgical product. Liturgical asceticism does not name two things, it names Christ's purity of heart become our own.

---

[6] John McGuckin, "Monasticism," in *The Blackwell Dictionary of Eastern Christianity*, ed. Ken Parry, David J. Melling, Dimitri Brady, and Sidney H. Griffin (Oxford: Wiley-Blackwell, 1999), 321.

[7] *Unseen Warfare: The Spiritual Combat and Path to Paradise of Lorenzo Scupoli*, ed. Nicodemus of the Holy Mountain, rev. Theophan the Recluse, trans. E. Kadloubovsky and G. E. H. Palmer (Crestwood, NY: St. Vladimir's Seminary Press, 1987), 71.

- Christian liturgical asceticism could not have existed before the Incarnation any more than iconography—and for the same reason.
- Liturgical asceticism is the discipline which capacitates a liturgist.
- If liturgy means sharing the life of Christ (being washed in his Resurrection, eating his body), and if *askesis* means discipline (in the sense of forming), then liturgical asceticism is the discipline required to become an icon of Christ and make his image visible in our faces.
- Liturgical *askesis* increases the measure by which we can participate in the liturgical life into which baptism initiated us.
- Liturgical asceticism corroborates the death of Christ in our own bodies.[8]

Now, I maintain that liturgical fasting is an instance of this. So let me turn to fasting as a Church discipline.

Repentant Fasting as a Therapeutic Struggle with Sin

The Church is a hospital for sinners. All the powers possessed by the Church—I mean her liturgy, her sacraments, the deposit of faith, the hierarchy, her magisterium—all these powers exist to cure the sinner. Why has Christ entrusted the Church with sacrament and liturgy? To cure sinners. With Scripture and creed? To cure sinners. With hierarchy and magisterium? To cure sinners. These ministries exist as medicaments for our wounds. I have named the three offices (*munera*) of the Church, which paragraph 783 of the *Catechism* says come from Jesus Christ as the one whom the Father anointed with the Holy Spirit and established as priest, prophet, and king: "The whole People of God participates in these three offices of Christ and bears the responsibilities for mission and service that flow from them." Jesus called himself the way, the truth, and the life, and now his body-in-the-world exercises the offices of governing, teaching, and sanctifying. And then the flip side is seen. As the cure takes hold, the hospital for sinners becomes a nursery for saints. A sinner undergoing the cure is a saint in the making. Salvation from sin is for the sake of a higher goal, namely deification. In Vladimir Lossky's words, "After the Fall, human history is a long shipwreck awaiting rescue: but the port of salvation is not the goal; it is the possibility for the shipwrecked to resume

---

[8] David W. Fagerberg, "A Century on Liturgical Asceticism," *Diakonia* 31, no. 1 (1998), 31–60.

his journey whose sole goal is union with God."⁹ Every activity of the Church is orientated to this ultimate eternal end. And she fulfills this task as truly in her office of governing as in her offices of teaching and sanctifying. Do not think the Church is being more truly herself when teaching and sanctifying than when disciplining. The fasting discipline she imposes exists for the same purpose: to lead to union with God. Now, the liturgical fast is a discipline of the Church. As a discipline imposed from one of the Church offices, liturgical fasting differs from other kinds of fasting which might be undertaken for voluntary or occasional reasons. Just as the Liturgy of the Hours is not private prayer but the prayer of the Church passing through the lips of an individual, even done in private, so liturgical fasting is not a private act but the conduct of the body being lived by an individual in sympathy with its head. There is an amazing corporate dimension to the liturgical fast.

The tradition speaks of fasting as a weapon for doing combat with sin. Isaac the Syrian says, "Let your weapons be tears and continuous fasting. . . . Understand what I say: there can be no knowledge of the mysteries of God on a full stomach."¹⁰ The Greek fathers used the word "passion" to name the problem. Today, in modern English, the word "passion" can be used either positively or negatively, as good or bad—a passion for art or a passion of lust. In the ascetical tradition, the idea of a passion usually meant a corrupted or misdirected human faculty. The faculties given by God are good, and remain good if oriented to the right end. But a faculty misdirected is a passion. As Maximus the Confessor says, a passion is "a movement of the soul contrary to nature. . . . Vice is the mistaken use of ideas from which follows the abuse of things. . . . As with everything, misuse is sin."¹¹ Since the Greek fathers thought of man possessing three faculties—appetite, spirit, reason—the passions could be organized according to whether they afflict the concupiscible, the irascible, or the rational faculty. In unfallen man, these faculties would be rightly ordered, as Maximus says. "The soul is moved reasonably when its concupiscible element is qualified by self-mastery, its irascible element cleaves to love and turns away from hate, and the rational element lives

---

⁹ Vladimir Lossky, *Orthodox Theology: An Introduction*, trans. Ian and Ihita Kesarcodi-Watson (Crestwood, NY: St. Vladimir's Seminary Press, 1978), 84.

¹⁰ Isaac the Syrian, Homily 4, in *The Ascetical Homilies of Saint Isaac the Syrian*, trans. Dana Miller (Brookline, MA: Holy Transfiguration Monastery Publications, 1984), 33.

¹¹ Maximus the Confessor, *The Four Hundred Chapters on Love*, in *Maximus Confessor: Selected Writings*, trans. George Berthold (Mahwah, NJ: Paulist Press, 1985), 48.

with God through prayer and spiritual contemplation."[12] But in fallen man, it is different, and so when Evagrius analyzed the wisdom of the desert athletes, he sorted the eight passions according to these three faculties. The first three in his list are distortions of our appetitive faculty (gluttony, lust, avarice), the second three are distortions of our enspirited faculty (sadness, anger, acedia), and the last two afflict our intellective faculty (vainglory, pride).

Asceticism is battle with the passions. So long as I see the world through the cataracts of sin, I see the world falsely. If I look at my neighbor's wife lustfully, or at the neighbor himself enviously, or at the goods of the earth avariciously, I am seeing the cosmos in distortion. The passions must be disciplined, and the wisdom of experience suggests how to do that. Maximus observes that "almsgiving heals the irascible part of the soul; fasting extinguishes the concupiscible part."[13]

The battle is spiritual, because the passions are a spiritual corruption of our faculties. But since we are talking about a human being, and not an angel, the body will be a field of battle. It is not a battle with the body (liturgical asceticism is not Manichaeism or Gnosticism, despite how this language might sound to our unaccustomed ears); the body is good. But it is a battle that involves the body. John Climacus says in *The Ladder of Divine Ascent*, "It is truly astounding how the incorporeal mind can be defiled and darkened by the body. Equally astonishing is the fact that the immaterial spirit can be purified and refined by clay."[14]

If the whole person has fallen—not just his matter, not just his spirit—then the remedy must be applied to the body as well as the spirit. The purpose of asceticism is not to free the soul from the body, but to free both the soul and body from the passions. Vladimir Solvoyof makes the point by saying, "The purpose of Christian asceticism is not to weaken the flesh, but to strengthen the spirit for the transfiguration of the flesh."[15] Being body-soul creatures, the remedy has to be applied to the soul *through* the body, by means of the body, along with the body. Ever since the harmony was disrupted, the faculties have been in disorder. Break the relationship with God above, and the faculties within become disordered. Hence the tension between soul and body that the philosophers only dimly understood, but talked about at length. The Christian philosophers understand

---

[12] Maximus the Confessor, *Four Hundred Chapters on Love*, 77.
[13] Maximus the Confessor, *Four Hundred Chapters on Love*, 77.
[14] John Climacus, *The Ladder of Divine Ascent*, trans. Colm Luibheild and Norman Russell (Mahwah, NJ: Paulist Press, 1982), 169.
[15] S. L. Frank, ed., *A Solovyof Anthology* (London: SCM Press, 1950), 119–20.

the problem more fully. In Step 15 of the *Ladder*, John Climacus laments about the failed harmony between spirit and body:

> By what rule or manner can I bind this body of mine? By what precedent can I judge him? Before I can bind him he is let loose, before I can condemn him I am reconciled to him, before I can punish him I bow down to him and feel sorry for him. How can I hate him when my nature disposes me to love him? How can I break away from him when I am bound to him forever? How can I escape from him when he is going to rise with me? How can I make him incorrupt when he has received a corruptible nature? How can I argue with him when all the arguments of nature are on his side? . . .
>
> He is my helper and my enemy, my assistant and my opponent, a protector and a traitor. I am kind to him and he assaults me. If I wear him out he gets weak. If he has a rest he becomes unruly. . . . What is this mystery in me? What is the principle of this mixture of body and soul? How can I be my own friend and my own enemy? Speak to me! Speak to me, my yoke-fellow, my nature! I cannot ask anyone else about you. How can I remain uninjured by you? How can I escape the danger of my own nature?[16]

It is not dualism, it is Christianity. It is not a battle of soul against body, it is a battle for righteousness, and both body and soul are involved. That is why fasting can be used to purify and refine the immaterial spirit. That is why fasting is a spiritual act, a spiritual struggle. John Climacus describes the effects of fasting this way in Step 14:

> Fasting ends lust, roots out bad thoughts, frees one from evil dreams. Fasting makes for purity of prayer, an enlightened soul, a watchful mind, a deliverance from blindness. Fasting is the door of compunction, humble sighing, joyful contrition, and end to chatter, an occasion for silence, a custodian of obedience, a lightening of sleep, health of the body, an agent of dispassion, a remission of sins, the gate, indeed the delight of Paradise.[17]

---

[16] John Climacus, *The Ladder of Divine Ascent*, 185–86.
[17] John Climacus, *The Ladder of Divine Ascent*, 169.

That, then, is the reason why the ascetics recommended bodily discipline. If it is difficult to grab hold of my thoughts because they are so quick and fleeting, I can nevertheless grab hold of my tongue and stop it for a time. Abba Isidore said, "Ever since I became a monk, I have been trying not to let anger rise as far as my mouth."[18] By holding my tongue, I gradually control my heart. How will I conquer the demons that stir up the passions? Abba John the Short says, "If a king wants to take a city whose citizens are hostile, he first captures the food and water of the inhabitants of the city, and when they are starving subdues them. So it is with gluttony. If a man is earnest in fasting and hunger, the enemies which trouble his soul will grow weak."[19]

I wish to reiterate: fasting is not a battle with the body, it is a battle with the passions that uses the body as a battleground. There is nothing wrong with money, sex, or beer; it is avarice, lust, and gluttony that is the problem. The monks were perfectly clear on that. A disciple of Abba Sisois said, "If in the meeting at church on Saturday and Sunday, a brother drinks three cups, is it much?" (They allowed wine during feast seasons.) "And the old man said: 'If there were no Satan, it would not be much.'"[20] If not for Satan's demons exciting the passions, the wine would not be a problem. But since we are prey to temptation, John Climacus says, "Control your appetites before they control you."[21]

> Whenever there is a comparison of ascetical values, the inner always trumps the outer. Once Epiphanius the bishop from Cyprus sent a message to Hilarion, and asked him, "Come, let me see you before I die." When they had met and had greeted each other, part of a chicken was set before them. The bishop took it and gave it to Hilarion. The hermit said to him, "No, thank you, abba. From the time I took the habit, I have not eaten anything that has been killed." Epiphanius said to him, "From the time I took the habit, I have let no one go to sleep who still had something against me, and I have never gone to sleep with an enemy in the world." Hilarion said to him: "I beg your pardon. Your devotion is greater than mine."[22]

---

[18] Benedicta Ward, trans., *The Desert Fathers: Sayings of the Early Christian Monks* (London: Penguin Books, 2003), 4.22.
[19] Ward, *The Desert Fathers*, 4.19.
[20] Ward, *The Desert Fathers*, 4.37.
[21] John Climacus, *The Ladder of Divine Ascent*, 167.
[22] Ward, *The Desert Fathers*, 4.15.

The professional faster in the desert sees the devotion of the bishop as greater, even though he is prevented by ecclesiastical responsibilities from fulfilling the stricter desert rule. Fasting is useless if it does not get to the heart of the person and uproot envy. "Abba Hyperichius said 'It is better to eat flesh and drink wine than to eat the flesh of the brothers by disparaging them.'"[23] Charity always trumps the ascetical rule.

> Abba Cassian said: "We came from Palestine to Egypt, and visited one of the fathers. After he had offered us hospitality, we asked him: 'Why, when you receive guests, do you not keep the fast? In Palestine they keep it.' He answered: 'Fasting is ever with me. I cannot keep you here for ever. Fasting is useful and necessary, but we can choose to fast or not fast. God's law demands from us perfect charity. In you I receive Christ: and so I must do all I can to show you the offices of charity. When I have bidden you farewell, I can return and make up my rule of fasting. The sons of the bridegroom cannot fast while the bridegroom is with them: when he is taken from then, then they can fast.'"[24]

The desert did have its superheroes of fasting, such as Abba Poemen, who admitted that when he was a young man, he used to fast three days on end, even for a week. But when questioned on it in his older age, he says, "The great elders have tested all these things, and they found that it is good to eat something every day, but on some days a little less. And they have shown us that this is the king's highway, for it is easy and light."[25] This may explain how an old man could fulfill both his duty of fasting and law of hospitality to John Cassian:

> Abba Cassian also said: "We came to another old man and he invited us to sup, and pressed us, though we had eaten, to eat more. I said that I could not. He answered: 'I have already given meals to six different visitors, and have supped with each of them, and am still hungry. Have you only eaten once and yet are so full that you cannot eat with me now?'"[26]

---

[23] Ward, *The Desert Fathers*, 4.51.
[24] Ward, *The Desert Fathers*, 13.2.
[25] Ward, *The Desert Fathers*, 10.46.
[26] Ward, *The Desert Fathers*, 13.3.

Liturgical Fasting as Sacrificial Worship

I have been describing a fast of repentance which functions as a therapy for sin. I can summarize it with the words of Kallistos Ware in his introduction to *The Lenten Triodion* of the Orthodox Church:

> The primary aim of fasting is to make us conscious of our dependence upon God. If practiced seriously, the Lenten abstinence from food—particularly in the opening days—involves a considerable measure of real hunger, and also a feeling of tiredness and physical exhaustion. The purpose of this is to lead us in turn to a sense of inward brokenness and contrition; to bring us, that is, to the point where we appreciate the full force of Christ's statement "Without Me you can do nothing" (John 15:5). If we always take our fill of food and drink, we easily grow over-confident in our own abilities, acquiring a false sense of autonomy and self-sufficiency. The observance of a physical fast undermines this sinful complacency.[27]

Said another way, I've been describing a sinner's fast. But I conclude there is another, additional explanation of fasting because I am aware of a fast by someone who was *not* a sinner. In Matthew we have the story of someone who was fasting because "man does not live by bread alone." You see how closely related are the fast of repentance and liturgical fasting; they are the same practice, but the subject doing it is different. When we find the words "man does not live by bread alone" on the lips of a sinner, it is a confession of idolatry: we have replaced our hunger for God with a hunger for finite things. But when we find these words on the lips of the Son of Man, it is a proclamation of the proper relationship between the things of earth and the things of heaven. And this is the final reason for fasting. In his liturgical fast, Jesus is praising the Father by sacrificial worship, doing as New Adam what the Old Adam failed to do. In his fast we see an eschatological declaration of the intended relationship of earth and heaven, the profane and sacred, the temporal and eternal.

Again I point out how closely related are these things. Kallistos Ware said the primary aim of fasting is to make us conscious of our dependence upon God. The sinner finds the path to this consciousness a path of brokenness and contrition, but Christ finds it to be a royal path from creation

---

[27] Archimandrite Kallistos Ware, "The Meaning of the Great Fast," in *The Lenten Triodion* (Boston: Faber and Faber, 1978), 16.

to Creator, the very path intended for Adam and Eve from the beginning. Aidan Kavanagh used to say liturgy is doing the world the way the world was meant to be done. Liturgical life is Christ's life in us, and he knew how to do the world. He knew the relative value of bread to the Word of God.

The sinner says, "Man does not live by bread alone," in order to break his false sense of autonomy and self-sufficiency, and then reinforces the confession with a fasting of repentance. The body cooperates with grace in rooting out our hubris and false autonomy. But when Christ says, "Man does not live by bread alone," having never left the bosom of the Father, he is articulating the true end for which man and woman were created. Remember that the Church is both a hospital for sinners and a nursery for saints. The sinner must use fasting for mortification, but the saint-in-training finds that fasting's true liturgical purpose is for deification. The repentant fast does battle with the passions, but only to enable the liturgical fast: we were not created for bread alone but for fellowship with the Trinity.

This liturgical fast—both as the sinner and as the saint practice it—seems to me different from the merely moral connotations we often associate with fasting. I will tell you when the thought first occurred to me. It was when I noticed that at the end of Lent we can have chocolate again! I make the point comically, but I am serious about the point I am making. This liturgical fasting must be different from moral improvement, because if we give up something for a moral reason, then we shouldn't resume the thing we have given up. For example, I sometimes hear people say that their Lenten fast this year will be to not get so angry at their kids—but when Lent ends, I hope they don't go back to being angry with their kids, whereas I will joyfully go back to my chocolate. Giving up something for Lent must be for a different reason than giving up something that's bad for you. We don't give up chocolate because it is bad, but for some other reason, and if we can pry out that reason, then we will understand fasting as liturgical asceticism.

I am treading very carefully here because I don't want to be misunderstood. Morality can be the handmaiden of deification, like philosophy can be the handmaiden of theology. The harmony between morality and liturgical asceticism is the harmony of nature to supernature. So I readily grant that there can be a moral element to the liturgist's asceticism, but moral improvement and a better human character is not the purpose of liturgical asceticism. The purpose of liturgical asceticism is deification, which first requires a negative moment of salvation and then starts a positive journey toward union with God. Because liturgical asceticism is orientated toward deification, moral reasoning alone cannot understand it, as Paul Evdokimov has pointed out:

> Asceticism has nothing to do with moralism. The contrary of sin is not virtue but the faith of the saints. Moralism exercises natural forces, and its fundamental voluntarism submits human behavior to moral imperatives.... On the other hand, the "virtue" of the ascetics has an entirely different resonance and designates the human dynamism set in motion by the presence of God.... Moral and sociological principles are powerless.... They cannot pardon or absolve, wipe out a fault or raise the dead.[28]

Put bluntly, and a little unfairly, but in a way that is nevertheless somewhat useful for the sake of clarity, I will say it is a moral act to renounce something because you believe it is bad, and it is an act of liturgical asceticism to renounce something even though you believe it is good. Jesus did not refrain from bread because he thought bread is bad, but for the simple fact that man does not live by bread alone. Morality urges renunciation of those things injurious to a person, so if an alcoholic gives up wine, I would call it a moral act. But that is not the reason why the Christian abstains from wine during Lent.

So here's our question: For what possible reason does someone give up chocolate during Lent if he believes chocolate is good, and he intends to take it up again on the very shining day after Lent ends? For some help with this I turn to an insightful article by Karl Rahner entitled "Reflections on the Theology of Renunciation." To begin with, Rahner also says, "Renunciation in the 'supernatural order' ... cannot be adequately explained ... from a standpoint of purely natural ethics."[29] To make his point, he invokes a scholastic distinction between two types of goods: those goods ordered to an end, called *bonum utile*, and those goods that contain meaning in themselves, called *bonum honestum*. The latter type are not "good for" something; they are good in themselves. Examples of *bonum honestum* are the marital union, a human being's freedom of development, or human autonomy. It misses the point to treat any one of these as a utilitarian good. We sense this if we ask, "What is marriage good for? Explain what's in it for me." It would be an insult to marriage to attempt

---

[28] Paul Evdokimov, *The Struggle with God* (Mahwah, NJ: Paulist Press, 1966), 139–40. Republished as *Ages of the Spiritual Life* (Crestwood, NY: St. Vladimir's Seminary Press, 1998).

[29] Karl Rahner, "Reflections on the Theology of Renunciation," in *Theological Investigations*, vol. 3, *The Theology of the Spiritual Life* (New York: Crossroad, 1982), 49.

a utilitarian answer (i.e., to see it as a *bonum utile*). So Rahner writes, "In a purely natural order there would therefore be no other values for the sake of which they [the *bonum honestum*] could be sacrificed."[30] Indeed, to give up a higher good for a lower one he calls "ethically perverse."

Therefore, Rahner asserts that Christian renunciation is not done because of any kind of resentful devaluation of natural goods, especially not of the highest natural goods. When the priest takes the vow of celibacy, it is not because he resents marriage and intends to devalue it. To the contrary, Church doctrine teaches that "Christian love, in its cosmic form, can also be exercised in the positive affirmation and realization of intramundane values (such as marriage, freedom, riches)."[31] So if liturgical ascetics do not give up the natural goods of marriage, freedom, and riches because they think these things are bad, how do we explain celibacy, vows of obedience, and poverty? How does it happen that a *bonum honestum* is ever renounced? If one only renounces a good for a higher good, then the highest natural good could only be renounced for a supernatural good.

However, there's one final consideration to make. The supernatural good in question is a good that is, as yet, still believed and hoped for. We don't yet have it in complete possession. Rahner writes:

> If . . . this higher value cannot be experienced in its own intrinsic reality but must be believed and hoped for . . . then this renunciation of one value in favor of the other takes on a characteristic proper to Christian renunciation and to it alone: the giving up of a value which can be experienced in favour of a value possessed only by faith and hope, and this is a realizing expression of the love of God, in so far as this love is eschatological and not so much in so far as it is also cosmic.[32]

Liturgical asceticism is the behavior we do in the face of the eschaton. We do experience the eschatological good in one way: we experience it liturgically. (That's why I choose to call what Rahner describes by the term "liturgical asceticism.") Liturgical fasting is an eschatological activity. The celibate who has renounced the *bonum honestum* of marriage is a walking billboard for hope and, as such, is a liturgical person. Liturgical fasting is an exercise of eschatological patience and hope. The liturgical fast is only

---

[30] Rahner, "Reflections on the Theology of Renunciation," 50.
[31] Rahner, "Reflections on the Theology of Renunciation," 50.
[32] Rahner, "Reflections on the Theology of Renunciation," 52.

secondarily about things; it is primarily a way of practicing time, i.e., living history in light of eternity. It is an exercise of liturgical patience, which Olivier Clément calls "a form of interiorized monasticism. . . . Patience puts its trust in time. Not merely in ordinary time, where death has the last word and where time erodes, separates and destroys everything, but time mingled with eternity, as it is offered to us by the Resurrection."[33] Every fast is an act of faith in the power of the Resurrection. In the fast of Lent, a Christian doctrine of history is being played out. Platonism offered to teach a person how to put up with time, but liturgical asceticism offers Christ, the wisdom of God, who redeemed time and made time redemptive. Even if the eschaton is not full in the sky yet, it has dawned, and every ascetical act of renunciation witnesses to that hope. For such patient hope God originally asked Adam and Eve, and they refused to give it. It was asked again of Christ, and he refused his Father nothing. That is why he is the New Adam, head of a new humanity.

Fasting can reveal a joy for which the human race was created, but which few know. So long as there is a trace of ego in the heart, humility will feel like humiliation. And, likewise, so long as there is a trace of ego in the heart, obedience will feel like forced constraint. Exactly this effect did the tempter want to bring about in the Garden of Eden. "Did God say you can eat?" he asked. Adam and Eve should have answered, "Yes we can! Look at all the trees we may eat from! They are all for us. Only not that one, that one single tree, because if we take it too early, without preparation and permission, and in any way but gift, then we will die." But the tempter turns the prohibition into a doubt and then into a dare: "Is God holding out on you? And if he is holding out on you, should you perhaps withhold your sacrifice of obedience to him?"

C. S. Lewis makes some astute observations about the human psyche by transplanting earth's story of Eden to another planet which hasn't yet suffered the Fall. In the second volume of his space trilogy, *Perelandra*, he depicts a battle for the soul of a Green Lady who is the Eve of this planet. The battle involves the Lady, a human named Ransom, and the devil speaking through a possessed human named Weston. Maleldil (the name by which God is known there) has made a watery planet and has given only one commandment: that the Woman should return to one of the floating islands each night and not spend the night on the fixed land. The devil works on her by suggesting that unless she disobeys this command, she will not become "older," as Maleldil desires her to become.

---

[33] Olivier Clément, *Three Prayers* (Crestwood, NY: St. Vladimir's Seminary Press, 2000), 79.

He further argues that the law is arbitrary, since this law does not exist on any other planet. Ransom struggles to refute the misleading logic by first summarizing it. The devil argues that this law is different because it is not the same for all worlds, and because it is different, therefore the Woman can disobey it. But then Ransom suggests there might be another reason why there is one law different from all other laws:

> "Say it" [the Lady asks].
> "I think He made one law of that kind in order that there might be obedience. In all these other matters what you call obeying Him is but doing what seems good in your own eyes also. Is love content with that? You do them, indeed, because they are His will, but not only because they are His will. Where can you taste the joy of obeying unless He bids you do something for which His bidding is the *only* reason? When we spoke last you said that if you told the beasts to walk on their heads, they would delight to do so. So I know that you understand well what I am saying."
> "Oh, brave [Ransom]," said the Green Lady, "this is the best you have said yet. This makes me older far: yet it does not feel like the oldness this other is giving me. Oh, how well I see it! We cannot walk out of Maleldil's will: but He has given us a way to walk out of *our* will. And there could be no such way except a command like this. Out of our own will. It is like passing out through the world's roof into Deep Heaven. All beyond is love Himself. I knew there was joy in looking upon the Fixed Island and laying down all thought of ever living there, but I did not till now understand."[34]

Thomas Aquinas notes in *Summa contra gentiles* that "we do not offend God except by doing something contrary to our own good."[35] Everything God commands is for our good. Every commandment we obey serves our own good. When God says, "Don't covet," it is like saying "Don't play in the street." But one commandment feels different. It is offered as an opportunity for self-gift, not merely for our protection. This commandment exists so that by keeping it we can take hold of a hand extended to us in fellowship. The joy to be had in keeping this type of law is a joy known only to lovers—to spouses, to parents, to friends, and especially to that

---

[34] C. S. Lewis, *Perelandra* (New York: Scribner, 2003), 101–102.
[35] Thomas Aquinas, *Summa contra gentiles* III, ch. 122, 2.

triune fellowship of lovers. It is the delight of obedience, of being bound in covenant. The Son's total delight is to do what his Father tells him. As the Green Lady found joy in looking at the Fixed Land but laying down all thought of living there, he found there is joy in looking upon the stones and laying down all thought of making them bread, simply because that is not the Father's will.

The Fall was an act of disobedience, so the reversal of that fall, in order that humanity might resume its ascent to heaven, required a radical act of obedience. We get a glimpse of that ascetical obedience. Jesus lived always in his Father's will; Mary gave her *Fiat*; the saints have made their will pliable by prayer, fasting, and almsgiving; liturgical asceticism trains us for a radically free obedience. Man was not made for the temporal alone, but for the eternal. We do not know what our asceticism would have looked like had the Fall not taken place. I think Adam and Eve had a discipline in the garden which could appropriately be called "liturgical asceticism," but it was exactly this that they failed to do. The Fall is the forfeiture of our liturgical career. Adam disobeyed in a garden; the New Adam obeyed in a desert. Adam had plenty to eat and still hungered for the one forbidden thing; the New Adam had nothing to eat but did not sin because he only hungered for one thing, his Father-God. For Adam, the command was a constraint; for the New Adam, fulfilling the command was a joy. Alexander Schmemann has defined original sin in terms of appetite. "In our perspective, the 'original' sin is not primarily that humans have disobeyed God; the sin is that they ceased to be hungry for God and for God alone, ceased to see their whole life depending on the whole world as a sacrament of communion with God."[36] The story of salvation can be told as a story of appetites—from the Garden of Eden, to the grace of manna, to Jesus's forty days, to the Eucharist, to the Messianic banquet.

The liturgical fast weans our appetites from the temporal, not because bread and chocolate are bad, but because there is a higher good we were created to hunger for and for which we must retrain our appetites. Neither the bread nor the stone from which it would have been made is sinful; only doing something outside of his Father's will would be sinful. Our asceticism now consists of restructuring our appetites after the Son, who had only one desire. For that to happen, his appetite must become our appetite. Such a process is called conversion, and the power that led us to the font is further fed when we eat him in Eucharist. We recover our

---

[36] Alexander Schmemann, *For the Life of the World* (Crestwood: St. Vladimir's Seminary Press, 1973), 18.

appetites by giving ourselves totally over to him, so that he can give us, with himself in the Spirit, over to the Father. Liturgical asceticism is sacrificial at the last.

So it turns out, in the end, that fasting isn't about us not consuming, it is about us *being consumed* by the love that flows between the persons of the Trinity. The basis of the liturgical fast we can learn from the mouth of a Talking Horse of Narnia named Hwin. She shakes all over when she meets Aslan for the first time and trots up to the great Lion. And she says "Please, you're so beautiful. You may eat me if you like. I'd sooner be eaten by you than fed by anyone else."[37] Such a sacrificial attitude can only be adopted when we are persuaded by practical discipline that man is not made to live by bread alone, but is made for greater ends. The liturgical fast lifts our eyes above every temporal horizon. When we see the Word of God in the flesh, then we realize that man is not made to live by bread alone.

---

[37] C. S. Lewis, *The Horse and His Boy* (New York: Macmillan, 1970), 193.

Liturgy and Theology

Schmemann's Cost
The Cost of Understanding Schmemann in the West*

I am grateful for this opportunity to make a small repayment of a debt I owe to a man I never met but who had a life-changing impact on my vision. I first met the works of Fr. Alexander through Fr. Aidan Kavanagh, who would become my thesis director. Fr. Aidan was on leave from teaching when I arrived at Yale, so I begged him for a directed readings course. He agreed on the condition that we read everything we could by Schmemann, for he was just finishing the Hale-Seabury lectures that would become his book *On Liturgical Theology*. So in those first weeks of my first semester studying under him, we went through most of Schmemann's material together, and I tell people that I spent the rest of my graduate studies trying to get the number of the bus that hit me. I had come as a systematician, with scalpel in hand, ready to dissect a liturgical cadaver to see the makeup of its internal organs, and Kavanagh introduced me to a thinker for whom liturgy was life. Kill it, in order to study it, and one would not be able to watch liturgy at work. Wrestling with Fr. Alexander's concept of liturgical theology changed everything for me, and I am thankful to be able to express my gratitude to the man I never met by standing at a podium in this institution to which he was so devoted.

I have left two intentional ambiguities in my title. The first is the word "West"—"understanding Schmemann in the *West*." I won't distinguish the Roman Catholic Church from Protestant ecclesial communities. I do not plan to specify whether this word indicates ancient Roman practicality, medieval university scholasticism, post-Enlightenment secularized culture, or a modern, low-grade anti-ecclesiastical prejudice in those academic theologies independent from the Church. I will, however, mention three conceptual uses of the term that I detect and find in this example. Orthodox scholars frequently note that a certain approach to the sacraments (along with the Latin language by which it was taught)

---

* David W. Fagerberg, "The Cost of Understanding Schmemann in the West," *St. Vladimir's Theological Quarterly* 53, no. 2–3 (2009): 179–207.

came to Russia from the west; they mean the word *geographically* here. The result is called the "Western captivity" of Orthodoxy, and here they mean something that altered Orthodoxy's *ecclesiastical cultural identity*. And this captivity is denounced as "a deeply 'westernized' theology."[1] Here the word is used pejoratively to describe something no longer orthodox. So "West" means geographical origin, or certain changes in Orthodox liturgy and theology, or something unorthodox, even if it can be found in Orthodox history. Almost every Orthodox theologian I've ever read or spoken to recognizes what is "Western" when he or she encounters it, and here I am going to see how close I can come to articulating their tacit understanding. Since I am a Western Christian myself, the defendant might have unique insights into the charge. I am less interested in finding out *what* the West has missed than *why* it has missed it.

The second ambiguous term in the title is the word "cost"—"the *cost* of understanding Schmemann." There may be similar or parallel costs also demanded of the Orthodox Church to understand Schmemann, but I am concentrating here on the West. The term comes to me from another of my mentors, Paul Holmer, who liked to comment, "You cannot peddle truth or happiness. What a thought cost in the first instance, it will cost in the second." Whatever it cost Irenaeus to think *recapitulation*, it will cost us to understand *recapitulation*. I want to explore what it would cost the West to understand what Schmemann thought liturgical theology is, but I leave it ambiguous whether that cost is a forfeit or an addition, a letting go or a picking up—a sacrifice of some categories or an embracing of larger ones. A term has different meanings in different language games, so even as the West hears Schmemann say "*leitourgia*" or "*lex orandi*," it must still pay the hermeneutical fee of listening to the grammar behind his words, namely, an Orthodox grammar. This causes me to be tentative in my approach, for as a Roman Catholic I am outside his Eastern Orthodox world. But my hope is that the contours of an object might be felt from both the inside and the outside, and I have tried to feel what Schmemann is describing without altering its shape. One final note: I have already presented my understanding of Schmemann's concept of liturgical theology elsewhere[2] and will avoid the tedium of simply summarizing it. Instead, I hope to

---

[1] Alexander Schmemann, Appendix "Sacrament and Symbol," in *For the Life of the World* (Crestwood, NY: St. Vladimir's Seminary Press, 1973), 135–36.

[2] See David W. Fagerberg, *Theologia Prima: What Is Liturgical Theology?* (Chicago: Hillenbrand Books, 2004), chaps. 3 and 7; and David W. Fagerberg, *Liturgy Outside Liturgy: The Liturgical Theology of Fr. Alexander Schmemann* (Hong Kong: Chorabooks, 2018).

locate this paper upon a source that was not available to me at that time, Schmemann's subsequently published *Journals*.

Theology as Vision

The West tends to think of theology as a mental activity. Probably this is because the people to whom the West gives the name "theologian" live in the academy. Theology is a science practiced in the hall of sciences, and even if an individual theologian is also urged to have faith-commitments in his or her heart, and to be active in service to the poor, the only reason for calling those people theologians is because of what they think about. Worship is taken to be either an expression of belief or an instrument for the creation of belief (orthodoxy serves orthopistis), and only if that believing requires a tune-up clarification does theology enter the picture. Liturgy is a place to stage the theological content we have deduced and believe, but theology's origin is not in liturgy, it is in texts, and its output is yet more texts for the next generation of theologians to critique and surpass. As Schmemann says in an early essay, "It is indeed the 'original sin' of the entire western theological development that it made 'texts' the only *loci theologici*, the extrinsic 'authorities' of theology, disconnecting theology from its living source: liturgy and spirituality."[3]

Schmemann is capable of understanding the term "theology" in this cognitive way; he does so in a definition in his early work *Introduction to Liturgical Theology*. "Theology is above all explanation, 'the search for words appropriate to the nature of God,' i.e. for a system of concepts corresponding as much as possible to the faith and experience of the Church."[4] But in a journal entry a dozen years later Schmemann writes:

> Pascha. Holy Week. Essentially, bright days such as are needed. And truly that is all that is needed. I am convinced that if people would really hear Holy Week, Pascha, the Resurrection, Pentecost, the Dormition, there would be no need for theology. All of theology is there. All that is needed for one's spirit, heart, mind and soul. How could people spend centuries discussing justification

---

[3] Alexander Schmemann, "Liturgical Theology, Theology of Liturgy, and Liturgical Reform," in *Liturgy and Tradition: Theological Reflections of Alexander Schmemann*, ed. Thomas Fisch (Crestwood, NY: St. Vladimir's Seminary Press, 1990), 42.

[4] Alexander Schmemann, *Introduction to Liturgical Theology* (Crestwood, NY: St. Vladimir's Seminary Press, 1975), 14.

and redemption? It's all in these services. Not only is it revealed, it simply flows in one's heart and mind.[5]

I think it would be wrong to use this as a brush by which to paint Schmemann (or Orthodoxy) as anti-intellectual. Instead, there are two things going on here. First, Schmemann is identifying theology's home, its native habitat. Theology is more a vision than a cogitation. All that theology would seek to explain in words is here in act—in the liturgical act of the Church celebrating Christ's paschal mystery. Schmemann is not opposed to theological discussion, he is opposed to letting theological discussion ever break free from a vision of the Trinity in action. I have recently taken to describing liturgy as *the perichoresis of the Trinity kenotically extended to invite our synergistic ascent into deification*.[6] Liturgy is the prolongation of the Son's agapic descent to enable humanity's Eucharistic ascent; it is our "translation" to heaven, to borrow the medieval term for picking up a relic and laying it in a new home. In Holy Week, God descends as low as he can go—to Hades—and we are raised up to eternal life. All that theology would talk about is contained in the vision of earth's transfiguration effected before our eyes. In another journal entry, written after spending two days discussing Orthodoxy and the West, Schmemann asks himself what is absolute in Orthodoxy. "I always come to the same conclusion: it is first of all a certain *vision*, an experience of God, the world, the man. The best in Orthodox theology is about that vision."[7]

The second thing going on in this quotation is the connection of theology with *theosis* (deification). The beginning of theology is not the card catalogue but doing battle with the passions; and the end of theology is not becoming a professor but becoming a saint. The image of God grows more into the likeness of God. And although Schmemann writes little about asceticism explicitly, he stands in a tradition for which *theologia* is at the end of an ascetical journey (after *praktike* and *physike*), and the vision at Holy Week stands upon eight weeks of Lenten discipline. Theology must either come from or lead to the altar of the Lord. I sense that when Orthodoxy calls something "scholastic" or "Western," it is for the suspicion that the system does not arise from the ascetic experience of the Church's

---

[5] Alexander Schmemann, *The Journals of Father Alexander Schmemann 1973–1983* (Crestwood, NY: St. Vladimir's Seminary Press, 2002), 13. I am grateful for my copy as a gift from Fr. John Leonard.

[6] David W. Fagerberg, "Liturgy as Icon of the Theological Imagination," *Louvain Studies* 34, nos. 2–3 (2010), 227–48.

[7] Schmemann, *Journals*, 89.

faith, and does not end in doxology. Orthodoxy does not pejoratively call something "scholastic" for being clear, organized, and precise; if that's what it means, then John of Damascus was a scholastic! Rather, scholastic means a system in which theories swirl around like academic dust bunnies but do not lead one toward deification. Theology is knowledge of God; real knowledge of God is full union with God; a scheme is called "scholastic" if it does not adequately express the realism of theosis.

I think this is what Schmemann intends when he repeatedly speaks of the reunification of theology, liturgy, and piety. They are three atoms that make up one molecule, and recovering their unity is the goal he identifies in his book on baptism:

> The goal of liturgical theology, as its very name indicates, is to overcome the fateful divorce between theology, liturgy and piety—a divorce which, as we have already tried to show elsewhere, has had disastrous consequences for theology as well as for liturgy and piety. It deprived liturgy of its proper understanding by the people, who began to see in it beautiful and mysterious ceremonies in which, while attending them, they take no real part. It deprived theology of its living source and made it into an intellectual exercise for intellectuals. It deprived piety of its living content and term of reference. . . . To understand liturgy from inside, to discover and experience that "epiphany" of God, world and life which the liturgy contains and communicates, to relate this vision and this power to our own existence, to all our problems: such is the purpose of liturgical theology.[8]

Individual v. Ecclesial Theology

In this triad, Schmemann does not mean what the West means when it starts with an isolated individualism. Piety is not one's subjective feeling, theology is not one's subjective reasoning, and liturgy is not one's subjective worship. When Schmemann talks about the experience of the Church, he does not mean taking a poll of the assembly's opinion because the Church

---

[8] Alexander Schmemann, *Of Water and the Spirit: A Liturgical Study of Baptism* (Crestwood, NY: St. Vladimir's Seminary Press, 1974), 12.

is not the sum of all believers, she is the mother of all believers. He writes of ecclesial experience several times in his *Journals*:

> The *experience* of the *Church*—*this* is what needs theological clarification; this is what is so difficult, because scientific theology says (in the textbooks) that the "Church believes" and that this belief is relegated to the realm of the authority of dogmas. In other words, the word "belief" itself does not have the notion or the reality of experience, so that the word "experience" sounds like some subjective moods, emotions, feelings.[9]

The "experience" is possessed by the whole Church, and this is Tradition. It is the normative, apostolic experience of the risen Christ in the Spirit, by which and to which we catechize and conform our personal experiences.[10] Liturgical theology is done with a sense of obedience to the Church. Again:

> I strongly feel that theology is the transmission in words—not of other words and beliefs, but of the experience of the living Church, revealed now, communicated now. The theology that is being taught has estranged itself from the Church and from that experience; it has become self-sufficient and wants above all to be a science. Science about God, about Christ, about eternal life; therefore it has become unnecessary chatter.[11]

Theology is a knowledge that must be imprinted in the mind of the theologian by God, the way baby ducklings are imprinted on a mother duck, so that the theologian will pursue God. The apophatic God who is being pursued is found in the hypostatic union, and this cataphatic kenosis sacramentally enables our participation. Liturgy is not a religion of Adam, it is the cult of the New Adam, and so the Holy Spirit will pass everything through the hypostatic union before it is used in liturgy—sacrifice, temple, priesthood, assembly are all different in Christ. This is the source of the cultic antinomy about which Schmemann speaks. Ecclesiology is

---

[9] Schmemann, *Journals*, 209.
[10] My gratitude to Fr. Calinic Berger for conversation on this point.
[11] Schmemann, *Journals*, 300.

Christology liturgically stretching forth in the Holy Spirit to its fullest length across history.

Theology is not thinking with an earthly mind about heavenly subjects, it is thinking in communion with the mind of Christ about all things, earthly and heavenly. So when Schmemann asks why our theological arguments seem so weak and ineffective, he answers, "Is it not because everything that is evident in religion cannot be proven, since the evidence is rooted in 'bright knowledge,' in communion with the 'mind of Christ'? And proofs, in order to be proofs, must operate in a dark knowledge, in the logic of this world."[12] These two kinds of knowledge may be what Archimandrite Sophrony is also describing in an epistemological contrast he makes:

> The usual way to acquire knowledge, the one we all know, consists in the directing of the intellectual faculty outwards where it meets with phenomena, sights, forms, in innumerable variety—a differentiation *ad infinitum* of all that happens. This means that the knowledge thus acquired is never complete and has no real unity. Insistently seeking unity, the mind is forced to take refuge in synthesis, which cannot help being artificial. The unity arrived at in this way does not really and objectively exist. It is merely a form of abstract thinking natural to the mind.
>
> The other way to acquire knowledge of being is to turn the spirit in and towards itself and then to God. Here the process is the exact reverse. The mind turns away from the endless plurality and fragmentariness of the world's phenomena, and with all its strength addresses itself to God in prayer, and through prayer is directly incorporated in the very act of Divine Life, and begins to see both itself and the whole world.
>
> To obtain knowledge after the first manner is natural to man in his fallen state. The second is the way of the Son of man.[13]

Theology is seeing the world in the light of Mt. Tabor, and this light still shines from the altar of the Lord. That is why liturgy is a *locus theologicus*. To possess this "bright knowledge" will require more than a scholarly preparation, more than an imaginative fancy; it will require a conversion

---

[12] Schmemann, *Journals*, 112.
[13] Archimandrite Sophrony, *The Monk of Mount Athos: Staretz Silouan 1866–1938* (Crestwood, NY: St. Vladimir's Seminary Press, 1989), 60.

of mind (*nous*). Theological episteme stands upon *askesis*. The capacity for liturgical theology depends upon a renewed mind, a *meta-nous*. Metropolitan Hierotheos cites examples of this theme:

> According to St. Maximus there is an attraction between a pure nous and knowledge [St. Maximus, *The Philokalia* 2, 56, 32]. The Holy Spirit finds the pure nous and "initiates it accordingly into the mysteries of the age to be" [Maximus, St. Thalassios, *The Philokalia* 2, 329]. *In this way the person becomes a theologian. For theology is not given by human knowledge and zeal, but by the work of the Holy Spirit which dwells in the pure heart.* The nous which has been purified "becomes for the soul a sky full of the stars of radiant and glorious thoughts, with the sun of righteousness shining in it, *sending the beaming rays of theology out into the world*" [Nicetas Stethatos, *Natural Chapters*, ch. 67]. Real theology is not a fruit of material concentration but a manifestation of the Holy Spirit. When a man's nous is purified then he is illuminated and if his nous has the capacity, that is, wisdom, he can theologise. *Therefore we say that his whole life, even his body itself, is theology. The purified man is wholly a theology.*[14]

This is an unusual grammar to Western ears: that our body itself should become theology, that theologizing requires a pure mind, that Mrs. Murphy (what Kavanagh called a practicing traditional liturgist) can be called a theologian by virtue of the liturgical ordering of her life. It means becoming what Abbot Vasileios calls "a theologian soul." "True theology is always living, a form of hierugy, something that changes our life and 'assumes' us into itself: we are to become theology. Understood in this way, theology is not a matter for specialists but a universal vocation; each is called to become a 'theologian soul.'"[15] There is an ascetical cost to liturgical theology.

Tradition as Something More Than History

This bright knowledge is thinking with the mind of Christ, so it can only be had in communion with the mind of the Church, in other words, by

---

[14] Metropolitan Hierotheos, *Orthodox Psychotherapy: The Science of the Fathers* (Levadia: Birth of the Theotokos Monastery, 1994), 147, italics added.
[15] Archimandrite Vasileios, *Hymn of Entry: Liturgy and Life in the Orthodox Church* (Crestwood, NY: St. Vladimir's Seminary Press, 1984), 27.

thinking traditionally. This is another way of describing what the fathers do (and so the patristic age did not necessarily expire in a certain century). If students lack this "bright knowledge," then simply increasing the number of patristic authors in the syllabus will not necessarily help. Schmemann writes, "It is my impression that with a few exceptions, the 'patristic revival' remains locked within the old western approach to theology, is a return much more to patristic *texts* than to the *mind* of the Fathers."[16] The Western approach to theology teaches one how to look at the texts of the fathers but stops short of teaching one how to think in union with the fathers; so also the Western study of liturgy teaches one how to look at the texts of the liturgy but stops short of liturgical theology. (And it does not significantly alter the situation to add ritual studies if the phenomenon of ritual is simply treated as another text for interpretation.)

For the West, tradition is a trajectory, little more than the sum of all the points that preceded the point on which we now stand. Understood in this way, tradition can be background, but cannot exert much influence. So concludes Georgios Mantzaridis:

> Western Christianity as a whole rejects tradition deep down. Of course, we cannot fail to distinguish "traditional" Roman Catholicism from "anti-traditional" Protestantism, but this distinction does not run very deep. Roman Catholicism neglected tradition as a source of unity based on memory.... Love of tradition in Roman Catholicism came to be identified, as was natural, with conservatism.... But conservatism proves itself to be inadequate....
>
> On the other hand, innovation abhors the decay associated with time.... Thus, a pattern of the unending reform of things is established and anything of any duration is considered wearisome.... This phenomenon emerged originally in Protestantism, in which, as we know, the view was held that the Church needs to be constantly reforming herself. *Ecclesia semper reformanda.* If the Church is not being reformed, then she cannot preserve her identity.[17]

---

[16] Schmemann, "Liturgical Theology, Theology of Liturgy, and Liturgical Reform," 42.
[17] Georgios Mantzaridis, *Time and Man* (South Canaan, AP: St. Tikhon's Seminary Press, 1996), 66.

The consequence in Catholicism, continues Mantzaridis, is to shift the emphasis "from that of unity based on memory to that of unity based on an institution.... The tradition of the Fathers was swept aside, and adherence to tradition came to mean agreement with the pope and his representatives."[18] And the consequence of Protestantism's constant reformation "leads not to organic development, but to actual alteration of the Church."[19]

Schmemann wants Tradition to exert a gravitational pull on our theology, our liturgy, and our piety. Tradition is a capacity, a faculty. So George Florovksy says, "Tradition was in the Early Church, first of all, an hermeneutical principle and method."[20] And so Vladimir Lossky famously distinguishes Tradition (capital *T*, singular) from traditions (small *t*, plural), in order to equate Tradition with the action of the Holy Spirit:

> It is not the content of Revelation, but the light that reveals it; it is not the word, but the living breath which makes the word heard at the same time as the silence from which it came.... The pure notion of Tradition can then be defined by saying that it is the life of the Holy Spirit in the Church, communicating to each member of the Body of Christ the faculty of hearing, of receiving, of knowing the Truth in the Light which belongs to it, and not according to the light of human reason.[21]

Schmemann says that when Tradition no longer exerts that pressure on our thinking and our worshiping, then it is mere traditionalism. "What needs to be said is that Orthodox traditionalism is inversely proportional to faithfulness, to *Tradition*.... Orthodoxy became entangled in the past, which it worshipped as tradition."[22] He calls this *Orthodoxism*. "I realize

---

[18] Mantzaridis, *Time and Man*, 66.
[19] Mantzaridis, *Time and Man*, 66. Andrew Louth has also discussed the question with his usual insightfulness and offers a similar diagnosis. "The Western Church has lost this sense of *sobornost* and either protects unity by authority at the expense of freedom—the Catholic way, not noticeably diminished since Vatican II—or affirms freedom to the point of destroying unity—the Protestant way" (Andrew Louth, "Is Development of Doctrine a Valid Category for Orthodox Theology?," in *Orthodoxy and Western Culture: A Collection of Essays Honoring Jaroslav Pelikan on His Eightieth Birthday* [Crestwood, NY: St. Vladimir's Seminary Press, 2005], 53).
[20] Georges Florovsky, "The Function of Tradition in the Ancient Church," in *Bible, Church, Tradition: An Eastern Orthodox View* (Belmont, MA: Notable & Academic Books, 1987), 79.
[21] Vladimir Lossky, "Tradition and Traditions," in *In the Image and Likeness of God* (Crestwood, NY: St. Vladimir's Seminary Press, 1974), 151–52.
[22] Schmemann, *Journals*, 89.

how spiritually tired I am of all this 'Orthodoxism,' of all the fuss with Byzantium, Russia, way of life, spirituality, church affairs, piety, of all these rattles."[23] Mere traditionalism means that instead of seeing with the fathers' vision, we become patrologists; and instead of seeing with liturgical vision, we become ritologists.

Ordo or Ortho?

For the West, tradition is a record of contingencies. That is why tradition cannot function normatively (how can historical accidents be a norm?), and theological specialists must be imported to evaluate the situation. Since the West thinks of tradition primarily in historical terms, it naturally uses historical method to examine tradition. This is like using chemistry to examine biology. Of course, historical examination of structural origin and development is crucial, or else we risk substituting our subjective theology of the liturgy for the Church's liturgical theology. History is crucial. But if unbalanced and unhinged from Tradition, then when it hears Schmemann speak of the *lex orandi*, it assumes he means an ancient and universal practice, and turns to historical methods in order to find that liturgical essence, defined as something traceable to liturgy's origins, as if there could be a single red thread running down the warp of the whole liturgical rug, stretching unbroken back to the ancient Church. But, alas, other historians are quick to point out that there is no such thread, and that ancient liturgical practice was not as uniform as we thought. Furthermore, since an essence is not easy to see under all that secondary subjective piety, the practiced eye of the academician is required. This is the service that the West believes the liturgical theologian provides to the Church. Thus Bernard Botte thought he was in agreement with Schmemann when the former wrote in 1968, "I fully agree with him on the role of liturgical theology. Its task is to recover the essential elements. History is not enough, for it supplies data but is not competent to issue value judgments. It is not enough to look to the past in order to find there an ideal age and suppress all that followed.... The essential here is that it be in continuity with the

---

[23] Schmemann, *Journals*, 146. Again, "In America, we often see the reduction of Orthodoxy to icons, to ancient singing, to Mt. Athos books about spiritual life. Byzantium is triumphing without a cosmic dimension. I can't avoid thinking that it is all a sort of romanticism—a love for that image of Orthodoxy, love because that image is radically different from the images of the contemporary world. Escape, departure, reduction of Orthodoxy" (*Journals*, 268).

initial impulse."²⁴ And Grisbrooke's voice chimed in the year after. "By whom is this understanding of the liturgical tradition to be attained? Presumably, by the whole body of the faithful, clergy and laity alike. By what means is it to be attained? Apparently, by instruction—spiritual and intellectual—given by a minority already enlightened, or on its way to enlightenment; that is, one must assume, by liturgical scholars."²⁵

Since I do not detect in any recent articles from the West a significant advance over the fundamental misunderstanding shared by Botte and Grisbrooke forty years ago, I will let Schmemann's reply to them still stand. First he writes:

> Grisbrooke, following in this Dom Botte, assumes that for me "the task of liturgical theology is to recover the essential and to relegate the 'accessories' to their place" and thus to prepare grounds for a liturgical reform that would restore the "essence" of the liturgy.... The fact, however, is that such is *not* my concept of liturgical theology."²⁶

And then:

> In the approach which I advocated by every line I ever wrote, the question addressed by liturgical theology to liturgy and to the entire liturgical tradition is not about liturgy but about "theology," i.e., about the faith of the Church as expressed, communicated and preserved by the liturgy.²⁷

If it's not too trite to play with neologisms, I suggest that while the West searches for an *ordo*, Schmemann searches for an *ortho*. He searches for what makes our *doxia ortho* (what makes worship *ortho*dox), but the Western liturgical historian translates that into a quest for a certain historical ordo. So enters the Western confusion of liturgical theologian and liturgical historian.

---

²⁴ Bernard Botte, "The Role of Liturgical Theology: A Debate on Liturgical Theology," in *Liturgy and Tradition: Theological Reflections of Alexander Schmemann*, ed. Thomas Fisch (Crestwood, NY: St. Vladimir's Seminary Press, 1990), 26.
²⁵ W. Jardine Grisbrooke, "Liturgical Reform: A Debate," in Fisch, *Liturgy and Tradition*, 33.
²⁶ Grisbrooke, "Liturgical Reform: A Debate," 38.
²⁷ Grisbrooke, "Liturgical Reform: A Debate," 40.

Development

The West defines life as growth, and growth as development, and development as change. That this chain of logic is not followed to the end by the East may be the most fundamental divide between East and West. If "development" means a change from one thing into another, then that is precisely denied by someone like Irenaeus, as Fr. John Behr notes in his study of the pre-Nicene fathers. "It is clear, then, that for Irenaeus 'tradition' is not alive, in the sense that it cannot change, grow or develop into something else."[28] Behr then includes a footnote from W. W. Harvey's edition (printed just twelve years after Newman's famous essay on development): "At least here there is no reserve made in favour of any theory of development. If we ever find any trace of this dangerous delusion in Christian antiquity, it is uniformly the plea of heresy."[29] For the fathers, development was a defense made by heretics. Truth doesn't change.

Irenaeus thought the Gnostics went wrong because although they had the Scriptures, they disregarded the order (*taxis*) and connection (*eirmos*) of the Scriptures. In other words, the heretics developed a different hypothesis. Behr gives contextual clues for what "hypothesis" meant for Irenaeus. In a literary context hypothesis meant the plot or outline of a drama or epic; in Aristotle it meant the first principles; the goal of health is the hypothesis for a doctor, and if one had a different hypothesis, one would prescribe a different diet. So Irenaeus says that the Gnostics have the same Scripture verses, like an artist might have the same mosaic tiles, but they have organized their verses according to a different hypothesis—and the image of a king is now turned into the image of a fox. But the Church's hypothesis is eternal and unchanging. Behr can summarize Irenaeus's basic perspective by saying, "Theological inquiry is not to be carried out by changing the hypothesis itself (thinking up another God or another Christ), but by reflecting further on whatever was said in parables, bringing out the meaning of the obscure passages, by placing them in the clear light of the 'hypothesis of truth.'"[30] And in another place, "The continually changing context in which the same unchanging Gospel is preached makes it necessary that different aspects of the same Gospel be drawn out to address contemporary challenges. However, while the context continually changes, the content of that tradition does not—it is

---

[28] Fr. John Behr, *The Formation of Christian Theology*, vol. 1, *The Way to Nicaea* (Crestwood, NY: St. Vladimir's Seminary Press, 2001), 38.
[29] Behr, *The Way to Nicaea*, 38n55.
[30] Behr, *The Way to Nicaea*, 38.

the same Gospel."³¹ If the West were more observant about this difference between context and content, it could avoid jumping to confusions. The living water never changes, but one can dig many wells.

Schmemann is aware of the historical level on which it can be said that liturgy develops, of course. So in the *Introduction to Liturgical Theology* he even writes, "The absence of development would be the sign of a fatal sclerosis."³² But the study of the Tradition is not a study of contingencies at work, it is finding the various contextual manifestations of the eternal content so that we, too, can be transformed by that truth now. If we believe in the Church, Schmemann writes, "then the study of her past has only one goal: to find, and to make ours again and again, that which in her teaching and life is truly *eternal*, i.e., which precisely transcends the categories of past, present and future and has the power to transform our lives in all ages and in all situations."³³ The goal of health is the hypothesis for a doctor, who then deliberates on how it is to be attained; the goal of deification—or supernatural health—is the hypothesis for a theologian, who then deliberates on how it is to be attained. And I propose that it is in this light that Schmemann understands the contested concept of *lex orandi*:

> What I tried to say in my book, and also in some other writings, is that the "essence" of the liturgy or *lex orandi* is ultimately nothing else but the Church's faith itself or, better to say, the manifestation, communication and fulfillment of that faith. It is in this sense

---

[31] Behr, *The Way to Nicaea*, 27. Louis Bouyer has a similar conclusion about development of doctrine with vividness. "No idea was more foreign to the ancients than the modern idea that the multiplication of definitions constitutes progress. This proliferation corresponds (in their view) to scars on the Body of truth, inflicted by the errors over which it triumphs. The *only genuine progress* in the knowledge of God, beyond what has been transmitted from the beginning by Christ and the apostles, results, according to the fathers, from the transition from faith to vision on the last day. The only anticipation that we can have of it is not in doctrinal development ... but in what they call "the science of the saints": the gnosis of Irenaeus, the mystical theology of Dionysius—the ineffable glimpse of the eternity of the blessed, which can be gratuitously communicated by God to those whose hearts and minds are sufficiently purified" (*The Church of God: Body of Christ and Temple of the Spirit* [Chicago: Franciscan Herald Press, 1982], 355).

[32] Schmemann, *Introduction to Liturgical Theology*, 16–17.

[33] Schmemann, *Of Water and the Spirit*, 150.

that one must understand, it seems to me, the famous dictum *lex orandi est lex credendi*.[34]

Suppose with me, then, that we take Schmemann at his word and treat *lex orandi* neither as a privileged thread discovered by the academic historian nor an abstract concept hatched by an academic theologian. Suppose, instead, *lex orandi* is the theological vision radiating from the Paschal mystery; the Tradition by which the Church lives; the hermeneutical principle by which we understand; a capacitation by the Holy Spirit by which we hear, receive, and know. *Lex orandi* is the hypothesis, the code, the grammar by which the Church reads Scripture traditionally, worships traditionally, believes traditionally—i.e., within the Tradition, in concord with the total experience of the Church. This is how I read a key passage in Schmemann's *Introduction*:

> To find the Ordo behind the "rubrics," regulations and rules—to find the unchanging principle, the living norm or "logos" of worship as a whole, within what is accidental and temporary: this is the primary task which faces those who regard liturgical theology not as the collecting of accidental and arbitrary explanations of services but as the systematic study of the *lex orandi* of the Church. This is nothing but the search for or identification of that element of the *Typicon* which is presupposed by its whole content, rather than contained by it.[35]

The ordo behind the rubrics, he says, is not accidental and temporary, it is unchanging ortho, a living norm, the logos of worship that is eschatological.

Eschatology: The Foundational Antinomy

Why does the West keep missing Schmemann's definition of liturgical theology? Because it still assumes that the role of liturgical theology involves finding a historical essence, then adding theological content to cult, all with the aid of a minority already enlightened. Schmemann, on the other hand, assumes that liturgical theology is the detection of Christianity's unchanging principle: eschatology. The mind of the

---

[34] Schmemann, "Liturgical Theology, Theology of Liturgy, and Liturgical Reform," 38–39.

[35] Schmemann, *Introduction to Liturgical Theology*, 32.

Church, its *lex orandi*, is eschatological. "*This* is the essence of Christianity as Eschatology. The Kingdom of God is the goal of history, and the Kingdom of God is already now *among us, within us*. Christianity is a unique historical event, and Christianity is the presence of that event as the completion of all events and of history itself. Here is, for me, *the whole meaning of liturgical theology*."[36]

To read life by the right hypothesis requires an eschatological light radiating from the sanctuary. This eschatological dimension pops up everywhere in the *Journals*:

> Yesterday, during the Liturgy (week of the Samaritan woman)—such a bright, firm sense of the presence, of truth, of light. Here, in the Liturgy, is *everything*, the "Spirit and Truth" which give birth to true disciples of the Father. Here is the *reality* of the Church, and here is where one must start its prophecy in the world. Last lecture this year: "*The Eucharist and Eschatology*." My whole heart is there.[37]

The West's anemic sense of eschatology in both its theology and in its liturgy makes it difficult for the West to understand what is at stake for Schmemann. Instead of understanding eschatology as the presence of supernatural joy, the West tends to make eschatology a doctrine of the last judgment. "Christianity ... has lost its eschatological dimension, has turned toward the world as law, judgment, redemption, recompense, as a religion of the future life; finally forbade joy and condemned happiness. There is no distinction here between Rome and Calvin."[38] Indeed, this loss of the eschatological grammar is the essence of scholasticism:

> Another preliminary question arises, about the essence of theology itself. It seems to me that in the West, theology, when it first became a science (i.e., since the appearance of scholasticism),

---

[36] Schmemann, *Journals*, 234. This has remained consistent for him. In *Introduction* he examines the collision of Christian *leitourgia* with the Jewish cultic practices out of which it came, and religious cultic practices which continued to support the Christian *leitourgia*. The cultic form is metamorphosized. And he writes, "Only by understanding the eschatological and ecclesiological basis of this 'metamorphosis' can we properly understand what constitutes historically the innate antinomy of the Christian *lex orandi*: its unquestionable continuity with Jewish tradition and its equally unquestionable newness" (*Introduction to Liturgical Theology*, 80).

[37] Schmemann, *Journals*, 165.

[38] Schmemann, *Journals*, 291.

became dependent on "this world"—on its categories, words, concepts, philosophies in the broad sense of the word.[39]

Schmemann seats his concept of liturgical theology upon an antinomy. Sometimes he calls it "the cultic antinomy" between *leitourgia* and religious cult,[40] and sometimes he is focused on the antinomous relationship between this present world and its eschatological end. Since he never pauses to define the term "antinomy," I will borrow a definition from the Russian tradition out of which Schmemann came. In *The Pillar and Ground of the Truth*, Pavel Florensky says antinomy arises from the conviction that "life is infinitely fuller than rational definitions and therefore no formula can encompass all the fullness of life."[41] (Similarly, liturgy is infinitely fuller than theological definitions and therefore no formula can encompass all the fullness of the Church.) The Spirit of Truth is one, Florensky insists, but it is not known as one when perceived by a human being who lives in time and space. We are finite, and for the finite knower, "Knowledge *of* the Truth becomes knowledge *about* the Truth. And knowledge about the Truth is *truth*."[42] Schmemann echoes this very language in a *Journal* entry about a faculty seminar in pastoral theology. "Very scientific, with Greek and psychological terminology and diagrams. . . . But the knowledge of these rules does not help, will never create pastors. Scholarly theologians do not understand, do not see it. The sum of scientifically stated truths does not discover nor reveal *Truth*. The sum of theories about God, does not give the knowledge of God."[43]

Florensky summarizes: "Antinomicalness does not say, 'Either the one or the other is not true.' It also does not say, 'Neither the one nor the other is true.' It only says, 'Both the one and the other are true, but each in its

---

[39] Schmemann, *Journals*, 279–80.

[40] The fact that the Church finally adopted the word *leitourgia* to name her cult "indicates her special understanding of worship, which is indeed a revolutionary one. If Christian worship is *leitourgia*, it cannot be simply reduced to, or expressed in terms of, 'cult.' The ancient world knew a plethora of cultic religions or 'cults.' . . . But the Christian cult is *leitourgia*, and this means that it is *functional* in its essence, has a goal to achieve which transcends the categories of cult as such" (Alexander Schmemann, "Theology and Liturgical Tradition," in *Liturgy and Tradition: Theological Reflections of Alexander Schmemann*, ed. Thomas Fisch [Crestwood, NY: St. Vladimir's Seminary Press, 1990], 40).

[41] Pavel Florensky, *The Pillar and Ground of the Truth: An Essay in Orthodox Theodicy in Twelve Letters* (Princeton: Princeton University Press, 1997), 108.

[42] Florensky, *The Pillar and Ground of the Truth*, 107.

[43] Schmemann, *Journals*, 229.

own way. Reconciliation and unity are higher than rationality.'"[44] What Schmemann desires to reconcile in unity is this world and its eschatological end, the old and the new. If we emphasize world to the exclusion of eschaton, we have history turned in upon itself and living according to its own mortal meaning; if we emphasize eschaton to the exclusion of world, we have a dramatic cultic ceremony that is irrelevant to life. But when the antinomy is firing with both pistons, then we have joy. A smile must be made with two lips, and the joy Schmemann is talking about cannot be made with world alone, or cult alone.

Schmemann's emphasis upon *leitourgia*, meaning the work of a few on behalf of the many, comes clear at last. "The Church itself is a *leitourgia*, a ministry, a calling to act in this world after the fashion of Christ, to bear testimony to him and His kingdom."[45] The Church as *leitourgia* is the presence of the Kingdom in the midst of history, so that history can find its meaning. Schmemann says that all his interest is directed toward the correlation of life's reality with what the liturgical cult celebrates.

Christian liturgy occurs as an arc of electricity between the two poles of world and Kingdom: move the poles too close together *or* too far apart, and the arc will not happen.[46] Western theology curricula have not forgotten the topic of eschatology, but they have tended to either relax the tension in the antinomy or overstrain it, by moving the Church too near the world or too far from it. Then liturgical theology does not spark. On the one hand, "The Protestant builds a useful, comfortable earthly life. In none of its aspects does it remind one of paradise, does it open it, or reveal it. The Protestant lives in the fallen world, not referred any more to the primordial, joyous, divine world. He is bound with the world by his reason, knowledge, analysis, but not faith, not a sacramental intuition."[47] On the other hand, the Catholic at least remembers—which is something, but not enough. In the "gilded, sometimes tastelessly heavily decorated churches, there is longing for paradise, and there are pieces of paradise, of joy." But Catholicism of late has followed suit "with a dull social message and service to the world."[48] On the one hand, "Protestantism was an attempt to save the faith, to purify it from its religious reduction. But the Protestants have paid a heavy price for denying eschatology and replacing

---

[44] Florensky, *The Pillar and Ground of the Truth*, 118.
[45] Schmemann, *For the Life of the World*, 25.
[46] The image of an arc between poles came to me first when reading Romano Guardini's twinned works, *The Church and the Catholic*, and *The Spirit of the Liturgy*.
[47] Schmemann, *Journals*, 125.
[48] Schmemann, *Journals*, 125.

it with personal individual salvation; and therefore, essentially, denying the Church."[49] On the other hand, when Schmemann watched Pope John II serve the Mass on his visit to New York in 1979, he recorded that his

> first impression is how liturgically impoverished the Catholic Church has become. In 1965, I watched the service performed by Pope Paul VI in the same Yankee Stadium. Despite everything, it was the presence, the appearance on earth of the eternal, the "super earthly." Whereas yesterday, I had the feeling that the main thing was the "message." This message is, again and again, "peace and justice," "human family," "social work," etc. An opportunity was given, a fantastic chance to tell millions and millions of people about God, to reveal to them that more than anything else they need God! But here, on the contrary, the whole goal, it seemed, consisted in proving that the Church *also* can speak the jargon of the United Nations.[50]

The West either loses the eschatological nature of the Church in becoming worldly wise, or it ceases to be the life of the world as it becomes heavenly minded. The foundational antinomy of liturgical theology is holding a correct tension between the two poles. Sacred and profane find their balance.

What the Church Offers the World

Throughout the *Journals* Schmemann finds different ways to summarize his position, as if coming to the same conclusion with equal freshness each time. I will pick this entry as a concluding summary:

> Christianity in general, and Orthodoxy in particular, are now undergoing a real test to determine what will enable them to remain alive in the world of today.... I hesitate to come forward with my feeling—it sounds arrogant—that I have an answer! In everything that I preach, or teach, or write, I want this answer to appear, hopefully to shine through.... It is simply a vision of life, and what comes from that vision is the light, the transparency, the referral of everything to the "other," the eschatological character

---

[49] Schmemann, *Journals*, 153.
[50] Schmemann, *Journals*, 229–30.

of life itself and all that is in it. The source of that eschatological light, the lifting up of all life, is the sacrament of the Eucharist.[51]

This is how theological vision is grounded in the liturgy: the church-at-Eucharist is the source of this eschatological light because here the Kingdom of God spiritualizes matter, reveals the meaning of history, and deifies man and woman. The *lex orandi* yields a doctrine of creation that asserts matter was made to be sacrament; it yields an eschatology that asserts everything is destined for glory; it yields an anthropology that asserts the image of God can attain the likeness of God (deification); it yields a Christology that asserts the reign of God brings with it obligations to the poor, imprisoned, and outcast; and it yields an ecclesiology that asserts the Church manifests the potency of the world. When Schmemann thinks about liturgy, he is thinking about the world in its course of redemption. That, indeed, is how he defines "church." "The church is not a religious establishment, but the presence in the world of a saved world."[52] *Leitourgia* is the Church's work on behalf of the world. In the liturgy, the world presents itself to be blessed, and God lifts the world to its spiritual fulfillment; the world is liturgy in its potency and the liturgy is the world in act.[53] The cost of understanding Schmemann is the cost of holding this antinomy in proper tension.

What Christianity offers to the world is joy. But salt that has lost its saltiness is good for nothing but being trampled underfoot. "What has Christianity lost so that the world, nurtured by Christianity, has recoiled from it and started to pass judgment over the Christian faith? Christianity has lost *joy*—not natural joy, not joy-optimism, not joy from earthly happiness, but the Divine joy about which Christ told us that 'no one will take your joy from you' (John 16:22)."[54] This must be joy on God's terms, not man's. Christianity must not sell its birthright for a bowl full of

---

[51] Schmemann, *Journals*, 24.

[52] Schmemann, *Journals*, 32. This echoes the definition Olivier Clément gives: "In its deepest understanding the Church is nothing other than the world in the course of transfiguration, the world that in Christ reflects the light of paradise" (*The Roots of Christian Mysticism* [New York: New City Press, 1993], 95).

[53] The thought is intended to mimic Maximus the Confessor's comment about sanctuary and nave in his commentary on the liturgy. "Thus, the nave is *the sanctuary in potency* by being consecrated by the relationship of the sacrament toward its end, and in turn the sanctuary is *the nave in act* by possessing the principle of its own sacrament" (italics added) ("The Church's Mystagogy," in *Maximus Confessor: Selected Writings*, trans. George Berthold [Mahwah, NJ: 1985], 188).

[54] Schmemann, *Journals*, 291.

temporary relevance. Adapting eschatological joy to the passing moods of the ages—in either our theology or our liturgies—will not gain credibility for Christianity. It is a false strategy to commit to the unending task of rewriting the content for each context. Schmemann says that capitulating theology to the categories and concepts of this world results in a "constant need of an adaptation, a verification—not of this world by the Good News of Christianity and the Christian experience, but *of* the Good News itself and its content—by this world and its "mutations."[55] These mutations, Schmemann says, produce a panic, and the panic leads to two orientations: either a dissolution of faith into worldly terms, or a spiritual escapism satisfied with cult. "The first choice is realized by reinterpreting faith (which, if understood correctly, must justify sex, abortion, euthanasia and revolution). The second choice is realized, for example, by reducing the whole Christian tradition, to, say, rubrics."[56] The Lion of Judah will not be retrained by our philosophies, nor restrained by our ritual catnip. Instead, "What is revealed surpasses and therefore tears apart life—the gift of joy 'which nobody will take away from you.' Genuine Christianity is bound to disturb the heart with this tearing—that is the force of eschatology. But one does not feel it in these smooth ceremonies where everything is neat, right, but without eschatological 'other worldliness.'"[57] The joy Schmemann describes comes with the price of a liturgical asceticism that pries open closed hearts.

For the West to understand Schmemann's idea, theology will have to receive its vision from the liturgical epiphany, and thus be able to look at all its subject matter with the eyes of the Dove. History will be seen against the horizon of eternity, matter will be seen sacramentally, each *imago Dei* will be seen in process to deified likeness to God. All theology will become Eucharistic, though the Eucharist will not be the only thing that theology studies. Once that happens, the theology can be as clear, organized, precise, and scholarly as you like.

Three Concluding Questions

I have not paused at any point to defend the West from any of these characterizations. That would be for another conference. All I have tried to do is make as pointed as possible what I hear behind the accusation when

---

[55] Schmemann, *Journals*, 279–80.
[56] Schmemann, *Journals*, 279–80.
[57] Schmemann, *Journals*, 122.

something is called "Westernized." I have tried to present that as a series of seven reductions: a holistic vision becomes a rational exercise, the theological vision becomes confused with the vision of theologians, tradition becomes precedence, ortho becomes ordo, tradition becomes contingency, the eschatological antinomy is relaxed, and the Church transforms the Gospel into either a relevant social message or an irrelevant cultic exercise. As a result, liturgy is thought to be an emotional appendage to theology, academics seek to add content to ritual studies, and liturgical theology is thought to be the task of finding a historical essence. In this way, I think the West fails to understand Schmemann's idea of liturgical theology.

But you will remember that I did distinguish three meanings of the concept "West"—geographical west, cultural West, and unorthodox West. With those three meanings in mind, I can pose three concluding questions.

First, need the geographical west be "Western?" Notice that it was neither geography nor history that constitutes scholasticism. Schmemann writes, "By 'scholastic' we mean, in this instance, not a definite school or period in the history of theology, but a theological structure which existed in various forms *in both the West and the East*, and in which all 'organic' connections with worship is severed."[58] And when Schmemann wants to talk about the corrosive effects of scholasticism, he offers us an example of the monopoly the scholastic type of theology has had. "A good example is the Eastern Orthodox Church, justly considered to be the liturgical Church *par excellence*." Why? Because "liturgical tradition has played practically no role, and has been almost totally ignored, even as a *locus theologicus*."[59] The sidelining of liturgical tradition has happened in both the East and the West, and should be repaired in both, and being geographically west need not stand in the way.

Second, I said "Western" means a culture, a style, a mind, which Orthodoxy feels as a captivity. Need the cultural West be "Western?" In other words, if the fundamental antinomy out of which Schmemann understands liturgical theology to be born is the presence of the eschatological in the world, may this antinomy be experienced in the cultural West? Schmemann reminisces in the first pages of his journal about an early experience of vividly coming to this sensation, and it was in the very cultural, Western city of Paris:

---

[58] Schmemann, "Theology and Liturgical Tradition," 13, italics added.
[59] Schmemann, "Theology and Liturgical Tradition," 13.

> During my school years in Paris, on my way to the Lycee Carnot, I would stop by the Church of St. Charles of Monceau for two or three minutes. And always, in this huge, dark church, at one of the altars, a silent Mass was being said.... Sometimes I think of the contrast: a noisy, proletarian rue Legendre ... and this never-changing Mass—one step, and one is in a totally different world. This contrast somehow determined in my religious experience the intuition that has never left me: the coexistence of two heterogeneous worlds, the presence in this world of something absolutely and totally "other." This "other" illuminates everything, in one way or another. Everything is related to it—the Church as the Kingdom of God among and inside us. For me, rue Legendre never became unnecessary, or hostile, or nonexistent—hence my aversion to pure "spiritualism." On the contrary, the street, as it was, acquired a new charm that was understandable and obvious only to me, who knew at that moment the Presence, the feast revealed in the Mass nearby. Everything became alive, intriguing: every storefront window, the face of every person I met, the concrete, tangible feeling of that moment, the relationship between the street, the weather, the houses, the people.

What was going on in the street was to be correlated with what was going on in that silent Mass, and Schmemann identifies this as his life's work, and gives it a name:

> This experience remains with me forever: a very strong sense of "life" in its physical, bodily reality, in the uniqueness of every minute and of its correlations with life's reality. At the same time, this interest has always been rooted solely in the correlation of all of this with what the silent Mass was a witness to and reminder of, the presence and the joy. What is that correlation? It seems to me that I am quite unable to explain and determine it, although it is actually the only thing that I talk and write about ("liturgical theology").... This correlation is a tie, not an idea; an experience. It is the experience of the world and life literally in the light of the Kingdom of God.[60]

---

[60] Schmemann, *Journals*, 19–20.

Schmemann experienced the antinomy that would become his life's work when a Western silent Mass was juxtaposed with a bustling, Western city. The cultural West need not stand in the way.

The third use of the term "West" I mentioned was the sense of being unorthodox. It seems to me that here "orthodox" is being used as a plumb line, and "Westernized" means those occasions when that line is transgressed. If something has been taught in Orthodoxy for centuries, how is it not Orthodox teaching? Because in this third sense, "orthodox" doesn't mean what we *do* find in the East; it means what we *should* find in the East. Orthodoxy is prescriptive—a canonical term indicating what ought to be. With that understanding, I ask if the West is by necessity "Western?" When Schmemann, and others, complain about Orthodoxy having been Westernized, they mean to support a reform that would restore orthodoxy to Orthodoxy. And in his first book, *Introduction to Liturgical Theology*, Schmemann acknowledges that such a current of reform runs in the Western liturgical movement:

> It should be added here that even though the liturgical revival as an organized movement arose and developed for the most part among non-Orthodox people in the West, it has nevertheless a deep internal bond with the Church in the East, and is therefore of special interest to Orthodox theologians. From a certain point of view and with a critical appraisal of each of its achievements, it can be regarded *as a kind of "Orthodox" movement in a non-Orthodox context*, since this is the restoration in the thought and life of the church of those emphases and categories which were in some measure lost by the Christian West.[61]

Is an Orthodox movement in a non-Orthodox context the same as saying a Western movement that is not Western? If once upon a time the East was Westernized for having let liturgy, theology, and piety drift apart, cannot the reverse also happen and the West be Easternized by bringing liturgy, theology, and piety back together? I leave that question for a later, ecumenical conference. For now I only wish to conclude by saying that in Schmemann's opinion, this would mean coming to understand liturgical theology as the place where the eternal antinomy of Christianity is reconciled:

---

[61] Schmemann, *Introduction to Liturgical Theology*, 13, italics added.

Here is, for me, *the whole meaning of liturgical theology*. The Liturgy: the joining, revelation, actualization of the historicity of Christianity (remembrance) and of its transcendence over that historicity....

Hence, the link of the Church with the world, the Church *for the world*, but as its beginning and its end, as the affirmation that the world is *for the Church*, since the Church is the presence of the Kingdom of God.

Here is the eternal antinomy of Christianity and the essence of all contemporary discussions about Christianity. The task of theology is to be faithful to the antinomy, which disappears in the experience of the Church as *pascha*: a *continuous* (not only historical) passage of the world to the Kingdom. All the time one must leave the world and all the time one must remain in it.[62]

---

[62] Schmemann, *Journals*, 234.

Schmemann's Anchor
The Anchor of Schmemann's Liturgical Theology[*]

I know many colleagues who in their dissertation have taken a deep dive into a subject or an author, never to return again to drink from those waters. Sometimes that is for the best (some authors who fascinate us during our doctoral teenage years are better left on the shelf when we grow up); sometimes it is realistic (we have sucked the topic dry); sometimes it is a sign of industriousness (finding new points on the horizon); sometimes it is a sign of fickle ambition (an academic must always be on the prowl for "the next big thing"). I am grateful to report that none of these circumstances have been the case for me because I was fortunate enough to have found a topic that continues to fascinate me, and an author whose guidance and counsel remain pertinent. Fr. Alexander was an essential guide when I began writing a dissertation simply titled "What Is Liturgical Theology?" and he has remained a reliable pedagogue for the thirty years since, while I have added clay to the bust I am sculpting. I can imagine a critic heckling from the wings, "Have you not advanced at all? Move on! We have heard about *lex orandi* before." But to me this sounds like saying to an iconographer, "Have you not advanced at all? Move on! We have seen the Theotokos before." Yes we have thought it and seen it before, but not exactly in this way. The icon is worth painting again with one's own brushstrokes, and some thoughts are worth brushing up against again with one's own words. Indeed, my experience when reading a great theologian is to find either my thoughts in their words, or their thoughts in my words. I have that same experience when reading Fr. Alexander; that's how I know he is a great theologian. So I return to him with regularity, and am honored to be able to come here and express my gratitude publicly.

Coming up with the title of a talk is a challenge because one must essentially write the paper months in advance of actually writing the paper, so when Fr. Hatfield asked for mine, I put the Muses to work on

---

[*] David W. Fagerberg, "The Anchor of Schmemann's Liturgical Theology: The Schmemann Lecture January 2010," *St. Vladimir's Theological Quarterly* 63, no. 4 (2019): 397–422.

it overnight. When I awoke, I found that they had placed in my mind a feeling, an intuition, an impression. It was the feeling of "an anchor." I felt that Fr. Alexander had anchored his liturgical theology to some bedrock, to some foundation that grounded and secured his perspective. People fail to understand his idea of liturgical theology if they let *lex orandi* float free. In this drift, its relationship to *lex credendi* is misunderstood. But *lex orandi* does not float free for Fr. Alexander, it is anchored. It has a foundation, a mooring, a sub-stance, if I may make a scholastic pun. Now, to only find out what that is! I wish the Muses had gone on to identify it, but that is the part of the labor they left for me. What is the fixed point that gives cohesion to Fr. Alexander's understanding of liturgical theology? We must do some archaeology.

Recently in Jerusalem there was a man who built his house on a site he strongly suspected had been inhabited during the Second Temple period, so this owner began digging under his own home. The entrance to his house was at street-level, but below it, underneath, he found a Hasmonean mansion. Imagine with me now "the house of Schmemann." It is his life's work, his intellectual construct, his theological paradigm. This house is what we want to explore today, and in order to do so, we must excavate. Most people enter Schmemann's thought at the street-level of liturgy, because for that he is famous. They expect this floor to be pretty and charming because they suppose he has built his whole house to lodge liturgy, and liturgy must be billeted in a house of mystical and classical adornments. But he himself strongly objects to supposing this is the only floor of his house, or supposing that his primary work concerns liturgical decor. Here are three examples of him objecting. First, "In the approach which I advocate by every line I ever wrote, the question addressed by liturgical theology to liturgy and to the entire liturgical tradition is not about liturgy but about 'theology.'"[1] Second, "In my own tradition, the Byzantine, this has meant, for example, the appearance of endless symbolic explanations of worship, and so the Eucharistic Liturgy that is the heart of the Church has been transformed in effect into a series of audio-visual aids."[2] And third, he confesses, "How spiritually tired I am of all this 'Orthodoxism,' of all the fuss with Byzantium, Russia, way of life, spirituality, church affairs, piety, of all these rattles. I do not like any one of

---

[1] Alexander Schmemann, "Liturgical Theology, Theology of Liturgy, and Liturgical Reform," in *Liturgy and Tradition: Theological Reflections of Alexander Schmemann*, ed. Thomas Fisch (Crestwood, NY: St. Vladimir's Seminary Press, 1990), 40.

[2] Alexander Schmemann, "Liturgy and Eschatology," in Fisch, *Liturgy and Tradition*, 96.

them, and the more I think about the meaning of Christianity, the more it all seems alien to me."[3]

The man who is famed as a liturgical theologian says his main interest is not liturgical embellishment. This first floor is not his total occupation. I therefore propose we do him an injustice if we fail to excavate down to the anchor of his thought. Like an excellent theological architect, he has carefully designed the skeletal structure of his whole house. I have concluded four strata to his thought. Here they are in summary, from top floor (at which we usually enter) to the foundational first floor (toward which we are working).

4. *Liturgical theology* (consisting of *lex orandi* and *lex credendi*)
3. rests upon *leitourgia* (which is different from our ordinary understanding of liturgy)
2. because it is anchored to *eschatology* (whence ecclesiology begins)
1. which is built upon *Christ*.

That is my summary blueprint of the house of Schmemann; what follows is each strata explored one by one.

Liturgical Theology

If one enters the Schmemannian digs, it is probably on the floor of liturgy, to see what the man has to say about liturgical theology. I will be cursory in my description here, because my other work has already given attention to it. Schmemann's understanding of liturgical theology continues to puzzle both liturgists and theologians, because instead of placing liturgy and theology side by side—the former being decorative illustration, the latter granting academic respectability—Schmemann proposes an ontological dependence of the one upon the other. Here are some examples: "Liturgical tradition ... is the ontological condition of theology, of the proper understanding of kerygma, of the Word of God, because it is in the Church, of which the *leitourgia* is the expression and the life, that the sources of theology are functioning precisely as sources";[4] "[the fathers] rarely speak of the Church and of liturgy in explicit terms because for them they are not an 'object' of theology but its ontological foundation";[5] he thinks problems arise "because theology ceased to seek in the *lex orandi* its source

---

[3] Alexander Schmemann, *The Journals of Father Alexander Schmemann 1973–1983* (Crestwood, NY: St. Vladimir's Seminary Press, 2002), 146.
[4] Alexander Schmemann, "Theology and Liturgical Tradition," in Fisch, *Liturgy and Tradition*, 18.
[5] Schmemann, "Liturgical Theology, Theology of Liturgy, and Liturgical Reform," 42.

and food, because liturgy ceased to be conducive to theology."[6] This idea of an ontological foundation is how he approaches a classic, traditional, yet today controversial, dictum. The essence of the liturgy is the Church's faith itself, and "it is in this sense that one must understand, it seems to me, the famous dictum *lex orandi est lex credendi*."[7] "The formula *lex orandi est lex credendi* means nothing else than that theology is *possible* only within the Church."[8] "The affirmation *lex orandi lex est credendi* means that it is again in the mystery of the Church that theology finds its inner fulfillment."[9] When we turn to the liturgy itself, we discover "the forgotten truth of the ancient saying: *lex orandi est lex credendi*."[10] Liturgy's ecclesial function is to reveal the faith of the Church by being "that *lex orandi* in which the *lex credendi* finds its principal criterion and standard."[11] "Theology must rediscover as its own 'rule of faith' the Church's *lex orandi*, and the liturgy reveal itself again as the *lex credendi*."[12] "Theologians have forgotten the essential principle that *lex orandi* constitutes the *lex credendi*; they have forgotten the absolutely unique function of Christian worship within all theological speculation."[13]

I believe he has made his point. But why is it so hard for us to take him seriously when he says this about theology?

Schmemann thinks that the alienation of *lex credendi* from *lex orandi* occurred when "the 'source' of theology, i.e., the Church's faith, began to be identified with a specific number of 'data,' mainly texts," and once faith was identified with propositions, there followed "the rejection from the theological process of any reference to or dependence upon experience. Yet it is precisely faith *as experience*, the total and living experience of the Church, that constitutes the source and the context of theology in the East."[14] In his *Journals* Schmemann records such a living experience. "Holy Week. Essentially, bright days such as are needed. And truly that is all that is needed. I am convinced that if people would really hear Holy Week, Pascha, the Resurrection, Pentecost, the Dormition, there would be no

---

[6] Schmemann, "Liturgical Theology, Theology of Liturgy, and Liturgical Reform," 46–47.
[7] Schmemann, "Liturgical Theology, Theology of Liturgy, and Liturgical Reform," 38–39.
[8] Schmemann, "Theology and Liturgical Tradition," 18.
[9] Alexander Schmemann, "Liturgy and Theology," in Fisch, *Liturgy and Tradition*, 64.
[10] Alexander Schmemann, "Symbols and Symbolism in the Byzantine Liturgy: Liturgical Symbols and Their Theological Interpretation," in Fisch, *Liturgy and Tradition*, 128.
[11] Alexander Schmemann, "Liturgical Theology: Remarks on Method," in Fisch, *Liturgy and Tradition*, 138.
[12] Schmemann, "Liturgy and Theology," 68.
[13] Schmemann, "Liturgy and Eschatology," 95.
[14] Schmemann, "Liturgy and Theology," 53–54.

need for theology. All of theology is there."[15] If the source of theology is not bare text, but involves faith as experience, then what does this make liturgical theology? "'Description' more than 'definition,'" he answers, "for it is, above all, a search for words and concepts adequate to and expressive of the living experience of the Church; for a reality and not 'propositions.'"[16] There is a correlation between life and the Eucharist, but when asked what that correlation is, he confesses, "It seems to me that I am quite unable to explain and determine it, although it is actually the only thing that I talk and write about ('liturgical theology'). It is not an 'idea': I feel repulsed by 'ideas'; I have an ever-growing conviction that Christianity cannot be expressed by 'ideas.'"[17] When he talks and writes about liturgical theology, he is engaged in a search for reality, a search for the connection between God, world, and life, and this is a more challenging undertaking. "To understand liturgy from inside, to discover and experience that 'epiphany' of God, world and life which the liturgy contains and communicates, to relate this vision and this power to our own existence, to all our problems: such is the purpose of liturgical theology."[18] "We need liturgical theology . . . as a slow and patient bringing together of that which was for too long a time and because of many factors broken and isolated—liturgy, theology, and piety, their reintegration within one fundamental vision."[19]

That is the floor plan of the top level of the house of Schmemann that we usually visit, but its layout is determined by the stratum below it: his definition of *leitourgia*.

Leitourgia

Here is the point at which I think many people take the wrong turn in interpreting Schmemann. They suppose that since *lex orandi* is liturgy, and since liturgy is ritual, and since ritual is a human product (because it is a human activity), to say theology rests upon *lex orandi* sounds like saying theology rests upon our own shoulders. At minimum this sounds tautological; at maximum it should sound blasphemous, because if human ritual actions are the ontological foundation of theology, then it appears that we've founded the Church's *lex credendi* upon ourselves. But Schmemann

---

[15] Schmemann, *Journals*, 13.
[16] Schmemann, "Liturgy and Theology," 54.
[17] Schmemann, *Journals*, 20.
[18] Alexander Schmemann, *Of Water and the Spirit: A Liturgical Study of Baptism* (Crestwood, NY: St. Vladimir's Seminary Press, 1974), 12.
[19] Schmemann, "Liturgical Theology, Theology of Liturgy, and Liturgical Reform," 46.

is not advocating that theology rests upon our composed rituals. In his liturgical theology, *lex orandi* is anchored to something firmer than the rickety notion of liturgy most of us carry in our minds, and I think he resorts to the Greek word *leitourgia* so often for the purpose of contrasting our understanding with the reality itself. He writes, "In the early Church ... even the term *leitourgia* was not, as it is today, a mere synonym of cult. It was applied indeed to all those ministries and offices within the Church in which she manifested and fulfilled her nature and vocation; it had primarily ecclesiological and not cultic connotations."[20] *Leitourgia* is "a corporate, common, all embracing action in which all those who are present are active participants";[21] is an experience of the Church "given and received in the Church's *leitourgia*—in her *lex orandi*."[22] The anchor of *lex orandi* is a more vigorous notion of *leitourgia*.

Although it is true that *leitourgia* is especially identified with the divine cult, Schmemann is adamant that we cannot equate the two because the Church's *leitourgia* is bigger than the Church's cultic liturgy that contains it:

> We know that originally the Greek word *leitourgia* had no cultic connotations. It meant a public office, a service performed on behalf of a community and for its benefit. In the Septuagint, the word acquired naturally a religious meaning, yet still not necessarily a "liturgical" one. It implied the same idea of service, applied now to the chosen people of God whose specific *leitourgia* is to fulfill God's design in history, to prepare the "way of the Lord." The early Christian use reflected the same meaning of *leitourgia*. The fact that the Church adopted it finally for her cult, and especially for the Eucharist, indicates her special understanding of worship, which is indeed a revolutionary one. If Christian worship is *leitourgia* it cannot be simply reduced to, or expressed in, terms of "cult." The ancient world knew a plethora of cultic religions or "cults"—in which worship or cultic acts were the only real content of religion, an "end in itself." But the Christian cult is *leitourgia* and this means that it is functional in its essence, has a goal to achieve which transcends the categories of cult as

---

[20] Schmemann, "Liturgy and Theology," 56.
[21] Alexander Schmemann, "Clergy and Laity in the Orthodox Church," *Orthodox Life* (Crestwood, NY: St. Vladimir's Seminary Press, 1959), https://oca.org/reflections/fr-alexander-schmemann/clergy-and-laity-in-the-orthodox-church, accessed July 31, 2018.
[22] Schmemann, "Liturgy and Theology," 55.

such. This goal is precisely the Church as the manifestation and presence of the "new eon," of the Kingdom of God. In a sense the Church is indeed a *liturgical institution*, i.e., an institution whose *leitourgia* is to fulfill itself as the Body of Christ and a new creation. Christian cult is, therefore, a radically new cult.[23]

The Church is indeed a liturgical institution, but that does not mean an institution of this world conducting endless cycles of liturgy. The reason the Church is called a liturgical institution is because she is in a constant state of passover, or pasch. The eternal passover will only come with the second coming of Christ, but here we are given foretastes of it.

If *leitourgia* originally meant a public work on behalf of a people, then to understand *leitourgia* we should be asking ourselves what work, by whom, on behalf of what people, and, most especially, toward what end? Israel had a *leitourgia* (and we don't mean the liturgy in the temple): its work was to prepare for the Messiah. The new Israel has a *leitourgia* (and we still don't mean the liturgy in the temple): its work, we shall see, is eschatological. The liturgical cult has the unique function of making the Church the "witness and participant of the saving event of Christ, of the new life in the Holy Spirit, of the presence in 'this world' of the Kingdom to come."[24] Christian *leitourgia* is not the addition of one more cult of Adam to the world's stockpile; it is the cult of the New Adam, perpetuated in his body, the Church.

The only way to grasp this is by what Schmemann calls "cultic antinomy." In this antinomy, the liturgy's inside is bigger than its outside: the *leitourgia* is bigger than the liturgy that contains it. "In this world, the *Eschaton*—the holy, the sacred, the 'otherness'—can be expressed and manifested only as 'cult.' . . . The Church must use the forms and language of the cult, in order eternally to transcend the cult."[25] The liturgical tradition of the Church is fundamentally antinomical because the Church does not gather for the purpose of celebrating the cult, she gathers to become, through cultic activity, what she really is. "The *leitourgia*, therefore, is not a cultic action performed in the Church, on its behalf, and for it; it is the action of the Church itself, or the Church *in actu*, it is the very expression of its life. . . . The *ecclesia* exists in and through the *leitourgia*, and its whole life is a *leitourgia*."[26] In one place Schmemann describes various cultic

---

[23] Alexander Schmemann, "Theology and Eucharist," in Fisch, *Liturgy and Tradition*, 79.
[24] Schmemann, "Liturgy and Theology," 56.
[25] Schmemann, "Theology and Liturgical Tradition," 17–18.
[26] Schmemann, "Theology and Liturgical Tradition," 17.

activities of the Church—baptism by water, coming together on the Lord's day, hearing God's word, eating and drinking at the altar table—and then concludes, "All this was not understood as mere 'cultic acts' but above all, as the fulfillment by the Church of her very nature, of her cosmical and eschatological calling.... The Church is the mystery of the new creation and she is the mystery of the Kingdom."[27]

If I can risk making my point clumsily, I will say that Schmemann is not talking about acts of liturgy; he is talking about liturgical acts of *leitourgia*. And if I may press my luck further, and create a verb, I will say that *leitourgia* is the action being performed when the Church "cults." By "culting" the Church becomes her true self, enjoys her true mystery, exercises her real *leitourgia*. The Church does not do cult, she uses cult to do *leitourgia*. And the *leitourgia* performed in her cult transforms the Church. "When I say that the entire liturgy is a *transformation*, I have in mind something very simple: that in the liturgy each of its parts, each solemn ceremony, each rite is transformed by the Holy Spirit into *that which it is*, a 'real symbol' of what it manifests."[28] This transformation is the reason why the liturgy can be said to be the ontological source of theology. "If ... it is the very function of the *leitourgia* to be the 'epiphany' of the Church's faith, to 'make the Church what she is,' then theology must find its way back to that source."[29] The Church's theological charism (and theology is a charism insofar as it is a Christian service, a *leitourgia*, a gift of the Holy Spirit[30]) comes from her fructifying experience of herself in the liturgy. The Church receives a vision from her self-experience in *leitourgia*, and that vision is theological. The Christian-at-liturgy receives a light-in-the-eyes which is an eschatological power of seeing through the material to the spiritual, through the visible to the invisible, through the created to the Uncreated. By *leitourgia* we are given the light, i.e., vision, by which to see and talk about the real subject matter of theology, which is God-man-world. The Church is cosmical and eschatological because at the very source and constitution of her life and faith she is given "the experience of the new creation, the experience and vision of the Kingdom which is to come. And this is precisely the *leitourgia* of the Church's cult,

---

[27] Schmemann, "Liturgy and Theology," 56.
[28] Alexander Schmemann, *The Eucharist* (Crestwood, NY: St. Vladimir's Seminary Press, 1987), 223.
[29] Schmemann, "Liturgy and Theology," 62.
[30] Schmemann, "Theology and Eucharist," 87.

the function which makes it the source and indeed the very possibility of theology."[31]

Theology seeks words adequate to the actions of God, but it is crucial to remember that the *opus Dei* is not only in the past and not only in the future. The work of God on behalf of his people toward the end of salvation can be experienced now, presently, this day, in the journey to the Kingdom that the Church experiences in her corporate procession and passage toward fulfillment. If today the field of liturgical studies does not attempt liturgical theology, that is due partly to where the interests of today's scholars lie, but due mostly to the mistaken detachment of liturgy from *leitourgia*. Liturgy absent *mysterion* is like the shell that remains after the oyster has died (and the pearl is long gone) and such a view of liturgy invites ritual studies instead of liturgical theology. If liturgy is detached from *leitourgia*, if cult is no longer a *leitourgia*-task, if liturgy is reduced to cultic categories alone, then of course scholars will run it through the sausage grinder of ritual studies. Yet even in such circumstances, Schmemann thinks some people will remain enamored of liturgy. "Paradoxical as it may seem, it is very often the liturgical 'conservative,' the passionate lover of rubrics and externals, the amateur of 'ancient and colorful' rites that is most hopelessly blind to the true meaning of these very rites, to the 'Truth and Spirit' which gave them birth and of which they are both manifestation and gift."[32] Such passionate lovers will fondle the liturgy, but fail to do justice to *leitourgia*. "One may be deeply attached to the 'ancient and colorful rites' of Byzantium or Russia, see in them precious relics of a cherished past, be a liturgical 'conservative'; and, at the same time, completely fail to see in them, in the totality of the Church's *leitourgia*, an all-embracing vision of life, a power meant to judge, inform and transform the whole of existence, a 'philosophy of life' shaping and challenging all our ideas, attitudes and actions."[33]

Liturgical theology must be ontologically fastened to *leitourgia*. "The theological and liturgical tragedy of the post-patristic age is that the Church's cult was deprived of its liturgical function, reduced to cultic categories alone,"[34] with the sad result that theologians now neglect to learn "the oldest of all languages of the Church, that of her rites, the rhythm in the ordo of her *leitourgia*."[35] In that rhythm of *lex orandi* we

---

[31] Schmemann, "Liturgy and Theology," 58.
[32] Schmemann, "Liturgy and Theology," 58.
[33] Schmemann, "Liturgy and Theology," 52.
[34] Schmemann, "Liturgy and Theology," 58.
[35] Schmemann, "Liturgy and Theology," 65.

find an all-embracing vision of life, we find a power that allows us to judge and inform and transform existence, we find eschatology—our next foundational stratum.

Eschatology

Question: To what is *leitourgia* anchored? Answer: Eschatology. "What eschatology does is to hold together things which otherwise are broken up and treated as separate events.... And when they are treated in that way, the true function of Liturgy is forgotten."[36] Since liturgy is the Church's specific and unique function, it is here "that the Church is informed of her cosmical and eschatological vocation, receives the power to fulfill it and thus truly becomes 'what she is'—the sacrament, in Christ, of the new creation; the sacrament, in Christ, of the Kingdom."[37] Minus eschatology, the Church will become "an organization among organizations, an activity among activities."[38] If the Church does not reveal and communicate the eschaton, then she "is but an institution among other human institutions."[39] This is a state of affairs about which Schmemann complains in his *Journals*. "Without putting the Eucharist at the very center, the Church is a 'religious phenomenon,' but not the Church of Christ," and in a moment of candor he adds, "If I have a vocation, it is here, in the fight for the Eucharist, against this reduction, against the de-churching of the Church."[40] An interesting phrase to describe a disastrous condition: de-churching of the Church because her liturgy does not reveal and communicate the eschaton. Instead, the liturgy becomes an activity among activities, which is why he diagnoses our problem as the omission "of the essentially eschatological nature of the *leitourgia*—its ultimate relation to and dependence upon the central object of Christian faith, i.e., the Kingdom of God."[41]

Someone will object that it is incorrect to say that we have forgotten eschatology. Is it not still included in our theological curriculum? Do we not have readings on the Last Things in our students' syllabus? Schmemann agrees that manuals of theology have included "a chapter or

---

[36] Schmemann, "Liturgy and Eschatology," 96.
[37] Schmemann, "Liturgy and Theology," 57.
[38] Schmemann, *Journals*, 327.
[39] Alexander Schmemann, "Prayer, Liturgy, and Renewal," *The Greek Orthodox Theological Review* 14, no. 1 (Spring 1969): 13.
[40] Schmemann, *Journals*, 310.
[41] Schmemann, "Liturgy and Theology," 66.

rather an appendix entitled 'de novissimis,' in which all kinds of information about the end of the world and what comes after it were given. What disappeared, however, was eschatology as precisely a dimension, a coefficient of the entire theological enterprise, shaping and permeating the whole Christian faith as its dynamic inspiration and motivation."[42] Under this metamorphosis in understanding, whereby a living and transformative power in history is changed into an apocalyptic condemnation of history, being pro-Kingdom came to mean being anti-world. This is one of the greatest tragedies of Church history, Schmemann thinks. "This eschatological character of the Christian *leitourgia* was little by little obscured in both theology and piety," with the result that the Church's worship lost "this eschatological, i.e., Kingdom-centered and Kingdom-oriented character of the liturgy that made it . . . the source of the Church's evaluation of the world, the root and the motivation of her mission to the world."[43] Now lost is the radical novelty that should be experienced every time the Church enters into the Kingdom on the eighth day. As a result, *leitourgia* is reduced to cultic dimensions and categories; theology comes to be concerned with obligation, efficiency, and validity; and liturgical theology corresponds to a non-ecclesiological and non-eschatological pious orientation.[44] Let us allow Schmemann to make his own summary:

> I can now make my point, which is very simple and which will, no doubt, appear naive to many a sophisticated ideologue of renewal. If [renewal] is to have a consistent orientation, and this means precisely a theology, this theology must be rooted, first of all, in the recovered Christian eschatology. For eschatology is not what people have come to think of it, an escape from the world, but, on the contrary, the very source and foundation of the Christian doctrine of the world and of the Church's action in the world. By referring the world every moment of its time, every ounce of its matter and all human thought, energy, and creativity to the "eschaton," to the ultimate reality of the Kingdom of God, it gives them their only real meaning, their proper "entelechy." Thus, it makes possible Christian action as well as the judgment

---

[42] Alexander Schmemann, "The 'Orthodox World,' Past and Present," in *Church, World, and Mission* (Crestwood, NY: St. Vladimir's Seminary Press, 1979), 28.
[43] Schmemann, "Prayer, Liturgy, and Renewal," 11.
[44] Schmemann, "Prayer, Liturgy, and Renewal," 12.

and evaluation of that action. Yet the "locus" of that recovery is the liturgy of the Church.[45]

What we witness in *leitourgia*, what we experience, what fills the Christian's vision, what the liturgical cult celebrates, what empowers our lives, is the Kingdom come. True, the eschaton is still coming but "the redemption occurs now, right now. This is Christian eschatology. It is not only an eschatology of the future."[46] The Kingdom can capacitate us to evaluate the world and take action in it because it does not simply await us in the future; we cross over into it through the liturgy already, now.

Schmemann thinks the tragedy of contemporary Christianity is that we have accepted an either-or alternative and abandoned the eschatological antinomy of both-and. We now assume we must make a choice between eschaton and time, Church and world, mystery and the mundane, liturgy and life. We assume that we must either leave history or settle into it as our home. This is a bifurcation he wants to destroy. Here is a lengthy quote from the *Journals* in which his resistance to this divisive thinking leads him to yet one more pronouncement on liturgical theology:

> Ultimately the whole novelty of Christianity consisted (consists) in destroying this choice, this polarization. *This* is the essence of Christianity as Eschatology. The Kingdom of God is the goal of history, and the Kingdom of God is already now *among us, within us*. Christianity is a unique historical event, and Christianity is the presence of that event as the completion of all events and of history itself....
>
> Here is, for me, *the whole meaning of liturgical theology*. The Liturgy: the joining, revelation, actualization of the historicity of Christianity (remembrance) and of its transcendence over that historicity.
>
> Hence, the link of the Church with the world, the Church *for the world*, but as its beginning and its end, as the affirmation that the world is *for the Church*, since the Church is the presence of the Kingdom of God.
>
> Here is the eternal antinomy of Christianity and the essence of all contemporary discussions about Christianity. The task of

---

[45] Schmemann, "Prayer, Liturgy, and Renewal," 12–13.
[46] Alexander Schmemann, "Between Utopia and Escape," lecture delivered March 22, 1981, transcribed by Martha Hoffmaster, http://schmemann.org/byhim/betweenutopiaandescape.html.

> theology is to be faithful to the antinomy, which disappears in the experience of the Church as *pascha:* a *continuous* (not only historical) passage of the world to the Kingdom. All the time one must leave the world and all the time one must remain in it.[47]

Antinomy is the coin of the realm in liturgy. The eschaton is coming, but it is already here, and the task of liturgical theology is to be faithful to the antinomy, even though the stress point is difficult for us. "This is the paradox, the antinomy, the message, which Christians could not endure because it was too much for them. It is much easier to have a little religion of the past, present and future, of commandments and prescriptions."[48] *Leitourgia* offers us something else, something bigger than this little religion. It offers us an experience of corporate passage from the old eon into the new eon, a liturgy based on divine action *now*, eternal life made manifest to us *here*. We touch it, we see it, we taste it in the eschatological antinomy the liturgy celebrates. The Church is not a little forum for social reforms, Schmemann says; rather, the Church's *leitourgia* is "the realized inaugurated eschatology of the Kingdom and, at the same time, the real knowledge of the Kingdom."[49] Out of such experiential knowledge, theology arises (that is, comes into being).

Leitourgia, we were told, is the work that God commissioned the Church to do in the world, on behalf of the world, for the world, and the nature of the Church as institution can be termed sacramental because the nature of that institution is one of perpetual passover, pasch, passage—a concept crucial to Schmemann. He says the dynamic essence of the Church is "passage from the old into the new, from this world into the world to come, from the kingdom of nature into the Kingdom of Grace."[50] He says the Eucharist is "the sacrament in which the Church performs the passage, the passover, from this world into the Kingdom, offers in Christ the whole creation to God, seeing it as 'heaven and earth full of His glory,' and partakes of Christ's immortal life at His table in His Kingdom."[51] He says that *leitourgia* is "a corporate procession and passage of the Church toward her fulfillment, the sacrament of the Kingdom of God."[52] He says

---

[47] Schmemann, *Journals*, 233–34.
[48] Schmemann, "Between Utopia and Escape."
[49] Schmemann, "Between Utopia and Escape."
[50] Alexander Schmemann, "Ecclesiological Notes," *St. Vladimir's Seminary Quarterly* 11, no. 1 (1967): 36–37.
[51] Schmemann, "Ecclesiological Notes," 37.
[52] Schmemann, "Prayer, Liturgy, and Renewal," 12.

the most valuable achievement of the Liturgical Movement was to discover "this 'paschal' dimension and root of the liturgy, its fundamental nature as passage and passover."[53] To call the Church sacramental, therefore, has less to do with a contrast between nature and grace, material and spiritual, and much more to do with a contrast between old and new, this world and the world to come, the kingdom of nature and the kingdom of grace. This is why the Eucharist is the true form of the Church, an expression Schmemann credits to Nicholas Afanasiev when "he developed the idea of the Church whose 'form' is to be found in its eschatological self-fulfillment at the Eucharistic gathering."[54] What we call the institution of the Church is the sacrament of the Kingdom, and she fulfills herself as the new life of the new creation.

The Church belongs to this world, yes, but it belongs to this world in order to reveal and manifest the true meaning of the world to itself. The world does not know why it is here; in the Eucharist we learn the reason. The cosmos does not know what it should be doing; in the Eucharist we are taught matter's purpose. Humanity has forgotten its Lord; in the Eucharist we meet him, join him, and resume our abandoned vocation as cosmic priests. The Church-as-institution is thus a sacramental sign of the world's true end: this is her work, her *leitourgia*. The Old Testament's *leitourgia* was to prepare the world for the Messiah; the New Testament's *leitourgia* is to liturgically celebrate an eschatological fact that leads the world out of the valley of the shadow of death. What the Church teaches about the Kingdom is the truth she experiences in passage to that Kingdom, therefore the experience of *lex orandi* establishes the content of *lex credendi*. The passage we experience in the Eucharist is the basis for how we think and speak about matter, world, time, self, sin, death, life—everything.

It should be evident, then, why liturgical theology is not primarily concerned with the liturgy. It is because liturgical theology is not narcissistic. Liturgical theology is not concerned with liturgy, but with the true objects of theology: namely, God, man, and the world, which are to be understood in a liturgical light. *Everything* (not just cultic liturgy) is judged in the light of the Kingdom of God that suffuses liturgy. The

---

[53] Schmemann, "Prayer, Liturgy, and Renewal," 14

[54] Alexander Schmemann, "Russian Theology: 1920–72. An Introductory Survey," *St. Vladimir's Seminary Quarterly* 16, no. 1 (1972): 182.

eschatological light that floods into us by the liturgy accompanies us into our daily life, and by that light we can discern the true value of all things:

> The rhythm of the Church, the rhythm of the Eucharist which comes and is always to come, fills everything with meaning, puts all things to their real place. Christians do not remain passive between one celebration and the next one, their "temporal" life is not empty, is not "diminished" by eschatology. For it is precisely the liturgical "eschaton" that ascribes real value to every moment of our life, *in which everything is now judged, evaluated and understood in the light of the Kingdom of God*, the ultimate end and the meaning of all that exists. There is nothing more alien to the true spirit of Orthodox liturgy than a certain superstitious "liturgiologism," or an "eschatologism" which reduces the whole Christian life to communion and despises everything else as "vain." Such liturgical "piety" does not realize that the true significance of the Eucharist is precisely that of judgement, of transformation, of making infinitely important, the whole life.[55]

Liturgical theology is about the life of the world, to borrow the title of Schmemann's most famous book.

The Kingdom is present on the Lord's Day when the Lord's people make memorial of the Lord's Paschal mystery. Schmemann thinks this triad was once self-evident and organic. The early Church experienced a "connection and interdependence within '*lex orandi*,' of the Lord's Day, the Eucharist and Ecclesia. . . . It was born of the Christian vision and experience of the World, the Church, and the Kingdom, of their fundamental relationship to one another."[56] Schmemann acknowledges that this connection still exists liturgically, but bemoans that it is not understood or experienced in the same way any longer. The connectedness remained part of the *lex orandi*, but the connection "ceased to be related in any way to the '*lex credendi*,' was no longer regarded as a theological datum and no theologian has even bothered to mention it as having any theological significance, as revealing anything about the Church's 'experience' of herself, the World, and the Kingdom of God."[57] If the link between *lex orandi* and *lex credendi* snaps, then we cease to experience the liturgy as

---

[55] Alexander Schmemann, "Fast and Liturgy: Notes in Liturgical Theology," *St. Vladimir's Seminary Quarterly* 3, no. 1 (1959): 7, italics added.

[56] Schmemann, "Liturgical Theology, Theology of Liturgy, and Liturgical Reform," 41.

[57] Schmemann, "Liturgical Theology, Theology of Liturgy, and Liturgical Reform," 41.

an epiphany of the cosmical and eschatological content of the Church's faith, and that has consequences. For piety, "the interest is narrowed the question of one's personal fate 'after death'";[58] for liturgy, "this was the beginning of an ever-deeper infiltration of 'illustrative symbolism' into the explanation of worship";[59] and for theology, the Church's "'*lex orandi,*' simply cannot be properly 'heard' and understood."[60] Liturgical theology broke down when it ceased being anchored to the liturgical experience of eschatology that illuminates God, man, and world.

The New Covenant's *leitourgia* is to perform an eschatological liturgy in the midst of the darkness for the world's salvation, therefore we will not be surprised to hear eschatological overtones when Schmemann describes the Church becoming "what she is." *Leitourgia* "eternally transforms the Church into what she is, makes her the Body of Christ and the Temple of the Holy Spirit";[61] it makes her "the sacrament, in Christ, of the new creation; the sacrament, in Christ, of the Kingdom";[62] it makes her "a realm of grace, of communion with God, of new knowledge and new life";[63] she is "the epiphany, the manifestation, the presence and the gift of the Kingdom of God, as its 'sacrament' in this world";[64] "the essential mystery of the Church [is being an] *experience* of the Kingdom of God, as its epiphany in 'this world.'"[65] The Church is the Kingdom sacramentalized in *leitourgia*. If the Eucharist is not cosmic in scope and eschatological in ambition, then it becomes one means of grace among others, aiming at individual edification and sanctification, and in that case, the Eucharist ceases to be an experience of the sacrament of the Church. The result is a theology exhausting itself "in purely formal and truly irrelevant definitions of sacrifice and transubstantiation, while piety little by little subordinates Eucharist to its individualistic and pietistic demands."[66] In such a state, the Church-at prayer cannot serve as the ontological condition for the Church's belief. *Lex orandi* can be the basis of *lex credendi* only where liturgy is experienced eschatologically as "the true epiphany of a new

---

[58] Schmemann, *The Eucharist*, 42
[59] Schmemann, *The Eucharist*, 44
[60] Schmemann, "Liturgy and Theology," 58.
[61] Schmemann, "Theology and Eucharist," 83.
[62] Schmemann, "Liturgy and Theology," 57.
[63] Schmemann, "Liturgy and Theology," 57–58.
[64] Alexander Schmemann, "The Problem of the Church's Presence in the World in Orthodox Consciousness," *St. Vladimir's Seminary Quarterly* 21, no. 1 (1977): 10.
[65] Schmemann, "The Problem of the Church's Presence in the World in Orthodox Consciousness, 10.
[66] Schmemann, "Liturgy and Theology," 60.

creation redeemed by Christ, the presence and power in 'this world' of the joy and peace and the Holy Spirit, of the new eon of the Kingdom."[67] "It is this experience which then illuminates the theological work proper, be it the exegesis of Scripture or patristic texts, or the elaboration in *theoprepeis logoi*, in words adequate to God, of the sacred doctrine, and of its application to the life and the problems of man."[68] Observe that he has identified a liturgical foundation for reading Scripture, and for doing theology, morality, and ethics.

I think this eschatological foundation is the source of the joy that Schmemann thinks should be the hallmark of the Church. In his *Journals* he reflects upon an experience from his youth in the Christian West (Paris) where he would stop by the Church of St. Charles of Monceau for two or three minutes on his way to the Lycee Carnot. The juxtaposition of the noisy, proletarian rue Legendre and this never-changing Mass was an experience he said remained with him forever, namely, "a very strong sense of 'life' in its physical, bodily reality, in the uniqueness of every minute and of its correlation with life's reality. At the same time, this interest has always been rooted solely in the correlation of all this with what the silent Mass was a witness to and reminder of, the presence and the joy."[69] Absent this, the Church has no witness to offer.

> What has Christianity lost so that the world, nurtured by Christianity, has recoiled from it and started to pass judgment over the Christian faith? Christianity has lost joy—not natural joy, not joy-optimism, not joy from earthly happiness, but the Divine joy about which Christ told us that "no one will take your joy from you" (John 16:22).... To the fallen world that has lost that happiness, but yearns for it and—in spite of everything—lives by it, Christianity has *opened up* and *given back* happiness; has fulfilled it *in Christ as joy*."[70]

Ecclesiology is eschatological because the Church has no other foundation, content, or purpose—no other *leitourgia*—than to communicate the transcendent reality of the Kingdom of God with the final joy it brings. "It is only when she performs and fulfills this 'passage,' when, in other terms,

---

[67] Schmemann, "Liturgy and Theology," 60.
[68] Schmemann, "Liturgy and Theology," 64.
[69] Schmemann, *Journals*, 20.
[70] Schmemann, *Journals*, 291–92.

she transcends herself as 'institution' and 'society' and becomes indeed the new life of the new creation, that she is the Body of Christ."[71]

Christ

When I started my excavation, this is all the further I expected to dig. I had wanted to ask what anchors Schmemann's liturgical theology and guessed it was the foundation of "eschatology." But while writing I concluded there is one final stratum to notice. The foundation of the house is itself built upon a granite ledge below. It is the rock of Christ. Liturgical theology is not only eschatological, it is also Christological because the Church has no foundation, content, or purpose outside of Jesus. For Schmemann, the cosmical, historical, and eschatological character of the Church-at-liturgy is anchored in Christ. "It is only because the Church's *leitourgia* is always cosmic, i.e., assumes into Christ all creation, and is always historical, i.e. assumes into Christ all time, that it can therefore also be eschatological, i.e., make us true participants of the Kingdom to come."[72] The *leitourgia* is the presence and communication of a Kingdom the Incarnate One brought, and therefore the uniqueness of the Christian *leitourgia* "lies in its stemming from the faith in the Incarnation, from the great and all-embracing mystery of the 'Logos made flesh.'"[73] Schmemann describes the Church as the mystery of a new creation, entered through baptism "by water and spirit in the likeness of Christ's Death and Resurrection," which gathers the faithful on the Lord's Day to hear His Word, to eat and drink at His table in his Kingdom, to relate all time and cosmos with "Christ who is to 'fill all things with Himself': all this was not understood as mere 'cultic acts' but, above all, as the fulfillment by the Church of her very nature, of her cosmical and eschatological calling."[74] The Church finds her fulfillment in Christ. The liturgy, then, is about entering into Christ, which is entering into the Kingdom. Schmemann sees this in every Entrance Rite of the Divine Liturgy when the celebrant approaches the altar:

> It has been given all possible symbolic explanations, but it is not a "symbol." It is the very movement of the Church as *passage* from the old into the new, from "this world" into the "world to

---

[71] Schmemann, "Theology and Eucharist," 77.
[72] Alexander Schmemann, "Worship in a Secular Age," *St. Vladimir's Seminary Quarterly* 16, no. 1 (1967): 7.
[73] Schmemann, "Worship in a Secular Age," 6–7.
[74] Schmemann, "Liturgy and Theology," 56.

come" and, as such, it is the essential movement of the liturgical "journey." In "this world" there is no altar and the temple has been destroyed. For the only altar is Christ Himself, His humanity which He has assumed and deified and made the temple of God, the altar of His presence. And Christ ascended into heaven. The altar thus is the sign that in Christ we have been given access to heaven, that the Church is the "passage" to heaven, the entrance into the heavenly sanctuary.... It is not "grace" that comes down; it is the Church that enters into "grace," and grace means the new being, the Kingdom, the world to come.[75]

These are the terms under which liturgical theology should operate: terms in which symbol is real.

This creates a final antinomy. We have seen the cultic antinomy, wherein the *leitourgia* that transcends cult is expressed by cult; we have seen the eschatological antinomy, wherein the Kingdom still to come is already present; we have here a final Christological antinomy, wherein Christ, who has come to the world, has been rejected by the world, and yet still saves the world. Despite claiming that the sacramental Church exists "for the life of the world," Schmemann is sternly realistic about the condition of that world, and the reason why it needs salvation. Three examples. First, "Having rejected and killed Christ—its Creator, Savior and Lord, 'this world' sentenced itself to death, and does not have 'life in itself.'"[76] Second, "While [the world] can be improved, it can never become the place God intended it to be. Christianity does not condemn the world. The world has condemned itself when on Calvary it condemned the One who was its true self."[77] Third, a long passage:

> The body of Christ is not and can never be of this world. "This world" condemned Christ, the bearer of new life, to death and by doing this it has condemned itself to death. The new life, which shone forth from the grave, is the life of the "new eon," of the age, which in terms of this world is still "to come." The descent of the Holy Spirit at Pentecost, by inaugurating a new eon, announced the end of this world, for as no one can partake of the "new life" without dying in the baptismal death, no one can have Christ as

---

[75] Alexander Schmemann, *For the Life of the World* (Crestwood, NY: St. Vladimir's Seminary Press, 1973), 31.
[76] Schmemann, *The Eucharist*, 34.
[77] Schmemann, *For the Life of the World*, 23.

his life unless he has died and is constantly dying to this world: "for ye are dead and your life is hid with Christ in God" (Col. 3:3). But then nothing which is of this world—no institution, no society, no church—can be identified with the new eon, the new being. The most perfect Christian community—be it completely separated from the evils of the world—as a community is still of this world, living its life, depending on it. It is only by passing into the new eon, by an anticipation—in faith, hope and love—of the world to come, that a community can partake of the Body of Christ, and indeed manifest itself as the Body of Christ. The Body of Christ can never be "part" of this world, for Christ has ascended into heaven and his Kingdom is Heaven.[78]

To be a liturgist, one must have died, be dead, and be constantly dying to this world. The eschatological liturgy that will save the world comes to the world from without, because nothing within this dead world can give the Body of Christ its life.

Here is the antinomy: the Body of Christ can never be part of this world, and yet it is in the world to bring the world salvation. The world in rebellion saw the son of the owner of the vineyard coming and said, "This is the heir; let us kill him, that the inheritance may be ours" (Luke 20:14). After we have killed the source of life, then there will be no more liturgy, no more Eucharist, no more peace, no more sacrament or sacrifice, no more reign of God over us. So Schmemann frankly points out that "the Church was born as a reality in opposition, externally visible—and even more, internally invisible—to this world."[79] Lose that opposition, and the hope of the world is lost. Lose that opposition, and the Church is de-churched. And, alas, this was a very great temptation. The "Church gradually became a religious servicing of the world";[80] "Christianity (not the Church in its mystical depth) has lost its eschatological dimension, has turned toward the world as law, judgment, redemption, recompense, as a religion of the future life.... Having ceased being eschatological, it made the world eschatological."[81] If we lose the true eschatology, then we fall for an ersatz eschatology: the world's utopias become an earthly eschatology. In a foolish effort to win back respect in the world's eye, Christianity "accepts this earthly eschatology, begins to convince itself and others that

---

[78] Schmemann, "Theology and Eucharist," 78.
[79] Schmemann, *Journals*, 250.
[80] Schmemann, *Journals*, 250.
[81] Schmemann, *Journals*, 291.

it was always striving for this earthly happiness, that neither Christ nor the Church ever taught anything else."[82]

The hope of the world lies in the Church's opposition to it; the life of the world is contingent upon Christians constantly dying to it; truth will only be found by leaving the world to stand in the *kairos* of liturgy:

> For there we stand before God, in Christ, who is the End, the *Eschaton*, the Fulness of all our humanity and in Him offer to God the only "reasonable service" (*logike latreia*) of the redeemed world—the Eucharist, and in the light of it see and understand and recapitulate in Christ the truth about God, man and the world, about the creation and fall, sin and redemption, about the whole universe and its final transfiguration in the Kingdom of God, and we receive this truth in participation of the Body and Blood of Christ, in the unending Pentecost that "guides us into all truth and shows us things to come" (John 16:13). The task of theology is to bear witness to this truth, and there is no end to this task. Each theologian will see it only partially and partially reflect it."[83]

Our liturgical life reflects the strangest paradox ever: the world killed Christ, and yet Christ gives life to the world. That is the perpetuation of the mystery of Cross and Resurrection.

The world cannot contain Christ, and therefore it is useless for the Church to try and adapt herself to the world. And yet—here is the antinomy again—if the Church were to isolate herself, she would cease to be Church:

> It is by being Mission, by loving those for whom Christ died, that the Church realizes herself as the Fulness. A Church that would isolate herself from the world and live by her eschatological fulness, that would cease to "evangelize," to bear witness to Christ in the world, would simply cease to be the Church—because the fulness by which she lives is precisely the agape of God as revealed and communicated in Christ. "Mission" cannot, therefore, be a static relationship with the world. It means fight with, and for, the

---

[82] Schmemann, *Journals*, 292.
[83] Schmemann, "Theology and Eucharist," 87.

world; it means a constant effort to understand and to challenge, to question and to answer.[84]

Perhaps our problem lies in being too eager to exchange the liturgy of the Church militant for the liturgy of the Church in glory. We must learn patience and perform our work, perform our *leitourgia*, where we are. To do so will require us to link faith and love with hope, and Christian hope is without foundation if it is not rooted in the Resurrection of Jesus. Ecclesiology and eschatology are linked in Christ's Resurrection. With full recognition of the treatment that Christ received from the world, he must remain the foundation of our eschatology, which is the foundation of our *leitourgia*, which is the foundation of the *lex orandi*, on which the Church's *lex credendi* rests.

That is the house that Fr. Alexander built.

---

[84] Alexander Schmemann, "The Idea of Primacy in Orthodox Ecclesiology," *St. Vladimir's Seminary Quarterly* 4, no. 2–3 (1960): 61.

Liturgy and Its Celebration

Scripture
Theologia Prima: The Liturgical Mystery and the Mystery of God*

The great tradition of the Church understands liturgy, Scripture, and theology in a way that is somewhat different from the way they are commonly understood today. I think it behooves us to figure out what that difference is. Toward that end, I would like here to think about the relationship of these three things within a larger context. How does the mystery of God encountered in the *liturgy* affect our understanding of *theology* and *Scripture*?

Entering this world of discourse requires of us a conversion of mind. As is well known, the Greek word for conversion was *metanoia*, coming from *meta*, meaning "beyond" or "after," and *nous*, which is not so much "reason" as what Metropolitan Hierotheos calls "the eye of the heart."[1] If we want to see liturgy, Scripture, and theology differently, we must see them with a *meta-nous*, and that will change our rational understanding of them. The thesis I would like to explore here is this: in order to see each one of them more clearly, we must see them all together. To see each one correctly, we must see all of them as connected and bound to one another holistically. Our task is not so much to replace the curricula of liturgy, Scripture, and theology with a new content (like opening three shoeboxes to replace shoes with sandals). Our task is to let the connection between liturgy, Scripture, and theology be a path to a thickened understanding of each of them. That is what we have ceased doing because we no longer see these three in the light of the singular mystery of God.

Casting around for some metaphors to make my point, I have come up with two. The first one comes, as do so many of my mental images, from G. K. Chesterton. In *The Autobiography* he writes that he always understood there to be some truth in pagan philosophical systems, but says he became a Catholic because he believes these truths are also contained *and better*

---

* David W. Fagerberg, "Theologia Prima: The Liturgical Mystery and the Mystery of God," *Letter and Spirit* 2 (2006): 55–67.
[1] Metropolitan Hierotheos, *Orthodox Psychotherapy: The Science of the Fathers* (Levadia: Birth of the Theotokos Monastery, 1994) and *St. Gregory Palamas as a Hagiorite* (Levadia: Birth of the Theotokos Monastery, 1997).

coordinated in Catholicism. "That almost any other theology or philosophy contains a truth, I do not at all deny.... [But] I have only found one creed that could not be satisfied with a truth, but only with the Truth, which is made of a million such truths and yet is one.... Flowers grow best in a garden, and even grow biggest in a garden; and in the wilderness they wither and die."[2] Scriptural exegetes have some truths; liturgiologists also keep some truths in their back pocket; theologians keep their truths tidy in various systematic pigeonholes; but whatever truths they have will grow biggest when they are coordinated in the garden of Truth.

Chesterton remembers thinking it odd, even before his conversion, to remove one part of the Christian faith, namely Scripture, and isolate it from the rest, as if a part can be played off against the whole. It is absurd to take the Bible out of the Church, or to use the Bible to condemn the great tradition of the Church. He makes his point by condensing the sixteenth-century exaltation of the Bible to a single episode of a single afternoon:

> The ordinary sensible skeptic or pagan is standing in the street ... and he sees a procession go by of the priests of some strange cult, carrying their object of worship under a canopy, some of them wearing high head-dresses and carrying symbolical staffs, others carrying scrolls and sacred records, others carrying sacred images and lighted candles before them, others sacred relics in caskets or cases, and so on. I can understand the spectator saying, "This is all hocus-pocus"; I can even understand him, in moments of irritation, breaking up the procession, throwing down the images, tearing up the scrolls, dancing on the priests and anything else that might express that general view. I can understand his saying, "Your croziers are bosh, your candles are bosh, your statues and scrolls and relics and all the rest of it are bosh." But in what conceivable frame of mind does he rush in to select one particular scroll of the scriptures of this one particular group (a scroll which had always belonged to them and been a part of their hocus-pocus, if it was hocus-pocus); why in the world should the man in the street say that one particular scroll was *not* bosh, but was the one and only truth by which all the other things were to

---

[2] G. K. Chesterton, *The Autobiography*, in *The Collected Works of G. K. Chesterton* (San Francisco: Ignatius Press, 1988), 16:328–29.

be condemned? Why should it not be as superstitious to worship the scrolls as the statues, of that one particular procession?[3]

Ever since this brawl in the streets of the sixteenth century, it is as if Protestants and Catholics have thought they must scuffle over the remaining debris. They have sounded like children choosing up teams for a game of kickball: "We'll take Scripture, faith, and grace." "Then we get the Pope, Mary, and the other five sacraments." There is a problem with allowing these fault lines to continue. It just may be that a particular scroll only blooms if it remains securely rooted in the whole Scripture; and the whole Scripture may only be intelligible if read as the marching orders for a liturgical procession; and the theology that comes from this liturgical life is about participation in the life of God. Liturgy, Scripture, and theology must be seen in light of the mystery of God.

I submit to the reader a second metaphor. This one entails some risk, because it comes from a world of science I have not dealt with since high school. As I remember it, when one hydrogen atom is bonded to another hydrogen atom, and those are bonded to an oxygen atom, the end molecule is substantially different from the atoms. The three atoms are gasses; the molecule H_2O is a liquid. To produce the liquid, one doesn't change one of the atoms to look like a different box on the Periodic Table of the Elements. Instead, one brings these three atoms into conjunction with each other to make a compound. Let the three atoms lose contact with each other and there won't be a liquid anymore, only gasses. Let liturgy, Scripture, and theology lose contact with one another, and instead of something refreshing you have something rather gaseous. This sometimes happens in the academy, where associating *Scripture* study with the mystery of God is assumed to corrupt the objectivity of the examiner; and *liturgy* is disassociated from the mystery of God and turned into a history of sacramentaries or a phenomenology of rite; and *theology* puts the mystery of God under a slide for our controlled examination.

Gathering my metaphors together, I can say that I would like to replant our scattered truths about liturgy, Scripture, and theology in a single garden of Truth. I would like to pick up the scattered pieces of our stumbled liturgical procession and return the scroll of Scripture to the arms

---

[3] G. K. Chesterton, *The Catholic Church and Conversion*, in *The Collected Works of G. K. Chesterton* (San Francisco: Ignatius Press, 1990), 3:73.

of liturgical theologians. I would like to first consider liturgy, Scripture, and theology on their atomic level, and then make some comments on the molecular level about their relationship to the mystery of God.

One Liturgy, on Earth and in Heaven

There are not two liturgies, one on earth and one in heaven. There is one liturgy, on earth and in heaven. The liturgy of the Church is the heavenly liturgy as it is practiced on earth, and it is crucial to restore this eschatological dimension to our practice of liturgy. In the liturgy we do what the angels do, namely, lose ourselves in a joy that erupts in praise. St. John Chrysostom said joy issues when the lover receives the beloved. In that case, the liturgy issues when the Church receives her beloved. The liturgy is our trysting place with God. According to the dictionary, a tryst is "an agreement, as between lovers, to meet at a certain time and place." Exactly! God, our Divine Lover, has agreed to meet us on holy ground for communion, and from that encounter with the Father through the risen Christ, the Holy Spirit creates "theologian souls."[4]

In order to identify this reality, we call the liturgy "sacramental." Paul Evdokimov speaks of sacraments as "an action of 'punching holes' in the closed world by powerful explosions from the Beyond." By the sacraments we are taught "that everything is destined for a liturgical fulfillment."[5] So the Divine Liturgy, the liturgy of the hours, the sacraments and sacramentals, and our personal liturgies of devotion, piety, and ministry to charity, are all points at which the reign of God presses through the partition that sin has constructed. The kingdom of God approaches us in liturgy in a way that is material, communal, and ritualistic, which is why the Church is a sacramental, political, and social entity.

"To swim" is a verb and "swimmer" is the noun. "To run" is a verb and "runner" is the noun. "Liturgy" is a verb and "Christian" is the noun. Liturgy is the activity of Christians, and Christians become what they do. My teacher Aidan Kavanagh also used to say, "I don't go to Mass because I'm Catholic; I'm Catholic because I go to Mass."

Imagine liturgy in the Church as blood is in the body. Or, better still, imagine liturgy in the Church as soul is in the body—what the scholastics meant by *anima forma corporis*. Étienne Gilson clarifies the meaning of

---

[4] Archimandrite Vasileios, *Hymn of Entry: Liturgy and Life in the Orthodox Church* (Crestwood, NY: St. Vladimir's Seminary, 1984), 23.
[5] Paul Evdokimov, *The Art of the Icon: A Theology of Beauty* (Redondo Beach, CA: Oakwood, 1990), 117.

the term *forma*. For St. Thomas Aquinas, he writes, "The soul does not first make a body move, it first makes it a body. A corpse is not a body. The soul makes it exist as a body."[6] Applied to our case, the liturgy is the form of the Church. The liturgy makes the assembly exist as the body of Christ. An assembly by itself is not a body. The liturgy does not first make an assembly move, it first makes it the body of Christ. The Eucharist makes the Church, as Henri de Lubac has reminded this generation.

Leitourgia originally meant a work done by a few on behalf of the many. "It denoted a work (*ergon*) undertaken on behalf of the people (*laos*). Public projects undertaken by an individual for the good of the community in such areas as education, entertainment or defense would be *leitourgia*."[7] Christ undertook a work on behalf of the vital interests of the clan to which he chose to belong—the family of Adam and Eve—and his liturgy continues in the activity of his body. We are the body of Christ because this activity continues in us. By baptismal grace we are incorporated into the sacred humanity of Christ, his Spirit is poured into our bodies, and we are made one of a new race. Baptism makes a new people called into existence for the very purpose of continuing the work of Christ. *Leitourgia* is Christ's work become ours.

Liturgy is not, then, a performance of *our* religion. Liturgy is the religion of Christ—the religion he enacted in the flesh before the Father—perpetuated. The religion that Jesus did in his humanity, he left to his Church to continue performing. We join Jesus in his liturgy to the Father and on behalf of the many. That would be why Pope Pius XII defined liturgy this way: "The sacred liturgy is . . . the public worship which our Redeemer as Head of the Church renders to the Father, as well as the worship which the community of the faithful renders to its Founder, and through Him to the heavenly Father. It is, in short, the worship rendered by the Mystical Body of Christ in the entirety of its Head and members."[8] It is not a thing that Jesus left to his Church, but himself. And he is, himself, the mediator of the Father's grace to us, and the mediator of our thanksgiving to the Father, all in the Holy Spirit. Liturgy is best understood as a relationship. Liturgy is participating in the relationship of love that flows between the persons of the Trinity.

---

[6] Étienne Gilson, *The Christian Philosophy of St. Thomas Aquinas* (Notre Dame, IN: University of Notre Dame Press, 1956), 187.
[7] Lawrence Madden, "Liturgy," in *The New Dictionary of Sacramental Worship*, ed. Peter Fink (Collegeville, MN: Liturgical Press, 1990), 740.
[8] Pope Pius XII, Encyclical Letter on the Sacred Liturgy *Mediator Dei* (1947), §20.

Scripture, an Invitation to Enter Sacred History

I therefore consider Christ to be the premier liturgist, and baby liturgists are born in the baptismal font when they are grafted into his life. The entire economy of salvation, as it is recorded in Scripture, has had as its purpose to produce liturgists. Obviously this only makes sense with a thickened definition of "liturgist" because what need has the world for more cantors and thurifers? But if liturgy is, as defined above, the extension of the Father's love to the world through the body the Holy Spirit has knitted together in the waters of the font, then we can say the entire economy of salvation recorded in Scripture exists to bring mankind into liturgy.

This makes the Bible something more than a book of religious propositions. The Bible is neither a catechism nor a morals manual. It is a record of the self-disclosure of God, made in history because we are historical beings. Furthermore, it is an invitation to step into that history. The revelation of God is not in the words of the book, the revelation of God is in the history recorded by the inspired words of the book. When we approach the Scriptures, we search for a person, not for a proposition. Luther said the Bible is the manger in which the Christ-child is laid, and we should never confuse the straw with the baby.

Augustine famously said, "In the Old Testament the New lies hid; in the New Testament the meaning of the Old becomes clear."[9] Marcion tried to take a hatchet to this reciprocal correlation and divide the New Covenant from the first Covenant. If he had succeeded, we would not have been able to understand either covenant, because we cannot understand Christ apart from the Old Testament covenant, or what the Old Testament was driving at without seeing Jesus as its omega point.

It is crucial that Christians discover the relationship of the Church to the Old Testament. Remember that the top row of the Orthodox iconostasis contains icons of the "Church of the Old Testament." Charles Journet said, "The Church made its appearance in time before Christ did. The frontier of the Church passes through each one of those who call themselves her members."[10] The Church may have been born at Pentecost to become a public, visible thing, but its moment of conception was

---

[9] Augustine's "old saying" is quoted in *CCC*, §129.
[10] Charles Journet, *The Church of the Word Incarnate* (New York: Sheed and Ward, 1955), xxvii.

earlier.¹¹ Israel is the womb for the human race, and the Church of the Old Testament is the Church *in utero*.

"Typology" is the name for this connection between the testaments. Jean Daniélou calls typology "the science of the similitudes between the two testaments."¹² When the yellow paint of Scripture meets the blue paint of Jesus, the green paint that results is called typology. Typology is the mystical art of finding Christ foreshadowed in the Hebrew Scriptures, and finding the Scriptures illuminated by the eschatological outpouring of the Spirit.

Since Jesus himself understood his identity in light of the Old Testament, what would it mean to us when he called himself the "bread of life" if we did not know Exodus 16? Or the "lamb of God," without Exodus 12? How could we understand sacrifice without the book of Leviticus, or the Son of Man without Isaiah and Daniel? Typology sees Christ in the light of Scripture and reads the spiritual meaning of the letter in light of the mystery made flesh. This is what the Apostles did. The Apostles' preaching is nothing but this. And when the Apostolic faith was written down, it composed the New Testament.

So the New Testament is neither an addendum to nor a replacement of the Scriptures; there are not two Bibles. The New Testament is apostolic witness to the hour when the Word of God spoken in the Old Testament became flesh. The authority of the New Testament derives from the Apostles' authority. They are the twelve pillars of the Church's Scripture and her tradition. The Church is Israel renewed (which is a better way of saying "a new Israel"). In the words of Alexander Golitzin, "The Church is nothing more nor less than Israel in the altered circumstances of the Messiah's death, resurrection, and the eschatological outpouring of his Spirit."¹³ The Old Testament and the New Testament are like the two

---

¹¹ "Doubtless, the Holy Spirit was already at work in the world before Christ was glorified. Yet on the day of Pentecost, He came down upon the disciples to remain with them forever (cf. John 14:16). The Church was publicly displayed to the multitude" (Second Vatican Council, Decree on the Church's Missionary Activity *Ad Gentes* (1965), §4, in Austin Flannery, ed., *Vatican Council II: The Conciliar and Post Conciliar Documents*, rev. ed. [Northport, NY: Costello, 1988], 816–17).

¹² Jean Daniélou, *The Bible and the Liturgy* (Notre Dame, IN: University of Notre Dame Press, 1956), 4.

¹³ Alexander Golitzin, "Scriptural Images of the Church: An Eastern Orthodox Reflection" (unpublished paper, 2001), available at https://freerepublic.com/focus/f-religion/2350866/posts.

cherubim facing each other, sitting atop the ark of the covenant, God's throne, looking at the Lord seated between them.[14]

Pope Benedict XVI says, "Apostolic succession is essentially the living presence of the Word in the person of the witnesses."[15] And that is the same reason why Karl Rahner insists on understanding the apostolic succession as a living experience. "It is not only propositions about their experience that the apostles bequeath, but their Spirit, the Holy Spirit of God, the very reality, then, of what they have experienced in Christ. Their own experience is preserved and present together with their Word."[16]

The First Letter of John provides a definition of apostolic tradition when it defines the aim of the Apostles. "That which we have seen and heard we proclaim also to you, so that you may have fellowship with us; and our fellowship is with the Father and with his Son Jesus Christ" (1 John 1:3). The twelve pass on what they have seen and heard, not so we can know what they saw and know what they heard, but so that we too may participate in the Son. If the witness recorded in the New Testament does not lead to the spiritual fellowship the Apostles had with the Father through his Son Jesus Christ, then we are misreading the whole Scripture. It becomes dead letter. It is not theological. It is not read liturgically.

The content of Christian tradition is proclaimed by the Church in the liturgy as the rule of faith. Such a tacit knowledge of the Church's rule of faith is called by Andrew Louth our participation in tradition, and it emerges, he writes, from the silence of prayer. "Prayer is seen in the fathers to be, as it were, the amniotic fluid in which our knowledge of God takes form."[17] Liturgical prayer is the mother of theology.

---

[14] The thought is from a homily by St. Gregory the Great: "In the two angels [who appeared in Christ's tomb] we can recognize the two Testaments.... They have come together where the Lord's body is, because, by announcing in convergent fashion that the Lord took flesh, died, and rose again, the two Testaments are as it were seated, the Old at his head and the New at his feet. That is why the two cherubim who protect the mercy seat face each other.... Cherub indeed means fullness of knowledge.... When the Old Testament foretells what the New Testament declares accomplished in the Lord, they face each other like the two cherubim, their gaze fixed on the mercy seat, because they are looking at the Lord between them and they... are recounting in harmony the mystery of his loving purpose" (quoted in Olivier Clément, *The Roots of Christian Mysticism* [New York: New City, 1996], 98).

[15] Joseph Ratzinger, "Primacy, Episcopate, and Apostolic Succession," in Karl Rahner and Joseph Ratzinger, *The Episcopate and the Primacy* (New York: Herder & Herder, 1962), 54.

[16] Karl Rahner, "The Development of Dogma," in *Theological Investigations*, vol. 10, *Writings of 1965–1967 II* (New York: Seabury, 1974), 68.

[17] Andrew Louth, *Discerning the Mystery: An Essay on the Nature of Theology* (New York: Oxford University Press, 1983), 65.

Theology, the Science of the Scriptures

The Western Church, straight up to Thomas Aquinas, called theology "the science of the Scriptures." Theology is not necessarily constructed by a lone PhD in an office lined with academic books because academic theology is only one species in the genus of theology. The kind of theology meant here consists of the ability to find Christ in the Scriptures, and to read the ecclesiological, moral, and eschatological meanings contained in the letter (these were the three "spiritual meanings" in tradition, called the typological, tropological, and anagogical). According to Yves Congar, the medieval Church understood theology to be "an extension of faith, which is a certain communication and a certain sharing of God's knowledge." Theology includes "the construction of God in us, or rather the construction of Christ in us."[18]

Theology's more relevant practitioner is Mrs. Murphy, who has been capacitated by the mystery of God in the liturgy to see the world in the light of Mount Tabor. She may not be able to say something about other theologians, but she can do something more important: she can say something theological about everything else in the world. The person who has been capacitated by liturgy to read the Scriptures in the light of Christ sees all things with the eye of the dove, which is how St. Gregory of Nyssa spoke of "spiritual sight": it is seeing by means of the Holy Spirit. Becoming a theologian is therefore the calling and a responsibility of every baptized Christian.

The content of Christian tradition is tracked in the pages of Scripture. Being a tracker means knowing how to read trails; being a theologian means knowing how to read Scripture. And who are we tracking? The *Logos*. And where does he lead us? To *Theos*, to God the Father. And by what power can we do this? Not our own; the Holy Spirit must illuminate the process. Tomáš Špidlík's work on spirituality notes that the Church fathers "understood the practice of theology only as a personal communion with *Theos*, the Father, through the *Logos*, Christ, in the Holy Spirit—an experience lived in a state of prayer."[19] That is why prayer is the amniotic fluid for theological knowledge.

Being a theologian means being able to use the grammar learned in liturgy to speak about God. Even more, it means speaking of God. Yet even more, it means speaking with God. That is why Evagrius of Pontus calls

---

[18] Yves Congar, *A History of Theology* (New York: Doubleday, 1968), 261.
[19] Tomáš Špidlík, *The Spirituality of the Christian East*, trans. Anthony P. Gythiel (Collegeville, MN: Cistercian, 1986), 1.

prayer theology: "If you are a theologian you truly pray. If you truly pray you are a theologian."[20] And before there were universities with theology faculties, it was possible to learn and to use this theological grammar. *Theologia* stood at the end of a process of asceticism that conformed a life to Christ. The starting point of theology was not the library card catalogue, but the Eucharist, the grammar of faith learned in the *lex orandi* ("law of prayer") of liturgical life.

For the fathers, theology meant a knowledge of God which comes from an illumination of the soul by the Holy Spirit, and this is the very substance of the soul's deification. Theology is not only knowledge about God; it is the supernatural communication of God's very life. Irenaeus called the Son and the Holy Spirit the two hands of the Father. What does the Father want to do with his two outstretched hands? I picture God, who once formed man by crouching over the clay of the earth and sculpting it into a human form (see Gen 2:7), now wanting to finish his handiwork. The Father reaches out through the Son and the Holy Spirit to bring us to completion. The image grows further into the likeness of God. Within this context, theology is less the fruit of a graduate program at university and more the fruit of a rightly ordered existence. Theology is as much a practice as a cognition.

The Mystery of God's Will

Now we want to find some water. We must turn from the atomic level to do molecular theology. We want to find out what bonds these atomic elements of the Church. How are liturgy, Scripture, and theology unified, and what prevents them from drifting apart? We want to avoid loss of harmony lest we lose the mystery itself. Why is there a salvation history recorded in Scripture, and a Church which performs liturgy, and theologians formed for Mount Tabor?

The *Catechism of the Catholic Church* suggests the following reason for the inauguration of the economy of salvation: "Disfigured by sin and death, man remains 'in the image of God,' in the image of the Son, but is deprived 'of the glory of God,' of his 'likeness.' The promise made to Abraham inaugurates the economy of salvation, at the culmination of which the Son himself will assume that 'image' and restore it in the Father's

---

[20] Evagrius, *The Praktikos and Chapters on Prayer*, trans. John Bamberger (Collegeville, MN: Cistercian Publications, 1981), 65.

'likeness' by giving it again its Glory, the Spirit who is 'the giver of life.'"[21] Man and woman, the image of God, are to grow into the likeness of God, and this is the reason for all of salvation history, this is our liturgical life, and this is theology in motion. But what is the mysterious charge that bonds these three together?

Let me suggest an answer by means of an imaginary illustration. Suppose with me that you had a friend to whom you lent a copy of the Bible because he had never seen one before. He was curious about the Christian Bible, so you invited him to examine one. A week or so later you ask, "What did you think of it?" and suppose he soberly answers, "It is a great book. I've never seen such sturdy binding, and I thought the typography elegant, and the paper is certainly top quality." If your friend said something like that, I should suppose that he was not attending to the book as a Bible but attending to the book as a book. Maybe he was a bookbinder by profession; maybe he sold paper and ink and covers for books; maybe he was a Bible collector and knew all about rare Bibles. Whatever the case, he would not be attending to the Bible as a believer, but as a bibliophile.

Suppose with me further that the Bible was lent to another person who, after careful examination, looked up with a furrowed brow and pointed out a chronological discrepancy in Second Kings, or an error about the Hittites which more recent archeology has now corrected. That person would be attending to the Bible as a historian. Or suppose a reader mused about Abraham's conflicted mind during his trip up Mount Moriah with Isaac, or opined about whether it was sexual insecurity which caused Solomon to aspire to a greater harem than the King of the Euphrates had; then we would think this person was attending to the book as a psychiatrist. A scientist could attend to the cosmological descriptions in Genesis, a sociologist to the kinship structure of Israel's patriarchal era, a Hellenist to the parallels between Jesus and a wandering cynic, a comparative religionist to the subtle similarities between Israel's temple cult and Hindu sacrifice—in any of

---

[21] *CCC*, §705.

a hundred ways a person could attend to the book in a different way from what we might have expected.[22]

Now we can see the question I want to ask: To what would one have to be attending in order to experience the Bible as Scripture? This same question should have two other echoes. To what would one have to be attending in order to experience the ritual as liturgy, and the words as theology? How do we approach liturgy, Scripture, and theology in order to receive them from God?

In each case, I submit, we have to attend to the mystery of God. And we experience the mystery of God as our deification, our growth in holiness, our increased union with God. What we have been talking about throughout is the Church as she manifests herself in liturgy, Scripture, and theology. The Church is the mystery of God coming to fruition. Paul unpacks it this way in Ephesians:

> For [God] has made known to us in all wisdom and insight the mystery of his will, according to his purpose which he set forth in Christ as a plan for the fulness of time, to unite all things in him.... [He has abolished] in his flesh the law of commandments and ordinances, that he might create in himself one new man in place of the two.... [This mystery] was not made known to the sons of men in other generations as it has now been revealed to his holy apostles and prophets by the Spirit; that is, how the Gentiles are fellow heirs, members of the same body, and partakers of the promise in Christ Jesus through the gospel." (Eph 1:9–10; 2:15; 3:5–6)

The mystery is the Father's will. The mystery is the Father's will to join humankind into the perichoresis, the dynamic interpenetration and mutual reciprocity that flows between himself and the Son and the Holy Spirit. The mystery is Christ, who enacts that will. And the Church is where Christ (the mystery of God) and the Holy Spirit (the breath of God) are accomplishing God's will.

All this the Church has included in its understanding of "tradition." Louis Bouyer identifies four strands of meaning in the way the Church has used the term: First of all, tradition is the rule of faith, the synthetic statement of what every Christian and the whole Church, at all times

---

[22] David Fagerberg, "On the Reform of Liturgists," *Antiphon* 5, no. 1 (June 2000): 5–7.

must believe. It is also the Scripture, the Old Testament first of all, but also what the Apostles had expressed, together with the gospel of Christ which he himself proclaimed. It is further the organized and organic life of the Church in her hierarchical structure and her liturgical structure. Finally, tradition is the incarnate life of charity, the life of the Spirit, the Spirit of God which is the Body of Christ.[23]

Jean Daniélou's lovely little book on the angels cites St. John Chrysostom when the latter describes the angels' reaction when the mystery was revealed to heaven, that is, when the incarnated one ascended into heaven. Chrysostom writes:

> St. Paul speaks here [in Ephesians 3] of a mystery, because not even the angels knew it. The angels only knew that the Lord had chosen His people as His portion (Deut. 32:8).... That is why we need not be surprised that they did not know this [mystery], since, properly speaking, it is the gospel. God had said he would save his people Israel, but had said nothing about the nations. The angels knew that the nations were called, but could not imagine that they would be called to the same end and would be seated upon the throne of God.[24]

The same thought was expressed in the West by St. Paschasius, who likened Jesus to a needle, whose eye was pierced by his passion, but who now "draws all after him, so repairing the tunic rent by Adam, stitching together the two peoples of Jew and Gentile, making them one for always."[25] To Chrysostom, this completely explains the behavior of the angels at the Ascension:

> Do you want to know how they rejoiced in the Ascension? Listen to the account in the Bible, "They rise and descend continuously." That is the behavior of those who want to contemplate a very special sight. They want to see the unheard-of spectacle of man appearing in heaven. That is why the angels are constantly

---

[23] Louis Bouyer, *The Church of God: Body of Christ and Temple of the Spirit* (Chicago: Franciscan Herald, 1982), 10–11. See also, Jean Daniélou, *God and the Ways of Knowing* (New York: Meridian Books, 1967), esp. chap. 5.

[24] Jean Daniélou, *The Angels and Their Mission* (Westminster, MD: Newman, 1957), 33.

[25] Quoted in Henri de Lubac, *Catholicism: Christ and the Common Destiny of Man* (San Francisco: Ignatius Press, 1988), 35.

showing themselves: when He is born, when He dies, when He rises into heaven.[26]

The angels were startled by the mystery because the mystery is, in Bouyer's words, "the secret plan of salvation which only God can reveal and which he reveals by carrying it out."[27] They rose up on tiptoes to see such a thing. Christ, our brother, brings human nature into heaven where we who cling to his Ascension by faith, having clung to his death and Resurrection by faith, can join the divine dance of love. The angels didn't want to miss it.

Jean Daniélou summarily says: "The Christian faith has only one object, the mystery of Christ dead and risen. But this unique mystery subsists under different modes: it is prefigured in the Old Testament, it is accomplished historically in the earthly life of Christ, it is contained in mystery in the sacraments, it is lived mystically in souls, it is accomplished socially in the Church, it is consummated eschatological in the heavenly kingdom."[28]

The Auto-graph of God

If you will understand my use of the term, I could propose that there is a difference between the way liturgy, Scripture, and theology are commonly understood today, and the way they are understood by the great tradition. The great tradition saw them as more *mystical* than we do. By "mystical" I do not mean baffling, bewildering, confusing. In the Christian tradition, *mysterion* means the Father's love for humankind revealed in and shared by Christ, and for something to be more mystical would mean something is drawn deeper into full, active, and conscious participation in salvation history.

If *Scripture* is read mystically, it will bring us before the mystery of God. That, claims Louth, was the real reason for typology or allegory, though few introductions to typology written today give this impression. "The traditional doctrine of the multiple senses of Scripture, with its use of allegory, is essentially an attempt to respond to the *mira profunditas* of Scripture, seen as the indispensable witness to the mystery of Christ. This is the heart of the use of allegory."[29] Bouyer adds that the mystical cannot

---

[26] Daniélou, *Angels*, 35.
[27] Louis Bouyer, *The Christian Mystery: From Pagan Myth to Christian Mysticism*, trans. Illtyd Trethowan (Edinburgh: T & T Clark, 1990), 133.
[28] Jean Daniélou, quoted in Robert Taft, "Toward a Theology of the Christian Feast," in *Beyond East and West* (Rome: Pontifical Oriental Institute, 1997), 29.
[29] Louth, *Discerning the Mystery*, 112.

be had outside the liturgy because "the mystical is the experience of what the Scriptures reveal to us in the Spirit who has given them to us and of what this Spirit communicates to us in the sacraments, in the Eucharist first and foremost."[30]

If *liturgy* is celebrated mystically, it will bring us before the mystery of God. "In the beginning was the Logos," John's Gospel tells us, "and he pitched his tent among us." The Logos is the Word in the sense of reason, principle, standard, or logic. He is the wisdom of the Father, the Father's thought. By the Logos the cosmos was made, and by the Logos all things hold together, from electrons to galaxies. The Logos is the reason of things, and the reason for things—their *telos*, their end, that toward which providence aims. What we have every eighth day, then, is a liturgy of the Logos and a liturgy of the Eucharist. Mystical liturgy would be a way into God's Logos, who is the mystery that invites the sons of Adam and daughters of Eve home to the Father's covenantal love.

If *theology* were to become more mystical, then we would understand it not as a rational science by us but as the Father's Logos shared with us. Blessed Columba Marmion asked, "What in fact is faith?" And he answered, "It is a mysterious participation in the knowledge that God has of himself. God knows himself as Father, Son, and Holy Spirit."[31] When we acknowledge Christ as divine, then our confession is an echo of the very knowledge that God has of himself.

The Church fathers thought of theology as knowledge of the Trinity. But this is more than information. Theology is the art of life—spiritual life, to be exact. Becoming a theologian soul means being further conformed to the God-man. We are to become an image of Christ, who was the image of the Father. We are to become an icon of the icon of God. To say that this process takes place all by grace is only to say that God is writing each of us as an image of his Son by his own hand. We are the Father's auto-graph: Christ the mystery is inscribed in us by the Holy Spirit.

---

[30] Bouyer, *The Christian Mystery*, 183.
[31] Columba Marmion, *Christ in His Mysteries* (St. Louis, MO: B. Herder, 1931), 237.

Sacrifice
Divine Liturgy, Divine Love: Toward a New Understanding of Sacrifice in Christian Worship*

Occasionally an author writes a line in an almost accidental fashion, in the heat of the moment, so to speak, and later the line looks different. At the time of writing, it looked like the climax of a train of thought, but later, even after the train has left the station, it seems to hold promise standing alone. Here is how it happened to me. It occurred in a chapter of my book *Theologia Prima* at a juncture where I was trying to explain Alexander Schmemann's idea of cultic antinomy. I wrote:

> So on the one hand, liturgy directs its participants to a goal different from the cultic goal of attaining contact with God [because Christ has effected union with God]. Everything that religious cult foreshadowed has had its fulfillment in Christ. He is the new temple and the new sacrifice, as well as the new altar, priest, king, prophet, Torah, Sabbath, and tabernacle. Everything we use in Christian liturgy has passed through the hypostatic union. The goal of liturgy, in Schmemann's words, is "the *Church* as the manifestation and presence of the 'new *aeon*' of the Kingdom of God." Christ did not found another religion; he founded a new age, the age of the Church, which is populated by a new race of people in unity with himself. This is his body, the *totus Christus*. . . . The liturgy is antinomous because what cult cannot contain is contained in liturgical cult, just as what heaven and earth could not contain was contained in the womb of the *Theotokos*.[1]

I can put a finer point on the line I am thinking of by restating it this way: all things must pass through the hypostatic union before they are of any

---

* David W. Fagerberg, "Divine Liturgy, Divine Love: Toward a New Understanding of Sacrifice in Christian Worship," *Letter and Spirit* 3 (2007): 95–113.

[1] David W. Fagerberg, *Theologia Prima: What Is Liturgical Theology?* (Chicago: Hillenbrand Books, 2003), 13–14.

use to us. That is my thesis in this article. Things are different after they have been assumed into Christ and touched by the hypostatic union (this phrase refers to the Incarnation as the union of two natures in one person, one hypostasis). Things are now joined to the activity of the God-Man. Their meaning is new because their context is new, and their context is new because they have a new alpha and a new omega, a new final cause and a new efficient cause.

I am not modest in the claim. I mean that *all things* in the Church must pass through the hypostatic union before we can use them at liturgy. This includes temples, vestments, altars, the priesthood, authority of both the monarchical and collegial variety, Sunday, feast days, canon law, hierarchy, fasting, charity, confraternal fellowships, architecture, music, art, and more. The natural accoutrements of religion can be found in the Church, but they do not function in the Church in the same way because they have been perfected. They have passed through the hypostatic union and are now part and parcel of the mystical body of Christ.

As I say, this idea could shine light in various theological directions. To take but one example, I might venture the hypothesis that this line explains the Christian interpretation of Scripture known as typology. Jean Daniélou defined typology as the "science of the similitudes between the two Testaments,"[2] but we must not take that to mean holding up one beside the other and looking back and forth, first at one, then at the other. It's rather a matter of seeing everything in the Old Testament pass through the hypostatic union as it arrives at the feet of the Christian interpreter. Typology is Scripture filtered through Christ. It is seeing the prophet Moses, the Jerusalem temple, the Passover lamb, the Red Sea passage, and the Sabbath rest as types of Jesus. Israel's history comes to us through the hypostatic union and constructs our ecclesiology, moral theology, eschatology, and sacramental mystagogy. But those are other topics.

Liturgy, the Life of Christ in His Body

The thesis I propose is that sacrifice must also pass through the hypostatic union before it can be of any liturgical use to us. This does not negate sacrifice, it perfects it; like Christ's divinity did not negate his human nature, it perfected it; like God's grace does not nullify our identity but perfects our humanity. The supreme act of human religion, sacrifice, passes

---

[2] Jean Daniélou, *The Bible and the Liturgy* (Notre Dame, IN: University of Notre Dame Press, 1966), 4.

through the hypostatic union and is elevated to be liturgical sacrifice. That's what it means, in my opinion, to call something "liturgical." Something is liturgical for being an exercise of Christ's mystical body. I know the term is sometimes used otherwise, as in the time someone said to me, "If you like liturgy, wait until you see a Notre Dame football game." In their language game, liturgy meant anything done in a fancy, regularized, orderly, ceremonial, formal way. But in my language game, ritual alone, without a divine content, does not a liturgy make. The word "liturgy" names more than ritual form; it names Christological content: the content of liturgy is the life of Christ extended to his mystical body. Therefore, in *Mediator Dei* Pope Pius XII defines the sacred liturgy by identifying three interwoven actions:

> [a] The public worship which our redeemer as head of the Church renders to the Father, as well as [b] the worship which the community of the faithful renders to its founder, and [c] through Him to the heavenly Father.
> It is, in short, the worship rendered by the Mystical Body of Christ in the entirety of its Head and members.[3]

This alters how we hear phrases like "liturgical theology" or "liturgical music." We do not mean a style. We mean a presence. The content of liturgy is the life of Christ extended to his mystical body, and the content of liturgical sacrifice will be the sacrifice of Christ continued in us, his mystical body.

Of late, I have been reading Emile Mersch's three classic works on the mystical body,[4] and nobody makes the connection to the hypostatic union closer and clearer than he does. A few quotes from his first volume, *The Whole Christ*:

> Christ has a twofold life on earth: one visible and historical, the other invisible and mystical; the first is the preparation for the second, and the second is the prolongation of the first. In the second, which is His mysterious existence in the depths of souls,

---

[3] Pope Pius XII, Encyclical Letter on the Sacred Liturgy *Mediator Dei* (1947), §20.
[4] Emile Mersch, *The Whole Christ: The Historical Development of the Doctrine of the Mystical Body in Scripture and Tradition*, trans. John R. Kelly, SJ (Milwaukee, WI: Bruce, 1938); *The Theology of the Mystical Body* (St. Louis, MO: B. Herder 1952); and *Morality and the Mystical Body* (New York: P. J. Kennedy & Sons, 1939).

Christ is far more active, far more truly alive than ever He was in the days when He walked and preached in Judea.

The Church is the continuation, the fullness, the pleroma of Christ. Christ's actions and sufferings are prolonged and consummated in the action of Christians.

The hypostatic union does not affect our Lord alone, but it is somehow prolonged in us, the members; we are the prolongation of the Head, and the hypostatic union renders us divine by reason of our continuity with the God-man.

The divine life we receive is the life given in all plenitude to Christ's human nature.

The same hypostatic union causes to flow into our human nature the life that it imparts to the humanity of Christ.[5]

Everything in Christianity derives from the union that Christ's sacred humanity had with the Word. Incarnation is the union of divine and human natures, not a docetic appearance of God in a costume of flesh. This union in one personal hypostasis has changed the relationship of God with man. In the words of St. Athanasius (d. 373): "The Son of God became the Son of man in order that the sons of men, the sons of Adam, might be made sons of God. . . . He is the Son of God by nature, we by grace."[6] In the words of St. Cyril of Alexandria (d. 444): "No created thing has the power to vivify. . . . The flesh of Paul, for instance, or of Peter, could not produce this effect in us, but only the flesh of our Savior, Christ."[7] In the words of St. Thomas Aquinas (d. 1274): "What is first in any genus is also the cause of whatever comes after it in the genus."[8]

The Church is mankind transfigured by the life of Christ, by the hypostatic union. This may be what Alexander Schmemann had in mind when he quipped that the Church is not an institution with sacraments, it is a sacrament with institutions. And I propose that the life of Christ has transfigured sacrifice. In the Church, all objects, persons, times, all theology, cult, and authority are liturgical for having passed through

---

[5] Mersch, *The Whole Christ*, 44, 131, 283, 304, 356.
[6] Quoted in Mersch, *The Whole Christ*, 284.
[7] Quoted in Mersch, *The Whole Christ*, 340.
[8] Quoted in Mersch, *The Whole Christ*, 465.

the hypostatic union, and for the same reason, and in the same way, the Church knows liturgical sacrifice. The essence of liturgical sacrifice is love, for Christ is all love for the Father, and the Father is all love for his only begotten Son, and through the Spirit this love reaches to all the members united to the head. By spiritual liturgy we participate in the perichoresis of the Trinity's love.

The Mass: Real Sacrifice and Mystical Immolation

There is a difficulty in going straight to this conclusion, however, because the word "sacrifice" has fallen into ill repute today. The source of that bad odor may go back several hundred years, and in order for the world to understand us when we talk about liturgical sacrifice, it behooves us to pause momentarily to notice the meanings that have accrued to the word "sacrifice." I will do so as briefly and quickly as possible, but there are three important persons I should like to mention before returning to divine liturgy and divine love.

The first author I want to mention is Maurice de La Taille. In his *The Mystery of Faith* (1915), he proposes that sacrifice consists of a threefold act, but that our modern definition has infelicitously reduced it to only the middle one. Sacrifice, fully considered, involves offering, immolation, and God's acceptance of the sacrifice. We, however, have placed all our attention on the middle act, immolation. We tend to reduce sacrifice to the death of the victim, but in fact all three component parts are essential.

De La Taille writes, "Neither the offering in itself alone, nor the immolation in itself alone suffices to confer victimhood; both are required." And again: "If God rejects it, the gift will not pass into the ownership of God.... For it is ratified as victim at the moment, and only at the moment, when it is accepted by God.... The sacrifice which is not ratified by God is void."[9]

Applied to Christianity, this means that the full paschal sacrifice involves Christ, the great high priest, who offered the sacrifice of himself at the Last Supper. Christ is also the victim and paschal lamb, who suffered immolation on the Cross. That God the Father received and ratified his

---

[9] Maurice de La Taille, *The Mystery of Faith* (New York: Sheed and Ward, 1940), 1:14–15. Add to this thought the words of Gerhard von Rad: "Sacrifice was, and remained, an event which took place in a sphere lying outside of man and his spirituality: man could as it were only give it the external impulse; its actual operation was not subject to the control of his capacity or capabilities: all this rested with Yahweh, who had the power to accept the offering and let it achieve its purpose" (*Old Testament Theology* [New York: Harper & Row, 1962], 253).

Son's sacrifice is proven in the Resurrection. "Now in the Resurrection, Christ's Victim has passed over to God; Christ's Victim is received by God; Christ's Victim, food of God so to speak, is absorbed in the uncreated fire of the divine glory.... The acceptance in the consumption of the victim by earthly fire was figurative only. Whereas the glorification of Christ was true acceptance."[10] We celebrate these three moments of sacrifice with particular fullness on Maundy Thursday, Good Friday, and Easter Sunday.

De La Taille's work was beneficial as a course correction to a Catholic apologetic that had emphasized immolation in too exclusive a manner. When the Protestant reformers objected to calling the Mass a sacrifice, a series of apologists rose up to affirm the truth that the Mass is a genuine sacrifice, but they did so by focusing almost exclusively on immolation. The result tended toward an attempt to prove a fresh immolation of the victim on each altar, at each Mass. If sacrifice meant immolation, then to prove Protestants wrong when they said there was no sacrifice at the Mass, one tried to prove there was a fresh immolation at each Mass.

De La Taille patiently works through various theories that were tried. Some looked to the fraction rite, suggesting the body of Christ was broken and immolated anew. Some looked to the communion rite, whereat we chew the body and it is corrupted in our intestines afterward. But most looked to transubstantiation. Immolation came to be defined as moving from a superior status to an inferior one, and what more inferior state could the risen Christ suffer than having his glorified body reduced to an insensitive state under the accident of bread? This state was considered to be an even greater humiliation than the Cross, because at least on the Cross Christ's body still exerted its connatural function.

In passing, I mention two potential benefits of de La Taille's thesis. First, on the ecumenical front, it might address certain Protestant concerns. Catholics can say clearly that the sacrifice of the Mass does not add to the once-for-all character of the sacrifice on the Cross, a principle that is at the foundation of Protestant theology. Second, there has been strenuous resistance by some Catholics toward veneration of the Blessed Sacrament, and I have to wonder if they perhaps associate all tabernacle piety with this emphasis on Christ's wretched immolation.

Some of the explanations became quite vivid in expression. Remember, the Catholic apologists rightly wanted to assert that the Mass is a sacrifice, but since they thought this meant immolation, they sought to prove the

---

[10] De La Taille, *The Mystery of Faith*, 1:193.

risen Christ's renewed immolation by talking about him undergoing a constricted, lessened, reduced status at transubstantiation. One apologists points out that Christ's resurrected body could exercise its glorified senses, but when he assumes a mode of existence under the species of bread and wine, "he is bereft of the acts connatural to corporal life. . . . Jesus is constituted there [in the host] after the manner of an inanimate thing, as far as regards any act connatural to the sensitive life, which state, in comparison with the connatural state, is a kind of exinanition [an enfeebling]."[11] Another apologist writes:

> In the Eucharist (what a humiliation!) Christ so humbled himself and chose a state so abject that, apart from a singular miracle, He is like a dead trunk or a log, he can no longer obtain knowledge through acquired images, nor any longer can he, in the light of that knowledge, make acts of the will, likewise he has no more power to feel or move in any way whatever than he would have if he possessed no faculty of reason, sense, or motion. . . . Could anything be added to the supreme humiliation of Christ in the Eucharist, since he lies there like a dead trunk or a log, a state not realized even on the cross? For there, in the midst of his torments, his senses still exerted their connatural function. . . . Hence this state of Christ is by far the most wretched, a greater humiliation than even his abject condition on the cross."[12]

I only pause to notice these apologists because this way of defending the Mass led to a certain kind of tabernacle piety that caused some members in the liturgical renewal movement in the middle part of the last century to strenuously oppose adoration of the Blessed Sacrament. But what would tabernacle piety look like if it was based on a more adequate theology of sacrifice, one which was not restricted to immolation, but was, as de La Taille was trying to bring us to see, a full movement of Christ the priest, Christ the victim, and the Father's reception?

But that, as I said, is a passing comment offered for your reflection. The use I wished to make of de La Taille here is to affirm with him that the

---

[11] Franzelin, quoted in Maurice de La Taille, *The Mystery of Faith* (New York: Sheed and Ward, 1940), 2:203.

[12] Renaud, quoted in de La Taille, *The Mystery of Faith*, 2:203–204.

Mass is a "real sacrifice but a mystical immolation." De La Taille quotes Peter Lombard to this effect:

> It is asked: is sacrifice or immolation the proper term for what the priest does, and is Christ immolated each day, or was He immolated once only? Our answer is briefly this: what is offered and consecrated by the priest is called a sacrifice and an oblation, because it is the memorial and the representation of the holy immolation made on the altar of the cross. And Christ died on the Cross once, and in Himself he was immolated there; but he is daily immolated in the sacrament, because in the sacrament was made the memorial of what was done once.[13]

The offering, the immolation, and the reception by the Father together make up the sacrifice. So, in the words of the Council of Trent (1545–1563), Jesus did what he did at the Last Supper in order that

> His priesthood might not come to an end with His death ... that he might leave to His beloved spouse the Church a visible sacrifice, such as the nature of man requires, whereby that bloody sacrifice once to be accomplished on the cross might be represented, the memory thereof remain even to the end of the world.... [He] offered up to God the Father His own Body and Blood under the form of bread and wine.[14]

Or, in the words of the Second Vatican Council document *Sacrosanctum Concilium* (1963): "At the Last Supper, on the night when he was betrayed, our Savior instituted the Eucharistic sacrifice of his Body and Blood. He did this in order to perpetuate the sacrifice of the Cross throughout the centuries."[15] Or, in the words of the *Catechism of the Catholic Church*:

> The sacrifice of Christ and the sacrifice of the Eucharist are *one single sacrifice*: "The victim is one and the same: the same now offers through the ministry of priests, who then offered himself on the cross; only the manner of offering is different." "And since

---

[13] Lombard, quoted in de La Taille, *The Mystery of Faith*, 2:210.
[14] Council of Trent, Session 22, chap. 1, in *The Canons and Decrees of the Council of Trent* (Rockford, IL: Tan, 1978), 144.
[15] Second Vatican Council, Constitution on the Sacred Liturgy *Sacrosanctum Concilium* (1963), §47, in *The Liturgy Documents*, 4th ed. (Chicago: Liturgy Training Publications, 2004), 1:13.

in this divine sacrifice which is celebrated in the Mass, the same Christ who offered himself once in a bloody manner on the altar of the cross is contained and is offered in an unbloody manner ... this sacrifice is truly propitiatory."[16]

The victim who is made present on the altar is an immolated victim, so when the Church gives him over to the Father, it is a real sacrifice. But the victim made present on the altar is already an immolated victim, so we do not add to his victimhood. That is how it can be affirmed, as Catholic teaching always has, that our "new" sacrifice of the Mass does not add something new (in the sense of "additional") to the Cross. "Hence whatever is new in the sacrifice of the mass in relation to the sacrifice of the Cross comes only from the Church, which now makes its own the offering made by Christ in the past, making it new only in so far as the power and the act of sacrificing passes from the Head to the body."[17]

Recovering the True Meaning of Sacrifice

The second author I want to mention is Royden Yerkes, who analyzes the ditch that divides the modern thinker from medieval, ancient, and biblical thinkers. As a young graduate student, Yerkes became increasingly uncertain about the explanation of sacrifice offered by prevailing nineteenth-century theories of religion, and later summarized his conclusions in a 1953 study entitled *Sacrifice in Greek and Roman Religions and Early Judaism*.

Yerkes contrasts the modern, secular connotations of sacrifice with the ancient, religious connotations. According to the prevailing modern definition, sacrifice may be material or immaterial and it must be valuable to the person making the sacrifice. Sacrifice is constituted by renouncing or giving up something, because the sacrificer is depriving himself of its use. The sacrifice is *by* somebody, *of* something, and *for* something, but never *to* anybody. Thus, the emphasis is upon the sacrificed thing's destruction; because of this, sacrifice denotes sadness and misfortune. Finally, the cost of the sacrifice should be compared with the value obtained because we desire to obtain as much as possible for as little as possible.

Yerkes concludes: "The word sacrifice has ... undergone a complete transformation of meaning. The general and popular use of the term today,

---

[16] *CCC*, §1367. The paragraph is quoting Council of Trent (1562); cf. Heb 9:14, 27.
[17] De La Taille, *The Mystery of Faith*, 2:193.

with a few esoteric exceptions, is wholly secular and describes some sort of renunciation, usually destruction, of something valuable in order that something more valuable may be obtained."[18]

In contrast, he notes the connotations associated with sacrifice in the ancient mind, Hebrew as well as Greco-Roman. The word was only used to describe religious rites and things; it had no secular usage. Sacrifice never connoted reluctance or deprivation or renunciation or sadness, but rather sacrifices were occasions of greatest joy and festivity and thanksgiving—gladly performed as expressions of the attitude of people toward their gods. Therefore, sacrifices were always as large as possible, because the larger the sacrifice, the greater the accompanying joy and festivity. Sacrifices were offered *by* men *to* their gods, and a sacrifice not offered to some person was inconceivable (the emphasis was on the *giving to* and not the *giving up*). While sometimes offered to procure boons, sacrifices were frequently offered as thanksgiving after the boon had already been received. The death of the animal was a necessary preliminary act but no particular significance was attached to the fact that the animal had died.

Thus Yerkes provides us with some vocabulary. "Any object which had been given to a god by repetition of prescribed words and with a prescribed ceremony was called *sacer*." Objects set apart were called *sacra*. The process of devoting things to the use of a god was described by the word *sacrificare* or its kindred *consecrare*.[19] This leads him to the definition of sacrifice as "to make a thing sacred" or "to do a sacred act."

The third and final author I want to mention is Louis Bouyer because he advances a clarification on this point. It was a clarification that he refined in his own mind over the course of his career. In a series of talks at Notre Dame, finally published under the title *Liturgical Piety* in 1955, he follows St. Augustine (d. 430) in saying sacrifice creates a people, and writes:

> Here is the deepest meaning of the word "sacrifice": *sacrum facere*, to make holy. What is the holy thing which is made, or the thing which is made holy as the final effect of God's Word proclaimed to the world? We can say that it is the people, for it is made a people in being made the people *of God*. This is precisely the conclusion reached by St. Augustine. . . . The sacrifice which is

---

[18] Royden Yerkes, *Sacrifice in Greek and Roman Religions and Early Judaism* (London: Adam and Charles Black, 1953), 2.

[19] Yerkes, *Sacrifice*, 6.

offered to God the Father in Christianity is finally the whole
redeemed city offering itself to its redeemer.[20]

But eight years later, in 1963, Bouyer published *Rite and Man*, which contains a more careful consideration and a more nuanced definition. Here he first reviews various theories about natural religion, and developments in the history of religions and psychology, and he arrives at the conclusion that "*sacrum facere* could not mean 'to make sacred' unless one had consciousness that the world was not sacred." In other words, one thinks one must go round with a sacrifice wand consecrating things only if one thinks the world is not sacred and needs man to effect its consecration. Such a consciousness does not belong to the most primitive, natural religious consciousness of man, Bouyer insists. Instead, it belongs to a later stage that is rather far removed from the sensibility of natural religion. Bouyer therefore refines his own, earlier definition of sacrifice:

> Originally, *sacrum facere* certainly did not mean "to make sacred" what supposedly was not sacred up to that particular moment, but rather quite simply "to do what is sacred" *in se ac per se*. For the ancient Latins, sacrifice was nothing more than the sacred act.... By definition, the "sacred" is that over which man has no control.[21]

Whence arose this erroneous illusion by men and women that the earth is theirs, and all the glory therein, and for God to have a piece of it—a mountain, a tree, a well, a sheep—the human being must make that thing sacred by sacrifice? Bouyer's answer is that sin has corrupted our understanding:

> [Modern persons] assume that reality was from the first profane and in order to have something sacred it was necessary to take

---

[20] Louis Bouyer, *Liturgical Piety* (Notre Dame, IN: University of Notre Dame Press, 1955), 160.

[21] Louis Bouyer, *Rite and Man: Natural Sacredness and Christian Liturgy* (Notre Dame, IN: University of Notre Dame Press, 1963), 80. Bouyer is familiar with de La Taille's work, and has this to say: "In his beautiful and profound study, *The Mystery of Faith*, Pere de La Taille maintains that in a state of integral nature the oblation would actually constitute the essence of a sacrifice, and that the painful immolation has only come in as a result of sin.... In favor of a general application of Pere de La Taille's thesis to the history of religions it might still be said that it corresponds well enough to the etymology of the word *sacrificium*, that is, *sacrum facere*, 'to make sacred.'... Unfortunately, however, this etymological interpretation bears the obvious stamp of an advanced stage of religious development." From here, Bouyer goes ahead to correct the definition he once shared with de La Taille.

hold of that which was profane and consecrate it. The truth, however, is the very opposite to this rather smug opinion. Not only was the sacred never made out of the profane, but, in fact, it is the profane that has come into being through a desecration of the sacred.[22]

Notice the inversion that sin has caused in our understanding. In fact, the sacred does not appear when the profane is consecrated; the profane appears when the sacred is desecrated. Bouyer goes on to analyze the source and effect of desecration:

> [Man] circumscribes a limited area in this reality as his own to the exclusion of God. At this moment the profane in contrast to the sacred makes its appearance. The more firmly a man establishes himself in the world as his own home, the more this area of the profane is extended. Moreover, the farther he extends the boundaries of his own piece of ground, the less interest he takes in the rest. A time finally comes when the profane practically seems to coincide with the real. The sacred is no more than a local survival. The rites then easily appear to man as the making of something sacred.[23]

Such is sinful man's outlook on the cosmos once his attitude toward sacrifice has been corrupted.

What Happens in the Sacrifice of the Liturgy

With these perspectives on sacrifice, we have positioned ourselves to consider what is really happening in the liturgical sacrifice. From de La Taille we want to remember that for a full understanding of sacrifice, the immolated victim must be both offered up (as Christ gave his Apostles the power to do) and accepted (as the Father has promised to do by commanding his angel to carry the sacrifice to his altar in heaven). Sacrifice is defined as a dynamic motion of relationship, not the killing of a static thing. From Yerkes we want to remember the gift quality of sacrifice. It is a gesture of thanksgiving wherein we emphasize *giving to*, not just *giving up*. From Bouyer we want to see how to reverse the egoism that first excludes

---

[22] Bouyer, *Rite and Man*, 80.
[23] Bouyer, *Rite and Man*, 80–81.

God from the world, and then offers him a place for local survival in a sacred sphere cut off from our so-called "real life."

I have asserted that sacrifice must pass through the hypostatic union to be used in liturgy. Sacrifice is the supreme act of religion, but our religion is transformed by Christ. Natural religion, with its sacrifice, is elevated by the instrumental causality of Christ's sacred humanity. The Christian liturgy does not do its own human religion—it does the religion of the Christ, who is God as human person. The Christian sacrifice is natural sacrifice restored and elevated by passing through the hypostatic union to be used in divine cult. Sacrifice is a uniquely human activity, but now that human nature has been united with the divine Word, our sacrifices are transfigured through Jesus.

To see this transfiguration, I would like to look at sacrifice through three lenses: the protological, the soteriological, and the eschatological—or, what should have been, what is, and what it is becoming. Protologically, because man is made in the image of God, and that means man's sacrifice will reflect relationship. Soteriologically, because man is a sinner, and that means his sacrifice, now become ineffective, will need redemption. Eschatologically, because what liturgical sacrifice communicates is not an improved natural religion, but Christ's supernatural religion.

First, protology affirms that sacrifice is a natural act of humanity's natural religion. The *Catechism* offers Augustine's definition as its own when it says: Sacrifice is "every action done so as to cling to God in communion of holiness, and thus achieve blessedness."[24] When we consecrate something, we are clinging to God. Mersch defines sacrifice "as the supreme act of religion," and then defines religion as "a conscious and deliberate straining of the creature toward the Creator, an aspiration toward God, a desire of nearness and union with Him, so far as this is possible for a creature."[25] Sacrifice acknowledges the primordial relationship of dependence upon God, leading Mersch to the vivid conclusion, "To exist is our first cult. Thereafter our entire existence can be a religion."[26] And, as usual, G. K. Chesterton can put this into words better than I can:

> [Greek sacrifice] did satisfy a thing very deep in humanity indeed; the idea of surrendering something as the portion of the unknown powers; of pouring out wine on the ground, of throwing a ring

---

[24] *CCC*, §2099, quoting St. Augustine, *The City of God* 10.
[25] Mersch, *Theology of the Mystical Body*, 580.
[26] Mersch, *Morality and the Mystical Body*, 8, 10.

> into the sea; in a word, of sacrifice. It is the wise and worthy idea of not taking our advantage to the full; of putting something in the other balance to ballast our dubious pride, of paying tithes to nature for our land....Where that gesture of surrender is most magnificent, as among the great Greeks, there is really much more idea that the man will be the better for losing the ox than that the god will be the better for getting it.[27]

This was sacrifice, protologically speaking. It was an expression of dependence and thanksgiving upon God. It was a secret connection between sacrifice and thanksgiving (*thusia* and *eucharistia*). If sacrifice is every action done so as to cling to God, as the *Catechism* says, then one would hope that one's whole life would be sacrificial—that every action in life would be done so as to cling to God.

This protological definition is included in liturgical sacrifice. Aidan Kavanagh used to speak of the person at liturgy being "stunningly normal." He writes, "A liturgy of Christians is thus nothing less than the way a redeemed world is, so to speak, done."[28] At the sacrificial action of the Mass, we stand again as man and woman were created to stand in Eden—that is, righteously, in right relationship to Creator above and creation below. Sacrifice is an act that comes out of relationship and expresses the divine-human relationship. The righteous person has an instinct to sacrifice, and a righteous person expects a response from heaven, as de La Taille reminded.

However, we don't do nature naturally anymore, so in the second place liturgical sacrifice will include a soteriological dimension. When mankind is sinful, as is actually the case, religious activity and sacrifice will include yet another factor. Sacrifice is "every action done so as to cling to God in communion of holiness." But for a sinner to cling to God, he must stop clinging to himself. The righteous offering pronounced over the victim expects a response from heaven. But our sacrifices are not offered righteously anymore. Our sacrifices are ineffective. The only righteous sacrifice, one that could receive a response from heaven, would be a sacrifice offered by a righteous man. And we know from Scripture that no man is righteous

---

[27] G. K. Chesterton, *The Everlasting Man*, in *The Collected Works of G. K. Chesterton* (San Francisco: Ignatius Press, 1986), 2:242.

[28] Aidan Kavanagh, *On Liturgical Theology* (Collegeville, MN: Pueblo, 1984), 100.

(Rom 3:10). So our offerings will have to be joined to the Righteous One (Acts 3:14; 7:52) by passing through the hypostatic union.

In order to cling to God in sacrifice, the sinner must not be afraid. Yet when the Lord God called to the man and asked, "Where are you?" the man answered, "I heard the sound of you in the garden, and I was afraid, because I was naked; and I hid myself" (Gen 3:9–10). The human race has been hiding in the bushes ever since, and only a corrupt form of sacrifice can come forth from a hiding place.

Sacrifice is supposed to be born of a desire to be near to God, but ever since our ancestors by disobedience seized what was not yet theirs to have, our sacrifice has been faulty. The very purpose of sacrifice has been inverted. We no longer desire to be near God, and mankind makes sacrifice in order to stay "safe" from God. If sinful man has circumscribed the world as his own, to the exclusion of God, then the first act of true religion must consist of man relinquishing his rash claims upon everything in the world. Because sin has entered the picture, sacrifice involves a prior, negative, soteriological act before it can be the positive act it was protologically intended to be. The sinner must resign his illusory control over his world, his life, himself, before the positive act of clinging to God in the communion of holiness can be made.

That is why sacrifice looks painful to us: because it will be painful to our old Adam! It will be positively mortifying! Sacrifice looks different under the law of sin than it looked in the garden of Eden, than it looks to the saints. That's probably why sacrifice appears to us as a "giving up"—because exactly the first thing we must do is to give up the profanity that attempts to circumscribe God to a local survival. The sinner's first act of sacrifice must be an act of surrender, an unclenching of his grasping hands. But this is exactly what the sinner is powerless to do. Archimandrite Boniface Luykx, of blessed memory, told me religion is building a road for God to come to you on. But the sinner is afraid of God coming to him, so he is afraid of religion, and he is inept at sacrifice.

Cosmic Priests and Divinized Sacrifice

We must remember how things had been brought to such a state, according to the salvation history we find recorded in Scripture. Before the high king, all creatures should bring their sacrifice. The sacrifices presented by the cherubim are accepted, as well as by the seraphim, archangels, and principalities. But where is earth's sacrifice? Where is the sacrifice from visible creation? The angel of that world (Lucifer) has begrudged the king and withheld it. So the king appoints a new priest, one made of flesh and spirit: Adam and Eve. They will be able to make the visible sacrifice because they belong to the visible world and are simultaneously endowed with spiritual soul. Man and woman are the cosmic priests. But they are too easily seduced away from their task by that rebellious prince of this world. The enemy finds it all to easy to give them easy amnesia and they forget their purpose. They no longer see the world as sacrament. They begin to look upon matter as something other than raw material for Eucharist. The cause of all sin is forgetting God, the Church fathers say, and by our weak-willed amnesia, the human race has discovered the reality of life apart from God; in other words, death.

What was God to do? More than we expect. (Isn't that always the way with grace?) Here enters our third lens, the eschatological understanding of sacrifice. The king's Son unites his own nature to these priests, and makes himself the victim. Thus, the sacrifice he gives back to Adam and Eve is a divinized sacrifice. He is the only priest, the high priest, the righteous priest, yet at the Last Supper he tells his Apostles they should continue doing what he has just done. They should offer him to the Father just as he is offering himself to the Father. He is the victim, but this is once for all, and because it is a righteous offering, it penetrates heaven, as the book of Hebrews says (Heb 9:23–24).

Sacrifice is restored, but—*O felix culpa!*—in a transfigured form. God gives himself to himself as the firstfruits of humanity's graced sacrifice. What the first Adam refused to do, the second Adam did willingly. Christ lived his life in total obedience to the Father, in total love to the Father, with total religion, in perfect sacrifice toward the Father, clinging at all times to the Father. And for this reason did he love us, too, as George MacDonald captures so well:

> The sons of men were his Father's children like himself; that the Father should have them all in his bosom was the one thought of his heart; that should be his doing for his Father, cost him what it might! He came to do his will and on the earth was the same as he had been from the beginning, the eternal first. He was not interested in himself, but in his Father and his Father's children.[29]

---

[29] George MacDonald, *Unspoken Sermons* (Whitethorn, CA: Johannesen Press, 2004), 2:172.

The liturgy therefore has twofold terrain—cultic and mundane. Jean Corbon[30] called them ritual liturgy and lived liturgy. It was sin that circumscribed an area to the exclusion of God; in Christ there is no sin, and therefore there was no area of his life that did not belong to the Father. There must not be any such area in our lives, either. Our whole life must be a clinging to God, as Christ's whole life was sacrificial. He was doing his Father's will as he loved the poor around him, so St. John Chrysostom (d. 407) reminded his parishioners that the ones seeking alms in the courtyard outside the church are a sacrificial opportunity:

> Do not protest! This stone altar is august because of the Victim that rests upon it; but the altar of almsgiving is more so because it is made of this very Victim. The former is august because, though made of stone, it is sanctified by contact with the body of Christ; the latter, because it is the body of Christ.... This altar you can see everywhere, in the streets and in the market place, and at any hour you may offer sacrifice thereon; for it too is a place of sacrifice.[31]

Christ is the firstfruits because he is the choicest part. The best lamb is offered on behalf of the flock; the best man is offered on behalf of humanity. As representative, God gives himself to himself (making no end to complications in the doctrine of Atonement). Christ took his humanity from us, the humanity in which all persons are united, and thus connected his sacrifice with every person redemptively. As Mersch says, Christ's reason for being "is to constitute the contact between God and men. His humanity is a means: the Word took it to use it, to sacrifice it, to exalt it too, under the title of first fruits of the human race."[32] And now, when the Church offers up the visible creation's sacrifice, it is only joining God's offering of himself to himself.

The priesthood of the Church is but a share in Christ's priesthood; the offering of the Church is but a share in Christ's self-offering. This is the basis of the priesthood of the Church, belonging to both the laity and the ordained, as the *Catechism* reminds us. "The whole community of believers is, as such, priestly. The faithful exercise their baptismal priesthood through

---

[30] See his *The Wellspring of Worship* (New York: Paulist Press, 1988).
[31] John Chrysostom, *Homilies on 2 Corinthians*, quoted in Mersch, *The Whole Christ*, 335.
[32] Mersch, *Morality and the Mystical Body*, 65.

their participation, each according to his own vocation, in Christ's mission as priest, prophet, and king."[33]

In order to equip and capacitate this common priesthood, Christ has instituted the ministerial priesthood, which is "directed at the unfolding of the baptismal grace of all Christians. The ministerial priesthood is a *means* by which Christ unceasingly builds up and leads his Church."[34] If there is a difference between these two kinds of priesthood, that difference "is not found in the priesthood of Christ, which remains forever one and indivisible, nor in the sanctity to which all of the faithful are called.... This diversity exists at the mode of participation in the priesthood of Christ."[35] This sacrifice, given by the Son to the Father, is the Church's liturgy. The liturgy is the work of a few on behalf of the many. At one time, it was the work of one man; every day more join Jesus's priestly act.

The regeneration of sacrifice is more than a soteriological solution; it is an eschatological accomplishment. It does more than untwist sin's snarl. The restoration is a transformation. We are not given back the first Adam's religion; we are given the God-Man's religion to practice. Blessed Columba Marmion writes, "The Church receives her mission from Christ: she receives the sacraments and the privilege of infallibility in order to sanctify men; but she has a part too in the religion of Christ towards his Father in order to continue upon earth the homage of praise that Christ in his sacred humanity offered to his Father."[36]

Adoration is the first act of religion, and now, because we are baptismally regenerated by the Holy Spirit, we adore the Father in the Son. To repeat Pius XII's definition of liturgy, the Church renders worship to her founder, and through him it goes to the heavenly Father, and thus the members participate in the worship which our redeemer renders to the Father as head of his mystical body. To borrow Marmion's words again:

> Christ does not separate himself from his mystical body. Before ascending into heaven, he bequeaths his riches and mission to his Church. Christ, in uniting himself to the Church, gives her his power of adoring and praising the Father; this is the liturgy. It is the praise of the Church united to Jesus, supported by Jesus;

---

[33] *CCC*, §1546.
[34] *CCC*, §1547.
[35] Vatican Congregation for the Clergy, *Instruction on Certain Questions Regarding the Collaboration of the Non-Ordained Faithful in the Sacred Ministry of the Priest* (1997), §1.
[36] Columba Marmion, *Christ the Life of the Soul* (St. Louis, MO: Herder, 1926), 284.

or rather it is the praise of Christ, the incarnate Word, passing through the lips of the Church.[37]

As I have tried to say it before, "Liturgy is not the performance of a human religion. Liturgy is the religion of Christ—the religion he enacted in the flesh before the Father—perpetuated."[38]

What was true of Christ by nature is true of us by grace. We are made members of the one who was the hypostatic union of human nature and Logos. So human beings are changed—now they are Christians. And our human religion is changed—now it is Christianity. Natural sacrifice is elevated and in the liturgy we step into the supernal relations of love between Father, Son, and Holy Spirit. To effect this unity was the whole purpose of the hypostatic union, says Mersch, and with his words we might end:

> Religion is a relation between man and God.... In the midst of us an individual has arisen, who, man and God at the same time, is the perfect priest. Let our religion be organized about this Emmanuel and in this Emmanuel, let it pass through him and it will pierce the skies and will penetrate the holy of holies.... And, in order to pass through him, our religion need not impose any mutilation on itself. Christ has assumed all our nature. There is then, nothing human which cannot be integrated into his religion.[39]

What has passed through the hypostatic union for our use passes again through the hypostatic union to pierce the skies and penetrate the holy of holies. Christ is the mediator of liturgical sacrifice.

---

[37] Columba Marmion, *Christ, the Ideal of the Monk* (St. Louis, MO: Herder, 1922), 297. Again, in *Life of the Soul*, 83: "Jesus Christ, when upon earth, offered a perfect canticle of praise to his Father; His soul unceasingly contemplated the divine perfections, and from this contemplation came forth his continual praise and adoration to the glory of his Father. By his incarnation, Christ associated entire humanity, in principle, with this work of praise. When he left us, he gave to his Church the charge of perpetuating, in his name, this praise due to His Father."

[38] Fagerberg, "Theosis in a Roman Key? The Conferences of Columba Marmion," *Antiphon* 7, no. 1 (2002): 30–39.

[39] Mersch, *Morality and the Mystical Body*, 29–30.

Sacrament
The Sacraments as Actions of the Mystical Body[*]

Sometimes in novels of fiction or fantasy the protagonist must engage in a contest of riddles in order to cross a bridge or win a prize. In *The Hobbit*, Bilbo Baggins continues such a contest against Gollum by asking, "What is a box without hinges, key, or lid, yet golden treasure inside is hid?" (I guess the book has been out long enough for me not to spoil it for anyone by divulging that the answer is an egg.) Now, if I were ever magically cast into a fantasy story and faced a troll who would not let me cross a bridge until I had answered his riddle, I believe the riddle I would receive would be this: "Are sacraments liturgical, or is liturgy sacramental?"[1]

That liturgy and sacraments should be entangled, I most fully agree. Christ, the Church, the liturgy, and the sacraments are all interrelated, like nesting cups, one inside the next.[2] First, Christ is sent by the Father, and, obedient always to his Father's will, he fulfills the divine plan for creation: he shatters the gates of Hades and gathers creation together for ascent back to the Father by sending the Holy Spirit to spiritualize things. Second, Church is Christ's mystical body, commissioned with the task of serving this redemption and sanctification. Georges Florovsky said, "The doctrine of the Church itself is but an 'extended Christology,' the doctrine of the *'total Christ,' totus Christus, caput et corpus*."[3] Third, liturgy is this Church in motion. It is the manifestation of the new creation that has been brought about by the paschal mystery, and it is shared by a social, sacramental body until the Lord of the Church returns as Lord of the world to hand all things over to the Father. And fourth, the sacraments

---

[*] David W. Fagerberg, "The Sacraments as Actions of the Mystical Body," *Communio* 39, no. 4 (Winter 2012): 554–68.

[1] Originally presented at the Academy of Catholic Theology, May 2012.

[2] This description echoes one I used in my entry on "The Sacramental Life," in *The Oxford Handbook of Catholic Theology*, ed. Lewis Ayres and Medi Ann Volpe (Oxford: Oxford University Press, 2019).

[3] Fr. Georges Florovsky, "The Ever-Virgin Mother," in *The Mother of God: A Symposium*, ed. E. L. Mascall (Westminster, MD: Dacre Press, 1959), 52.

serve our liturgical life by accompanying us from the cradle to the grave, capacitating us for an earthly liturgy in tune with a heavenly liturgy. There are not two liturgies, one in heaven and one on earth; there is one liturgy, in heaven and on earth. The sacraments communicate divine life: they inaugurate it, heal it, and order it—which is just how the sacraments have been categorized in the *Catechism* at paragraph 1211: sacraments of initiation, sacraments of healing, and sacraments at the service of communion and the mission of the faithful.

So we know that liturgy and sacrament are related, even interrelated, but what does each contribute to the other? That's the point of the troll's riddle. Are sacraments the central thing, and liturgy is just their form or style or setting—like a ring is the setting for a jewel? Or is liturgy the central thing, and it is garlanded and festooned with sacraments, some occasional, some regular, some rare? These alternatives, made in slightly sarcastic tone, fail because in them neither liturgy nor sacrament penetrates and conditions the other. I rather prefer their juxtaposition to result in each dilating the other. "Sacramental liturgy"—because liturgy is an *opus Dei*, and not Robert's Rule of Order for the Jesus club. "Liturgical sacraments"—because sacraments capacitate us for participating in the activity of the mystical body. So this paper is divided into these two parts: first, thinking about how a sacramental understanding would enlarge our concept of liturgy, and second, thinking about how a liturgical understanding would enlarge our concept of sacrament.

Sacramental Liturgy

The first task is to dilate our understanding of liturgy. You can get a sense of what people commonly mean by liturgy if you listen to what they say. I offer two anecdotal examples. One time a person said to me, when he heard that I was coming to Notre Dame, "You like liturgy, don't you? Wait until you see a football game there." Another time I was waiting in line with my colleagues to march into commencement exercises, all of us dressed in cap and gown, and the person behind me said, "You must like this sort of thing." From the fact that I studied liturgy, both of these people concluded that I would enjoy excessive pomp, useless formality, ritual etiquette, and extravagant ceremony. These are the shiny things they thought caught my attention in liturgical studies.

I do not deny that liturgy involves ceremony, but I have come to think that the ceremony is only the tip of the liturgical iceberg that is visible to us. In the Chronicles of Narnia, Lewis says first about a stable and then about Narnia itself, "Its inside is bigger than its outside," and I propose that the inside of liturgy is bigger than the ritual that holds it. I think this is what Alexander Schmemann was indicating when he spoke about "cultic antinomy." We want to discover what the visible cult above the waterline is connected to, and that would involve discovering connections between cult and cosmos, sacred and profane, church and world, ritual liturgy and lived liturgy. The liturgy is cosmic in scale and eschatological in scope.[4]

I do not object to using the term "liturgy" to mean the public collection of official services, rites, ceremonies, and prayers of the Church, but I no longer believe this is a sufficient definition. In what follows, I will offer three more adequate definitions, one of them my own. The first is from Pius XII's encyclical *Mediator Dei*, which contains this focus on Christ:

> The sacred liturgy is, consequently, the public worship which our Redeemer as Head of the Church renders to the Father, as well as the worship which the community of the faithful renders to its Founder, and through Him to the heavenly Father. It is, in short, the worship rendered by the Mystical Body of Christ in the entirety of its Head and members.[5]

This is the "work of God" in which the Christian liturgist participates upon being baptized into Christ and becoming his liturgical apprentice. Liturgy is not one of Adam's religions, liturgy is participating in the cult of the New Adam. Liturgy cannot be circumnavigated without Christology. The second definition comes from *The Liturgy of the Church*, by Virgil Michel, OSB, which contains this focus on the Trinity:

> The liturgy, through Christ, comes from the Father, the eternal source of the divine life in the Trinity. It in turn addresses itself in a special way to the Father, rendering him the homage and the glory of which it is capable through the power of Christ. The flow of divine life between the eternal Father and the Church is achieved and completed through the operation of the Holy Ghost.
>
> The liturgy, reaching from God to man, and connecting man to the fullness of the Godhead, is the action of the Trinity in the

---

[4] See David Fagerberg, "What Is the Subject Matter of Liturgical Theology?" *Roczniki Liturgiczno-Homiletyczne* 1, no. 57 (2010): 41–51.

[5] Pope Pius XII, Encyclical Letter on the Sacred Liturgy *Mediator Dei* (1947), §20.

Church. The Church in her liturgy partakes of the life of the divine society of the three persons in God.[6]

It would seem, then, that the liturgy originates in a place where scholars forget to look when they are investigating it. Liturgy's beginning is not ancient history, religious purity rituals, human need for fellowship; it is the Trinity. We join a liturgy already in progress. The liturgy is not the activity of the Jesus Club, it is coming to be connected into God's own perichoresis. What starts the liturgical ball rolling, the ignition switch in the liturgical engine, is not us, it is the Trinity. The bulb from which the liturgical tulip grows is not a human decision, but a divine decision that is intertwined with the reason why God created in the first place.[7]

In his *Four Hundred Chapters on Love* Maximus the Confessor counsels the reader, "Seek the reason why God created, for this is knowledge."[8] He seems to say that true knowledge would come from putting the ontological puzzle in roughly this form: What is God up to? Maximus offers an answer in this same work: "God who is beyond fullness did not bring creatures into being out of any need of his, but that he might enjoy their proportionate participation in him and that he might delight in his works seeing them delighted and ever insatiably satisfied with the one who is inexhaustible."[9] And he offers the same answer in different words in a different work:

> God made us so that we might become "partakers of the divine nature" (2 Pet. 1:4) and sharers in His eternity, and so that we might come to be like Him (cf. 1 John 3:2) through deification by grace. It is through deification that all things are reconstituted and achieve their permanence; and it is for its sake that what is not is brought into being and given existence.[10]

What is God up to? (That is true knowledge.) And Maximus suggests God is out to spiritually transfigure his world—what the Greek fathers

---

[6] Virgil Michel, O.S.B., *The Liturgy of the Church, according to the Roman Rite* (New York: Macmillan, 1937), 40.
[7] See David W. Fagerberg, *Mary in the Liturgy* (London: Catholic Truth Society, 2012).
[8] Maximus the Confessor, *The Four Hundred Chapters on Love*, in *Maximus Confessor: Selected Writings*, trans. George Berthold (Mahwah, NJ: Paulist Press, 1985), 76.
[9] Maximus, *The Four Hundred Chapters on Love*, 67.
[10] Maximus the Confessor, *Various Texts on Theology, the Divine Economy, and Virtue and Vice*, The First Century, in *The Philokalia*, ed. G. E. H. Palmer, Philip Sherrard, and Kallistos Ware

meant by *theosis*. And this cosmic *oikonomia* being worked by God is staged by the liturgy in microcosmic form. So the third definition I offer is the one I have been using of late: *Liturgy is the Trinity's perichoresis kenotically extended to invite our synergistic ascent into deification.* In other words, the Trinity's circulation of love turns itself outward, and in humility the Son and Spirit work the Father's good pleasure for all creation, which is to cause our ascent to participate in the very life of God; however, this cannot be forced, it must be done with our cooperation.[11]

I will try to make my point with another anecdote. I was once asked whether I could teach a course in liturgical history. I thought to myself: "Yes, I can. Liturgical history is an important topic; it deserves a course. Where shall I begin? I suppose with Abraham, leading to Moses's encounter at the burning bush, and then to Israel's kings and prophets preparing for the Messiah and the new Israel. No, wait. Probably the covenant with Noah needs to be mentioned. Well, actually, liturgical history began with the cosmic priesthood of Adam and Eve, and their fall was the forfeiture of their liturgical career, and the long story of salvation history was designed to restore man and woman to their liturgical state by becoming apprentices to Christ, the premier liturgist. That would be a *liturgical history*." Then I realized the person who asked the question only wanted to know if I could teach a course on the *history of the liturgy*.

Here's one more example. Anthropology is a study of *anthropos*, and it can be digging in the dirt for shards of a past civilization, or examining wooden face masks; a philosophical anthropology asks how *anthropos* is different from other animals; a social anthropology might conclude with Marx that man and woman's end is to serve the state, or with capitalism that their end is to grow the stock market. But Schmemann says the end of man and woman is a liturgical one:

> All rational, spiritual and other qualities of man, distinguishing him from other creatures, have their focus and ultimate fulfillment in this capacity to bless God, to know, so to speak, the meaning of the thirst and hunger that constitutes his life. "*Homo sapiens*," "*homo faber*" ... yes, but, first of all, "*homo adorans*." The first, the basic definition of man is that he is *the priest*. He stands in the center of the world and unifies it in his act of blessing God, of

---

(Boston: Faber and Faber, 1981), 2:173.

[11] What would be required of us to engage in this liturgy is the subject of my book *On Liturgical Asceticism* (Washington, D.C.: The Catholic University of America Press, 2013).

both receiving the world from God and offering it to God—and by filling the world with this eucharist, he transforms his life, the one that he receives from the world, into life in God, into communion with Him. The world was created as the "matter," the material of one all-embracing eucharist, and man was created as the priest of this cosmic sacrament.[12]

Liturgical history sees God drawing us forth into heaven's liturgy through the divine *oikonomia* that stretches from protology to eschatology. Liturgical anthropology sees man and woman as cosmic priests who were created to rule over creation in a dominion that was conditioned by their obedience to God. Liturgical cosmology sees matter as a sacramental touch by love's hand, a gift to use for sacrifice, the walls of a temple on earth where the heavenly angels can join us. And so forth. A similar Copernican revolution could be done with almost every field of theology.[13]

Liturgical history is more than a history of the liturgy, as Church is more than the Jesus club, as icon is more than picture, as homily is more than instruction, as Scripture is more than poetic wisdom and historical narrative, as symbol is more than sign—and as sacrament is more than souvenir. What the Church does in her sacraments is aligned to the divine intention that drives the whole enterprise, namely, a cause of deification. Gregory Palamas makes this point in one of his homilies on the parousia:

> The world was founded with this in view from the beginning. The heavenly, pre-eternal Counsel of the Father ... was for this end: to enable man at some time to contain the greatness of God's kingdom, the blessedness of God's inheritance and the perfection of the heavenly Father's blessing.... Even the indescribable divine self-emptying, the theandric way of life, the saving passion, *all the sacraments were planned beforehand* in God's providence and wisdom for this end.[14]

The telos of a knife is to cut, of a watch to tell time, of man and woman to be liturgical priests. The theandric way of life and all the sacraments were

---

[12] Alexander Schmemann, *For the Life of the World* (Crestwood, NY: St. Vladimir's Seminary Press, 1973), 15.

[13] See my *Liturgical Dogmatics: How Catholic Beliefs Flow from Liturgical Prayer* (San Francisco: Ignatius Press, 2021).

[14] Gregory Palamas, Homily Four, "On the Gospel Passage Describing Christ's Second Coming," in *Saint Gregory Palamas: The Homilies* (Waymart, PA: Mount Thabor Publishing, 2009), 28–29,

planned beforehand. Nicholas Cabasilas said the reason for creation was so that one day God could have a mother. Creation is the beginning of redemption, and redemption is the completion of creation, and at the end the Trinity will draw back into itself everything in creation that has been taken up into the wake of the ascension that Christ launched from Sheol. This is liturgical life, and it is something more than just temple etiquette. I have tried to apply *sacramental logic* to liturgy in order to make the point.

Liturgical Sacraments

Now to dilate our understanding of sacraments with a *liturgical logic*. We seek to define sacraments as something more than individual dosages of grace. The sacraments bring about liturgical life. Aidan Kavanagh used to say that liturgy is the faith of the Church in motion. By *faith* we step into the perichoresis of the Holy Trinity, so that our *hope* can be focused upon the eternal, and *charity* can steal its way into hearts of stone to make them live. The sacraments are contacts with the mystery that deifies. The life in Christ consists of union with him, and Christ bestows this new life through his mysteries, so Nicholas Cabasilas's opening sentence in his book on the sacraments is: "By them we are begotten and formed and wondrously united to the Savior."[15]

Interpreting his point, Panayiotis Nellas reminds us that according to St. Paul, the primary and highest mystery of our faith is Christ. "This primary mystery or sacrament which is Christ is refracted, according to Kavasilas [sic], and becomes concrete and active within time by being refracted through the sacramental mysteries, by which the Church is organized and by which it lives."[16] We speak of Christ being the primordial sacrament of the Father because when someone encounters Christ, he or she is encountering God. We furthermore speak of the Church herself being a sacrament, because in the Church one encounters Christ. If those first two steps in the sequence are correct, then it applies in the third as well, namely, in the seven sacramental rituals, we are encountering the Church, the mystical body. Going down the ladder we can say: Christ is the sacrament of God, the Church is the sacrament of Christ, and these seven are sacraments of the Mystical Body. Going up the ladder

---

italics added.

[15] Nicholas Cabasilas, *The Life in Christ* (Crestwood, NY: St. Vladimir's Seminary Press, 1974), 49.

[16] Panayiotis Nellas, *Deification in Christ: The Nature of the Human Person* (Crestwood, NY: St. Vladimir's Seminary Press, 1987), 142.

we can say: the rituals sacramentalize the Mystical Body, the Church sacramentalizes Christ, and Christ sacramentalizes the Father. Of course, the sacraments are the personal acts of Christ, but what they manifest is the Church, and in some sense can be called actions or expressions of the Church. Ex-pressed—the Church is "pressed out" through them. So Nellas describes the Church as dynamite (*dunamis*):

> The Church is not a static situation. It is a dynamic, transformative movement. It is the perpetual marriage in space and time of the Creator with His creation, the enduring mingling of the created with the uncreated. Through this unconfused mingling in Christ of created with uncreated nature, the created is subsumed into the flesh of Christ, is rehabilitated sacramentally, is transformed, become the body of Christ and lives as such.[17]

In even briefer words, he defines the Church as "creation grafted onto Christ and vivified by the Spirit."[18] And this links sacraments to their cosmic dimension. "The Church is *creation reassembled and restructured sacramentally*. It is higher than the first creation. The world is no longer the house of man only, but the house of the living God."[19] The sacraments are not Band-Aids for sin; rather, they are part of the reassembling and restructuring of creation called the Church, which includes the reconstruction of our own identity. God's *oikonomia* has been at work building a habitat for divinity! Such is the image described by the fifth-century Syrian poet-theologian Balai. He writes this hymn for the consecration of a Church:

> 9. That he may be accessible to earth-dwellers,
> he has built himself a house among those with bodies.
> He has established altars like mangers
> where the Church may feed on life.
>
> 10. Make no mistake, the King is here;
> let us enter the sanctuary and see him.

---

[17] Nellas, *Deification in Christ*, 143.
[18] Nellas, *Deification in Christ*, 142.
[19] Nellas, *Deification in Christ*, 145, italics added.

41. Where art thou, Lord? Behold, in heaven.
And where shall we seek thee? Behold, in the sanctuary.
Heaven is too high for us, we cannot reach it;
We see thee in thy Church, where we have access.[20]

The Church is a sacramental edifice, making God accessible to earth-dwellers.

Picking up on this same theme of deification, and explaining the sacraments as a means to it, Georgios Mantzaridis writes:

> Christ regenerated and deified in himself corrupted human nature, but not individual hypostases.... The sacraments of the Church make it possible for man to enter freely and personally into communion with the divinizing grace which the Logos of God bestowed upon human nature in assuming it. Through the sacraments corrupt man, sprung from the corrupted root of Adam, is united with the new root, that is, with Christ, and partakes of incorruptibility and a divine life.[21]

If the Church, as body of Christ, is creation reassembled and restructured sacramentally, then this must take place in each of the cells of the body. And I propose that asceticism has its place here—a sort that I am calling "liturgical asceticism" because it works for the capacitation of our liturgical life, and is accomplished sacramentally. If liturgy means sharing the life of Christ (being washed in his Resurrection, eating his body), and if *askesis* means discipline (in the sense of forming), then liturgical asceticism is the discipline required to become an icon of Christ and make his image visible in our faces.

There are many other motives for practicing an asceticism, but if the motive is to become by grace what Christ is by nature, then this asceticism should be called liturgical. It operates not out of our strength, but by relying upon the sacramental bestowal of the grace of Christ through the working of the Holy Spirit. And the sacraments should be seen as ordered to this purpose. Liturgy is participation by the believer in the perichoresis of the Trinity; asceticism is the capacitation for that participation. The mysteries reproduce the mystery of Christ in each believer.

---

[20] Translation by Robert Murray, *Symbols of Church and Kingdom: A Study in Early Syriac Tradition* (Cambridge: Cambridge University Press, 1975), 272–73.

[21] Georgios Mantzaridis, *The Deification of Man* (Crestwood, NY: St. Vladimir's Seminary Press, 1984), 42.

Blessed Columba Marmion writes that Christ attaches a grace to each of his mysteries in order "to help us to reproduce within ourselves His divine features in order to make us like unto Him."[22]

The way to the altar leads through the waters where the old Adam will be drowned, because the only way to the resurrection is through the Cross. The Church is the place where we can be sacramentally refitted to resume the liturgical journey to paradise, the journey that Adam and Eve abandoned. Vladimir Lossky writes, "After the Fall, human history is a long shipwreck awaiting rescue: but the port of salvation is not the goal; it is the possibility for the shipwrecked to resume his journey whose sole goal is union with God."[23] But there is this difference between the journey Adam and Eve should have taken, and the journey we now take: now we are in Christ, and Christ is in us. (Therefore the Easter Vigil exults *Felix Culpa*!)

Kavanagh used to define liturgy as "doing the world the way the world was meant to be done." It has occurred to me recently that he not only meant doing it with social justice; he also meant doing it sacramentally. The world's matter was intended to be sacramental and capable of becoming a temple. The reason the world groans in travail, as Paul tells the Romans, is because matter cannot fulfill its purpose due to Adam and Eve's failure as cosmic priests. The whole world was meant to have been an hierophany of grace, a sacramental encounter with God, but sin means we took the world as an end in itself and we are barred reentrance until we have regained control of our appetites and do the world the way it was meant to be done. The order of grace is sacramental because all matter is pliable in the hands of God and can be restored to its original liturgical function. All it takes is human petition and divine concession (which is called "epiclesis"). The sacramental restructuring of the world that is celebrated in the liturgy brings matter to completion, it does not vitiate it, and so Ratzinger can say that the transubstantiated Host is "the anticipation of the transformation and divinization of matter in the christological 'fullness.'"[24] And he can describe the Eucharist as "the real 'action' for which all of creation is in expectation. The elements of the earth are transubstantiated, pulled, so to speak, from their creaturely anchorage, grasped at the deepest ground of their being, and changed into the Body and Blood of the Lord. The New

---

[22] Columba Marmion, *Christ in His Mysteries* (St. Louis, MO: B. Herder), 233.

[23] Vladimir Lossky, *Orthodox Theology: An Introduction*, trans. Ian and Ihita Kesarcodi-Watson (New York: St. Vladimir's Seminary Press, 1978), 84.

[24] Joseph Ratzinger, *The Spirit of the Liturgy*, trans. John Saward (San Francisco: Ignatius Press, 2000), 29.

Heaven and the New Earth are anticipated."[25] Matter is sacramentally restored to its liturgical meaning, as Paul Evdokimov says:

> The final destiny of water is to participate in the mystery of the Epiphany; of wood, to become a cross; of the earth, to receive the body of the Lord during his rest on the Sabbath.... Olive oil and water attain their fullness as conductor elements for grace on regenerated man. Wheat and wine achieve their ultimate *raison d'etre* in the eucharistic chalice.... A piece of being becomes a hierophany, an epiphany of the sacred....
>
> Nothing in the world remains foreign to [Christ's] humanity, everything has received the seal of the Holy Spirit. This is why the Church in turn blesses and sanctifies all of creation: green branches and flowers fill the churches on the day of Pentecost; the feast of Epiphany has its "Great Blessing of the Waters and all Cosmic Matter"; at the *litya* during vespers, the church blesses wheat, oil, bread and wine; ... Cosmic matter thus becomes a conductor of grace, a vehicle of the divine energies.[26]

None of this is possible so long as the passions disturb our right relationship with the cosmos, which is why liturgical asceticism is also involved in a recovery of sacramental liturgy. What cripples our liturgical posture is no material flaw, but a spiritual fall. Maximus the Confessor defines a passion as "a movement of the soul contrary to nature.... Vice is the mistaken use of ideas from which follows the abuse of things."[27] Peter of Damascus concurs, "It is not the thing itself, but its misuse that is evil."[28] In brief, there is nothing wrong with money, sex, or beer—the problem is with avarice, lust, and gluttony. We do not do the world as it was meant to be done, failing liturgy; and the cataracts of sin on our eye means the world no longer has transparency to God, failing sacramentality. Because the Fall has darkened the *nous* (mind), we now look at our neighbor with lust, we look at the goods of the earth avariciously or gluttonously, and we look at God as a threat to our freedom. But the sacramentality of the world would be completely different for the liturgical person.

---

[25] Ratzinger, *The Spirit of the Liturgy*, 173.
[26] Paul Evdokimov, *The Art of the Icon: A Theology of Beauty* (Redondo Beach, CA: Oakwood, 1990), 117–18.
[27] Maximus the Confessor, *Four Hundred Chapters on Love*, 48.
[28] St. Peter of Damaskos, *A Treasury of Divine Knowledge*, in *The Philokalia*, ed. G. E. H. Palmer, Philip Sherrard, and Kallistos Ware (Boston: Faber & Faber, 1986), 3:156.

Conclusion

In the sacraments we are reclothed with the robe of immortality that the Lord Adam and Lady Eve had lost in Eden. They were stripped of immortality and clothed in garments of skin (mortality). C. S. Lewis points out in *The Four Loves* that "the word naked was originally a past participle; the naked man was the man who had undergone a process of naking, that is, of stripping or peeling (you used the verb of nuts and fruits)."[29] If I have a thirst, and drink, then my thirst has been slaked; if I am going too fast in an automobile and depress the left pedal, then I have braked; and Adam and Eve were normal and nude, but after they sinned knew they had been naked. So Ephrem the Syrian summarizes the whole economy of salvation as a story of four robes. Here is Sebastian Brock's summary: the robes of creation, incarnation, baptism, and the resurrection of the dead:

> At the Fall, Adam and Eve lose the "Robe of Glory" with which they had originally been clothed in Paradise; in order to re-clothe the naked Adam and Eve (in other words, humanity), God himself "puts on the body" from Mary, and at the Baptism Christ laid the Robe of Glory in the river Jordan, making it available once again for humanity to put on at baptism; then, at his or her baptism, the individual Christian, in "putting on Christ," puts on the Robe of Glory, thus re-entering the terrestrial anticipation of the eschatological Paradise, in other words, the Church; finally, at the Resurrection of the Dead, the just will in all reality reenter the celestial Paradise, clothed in their Robes of Glory.[30]

The doffing of sin and donning of glory is the liturgical asceticism practiced by the Mystical Body of Christ in its sacramental life. Every Christian has been committed to this struggle since the day of his or her baptism. Nicodemus of the Holy Mountain reminds us that asceticism teaches about "an unseen and inner struggle which every Christian undertakes from the moment of his baptism, when he makes a vow to God to fight for Him, to

---

[29] C. S. Lewis, *The Four Loves* (New York: Harcourt, Brace and Company, 1960), 147.

[30] Sebastian Brock, introduction to Ephrem the Syrian, *Hymns on Paradise* (Crestwood, NY: St. Vladimir's Seminary Press, 1990), 67. The Office of Matins sings, "You took upon yourself the condemnation of those who were rejected and condemned, O Christ. And after being stripped, you were placed on the tree of the cross for those who had been stripped by sin" (*The Office of Matins*, 187).

The Sacraments as Actions of the Mystical Body

the glory of His divine name, even unto death."[31] If we associate the word *sacramentum* with the vow taken by a soldier upon enlistment in the army, then liturgical asceticism is simply the fulfillment of our baptismal *sacramentum*. Christians do not practice asceticism because they hate the world but because they believe it an anticipatory reflection of the Kingdom (i.e., a sacrament). Christians do not practice asceticism because they think this world ugly but because by its ordered use (i.e., as sacrament) it can become an encounter with the Kingdom. Vladimir Soloviev said, "The purpose of Christian asceticism is not to weaken the flesh, but to strengthen the spirit for the transfiguration of the flesh."[32]

Liturgy can now do the world the way the world was meant to be done.

- *That liturgy is sacramental* means its inside is bigger than its outside, the grace is bigger than the ritual that contains it.
- *That sacraments are liturgical* means that they are not just Band-Aids for sin in this life, they are ordered to deification.
- *Sacramental liturgy* is the barque of Peter that brings us to beatitude.
- *Liturgical sacraments* root us in the new Adam.

By the light which pours out of the doors of the temple to flood the world in transfiguring light, the members of the mystical body see the cosmos theologically, as sacramental gift from God and raw material for Eucharist; they see man and woman in their role as cosmic priests; they see time no longer as a whirlpool circling nothingness, but rather as a training school for eternal happiness. But, Cabasilas warns, we cannot conclude then what we do not begin now:

> The life in Christ originates in this life and arises from it. It is perfected, however, in the life to come, when we shall have reached that last day. It cannot attain perfection in men's souls in this life, nor even in that which is to come, without already having begun here.... It is this life which is the workshop for all these things.[33]

Therefore the gift of liturgical sacraments

---

[31] *Unseen Warfare: The Spiritual Combat and Path to Paradise of Lorenzo Scupoli*, ed. Nicodemus of the Holy Mountain, rev. Theophan the Recluse, trans. E. Kadloubovsky and G. E. H. Palmer (New York: St. Vladimir's Seminary Press, 1987), 71.
[32] Vladimir Solovyof, "The Jews," in *A Solovyof Anthology*, ed. S. L. Frank (London: SCM Press, 1950), 120.
[33] Cabasilas, *The Life in Christ*, 43.

Liturgy and the Cosmos

Liturgical Cosmology
Doing the World Liturgically: Stewardship of Creation and Care for the Poor[*]

I do not have the intelligence to mimic Thomas Aquinas all the way to the end, but I would like to mimic him briefly here at the beginning. You all know the layout of the *Summa*: he presents a question asking whether such and such is the case; he responds with a series of objections that either say "it seems so" or "it seems not," followed by a contrary opinion before he reaches his own conclusion with "I answer that...." And you all know that whatever is said in that first objection is the opposite of where Thomas intends to wind up. I briefly follow suit.

Question: "Whether there is a connection between liturgy and social justice, especially concern for the poor and stewardship of creation?" Objection: "It would seem not." (You now know where I intend to wind up.) I borrowed the wording of that question from the first email contact inviting me to participate in this conference, and I have been thinking about the connection ever since. But I am momentarily sidetracked by this Thomistic exercise to consider whether anyone would have objections to the proposition. I am sidetracked to ask why we would *want* there to be a connection anyway? Why regret the divide between liturgy and social justice? Why not leave concern for the poor and stewardship of creation to the moral theologians, and leave liturgy comfortably at home with its candles and choirs, its vestments and versicles? Why would the liturgical theologian want to butt his sacred nose into the profane world's business? Never mind *how* we are going to do it; first ask *why* we want to do it. After all, liturgy has to do with heaven, and social justice with the earth; liturgy with our soul, and social justice with our body; liturgy with our salvation, and social justice with our neighbor's good; liturgy is for the weekend, and social justice for the week. Why even include this paper in our conference?

Under one definition of liturgy, that might be hard to justify. A thin definition reads only the surface of liturgy, like someone looking at the

---

[*] David W. Fagerberg, "Doing the World Liturgically: Stewardship of Creation and Care of the Poor," in *Authentic Liturgical Renewal in Contemporary Perspective*, ed. Uwe Michael Lang (New York: Bloomsbury T&T Clark, 2017), 69–82.

surface of a pond but not seeing the teeming life of the underwater ecosystem. Can we see the teeming supernatural ecosystem beneath liturgy? If not, then we are hard-pressed to explain how liturgy can get past the threshold of the narthex out into the world. The symbolism of temple topography has understood the sanctuary as heaven, the nave as the Church, and the narthex as the threshold between Church and world. My set of questions was intended to ask whether liturgy has any contact with the world across this threshold. The narthex is the membrane between sacred and profane: Is it permeable? The Liturgical Movement persuaded us that liturgy overflows the boundary of the sanctuary to involve the nave, but has it persuaded us that liturgy overflows the boundary of the narthex to concern the world?

I will repeat the question: Is there a connection between liturgy and social justice, especially concern for the poor and stewardship of creation? And now "I answer that" it seems so, because Christ comes to make his mercies flow far as the curse is found; because cult is the basis of culture; because of the relationship between cult and cosmos; because the tip of the liturgical iceberg that we can see is connected to a divine economy below; because the liturgy needs the world as material for sacrifice and matter for sacrament; because after liturgy, we crave mission; because Christ heads a parade from the empty tomb, through the dislocated gates of Hades, to the heavenly Jerusalem, and this liturgical procession marches straight through the valley of the shadow of death; because liturgy makes the Church, and the Church's reason for being is as a herald of salvation; because the *sphragis* has inscribed the Paschal Mystery on our brow as a phylactery; because the Church-at-liturgy is not a new world, it is the world renewed; because liturgy is to world as form is to matter; because the coin of the realm in liturgy is grace, and grace perfects nature; because we must be able to see the supernatural end of our creation in order to do justice to nature at the moment; because without the rational tongue of liturgists, mute matter could not symphonize with the angels; because of incarnation in a body and resurrection of a body; because liturgy puts man and woman in their true cosmic location. Let us give Benedict XVI the final word:

> The true liturgical action is the deed of God, and for that very reason the liturgy of faith always reaches beyond the cultic act

into everyday life, which must itself become "liturgical," a service for the transformation of the world.[1]

Cult, liturgy in the proper sense, is part of this worship, but so, too, is life according to the will of God. . . . Ultimately, it is the very life of man, man himself as living righteously, that is the true worship of God, but life only becomes real life when it receives its form from looking toward God. Cult exists in order to communicate this vision and to give life in such a way that glory is given to God.[2]

If the idea of a square triangle sounds more intelligible than liturgical action reaching beyond cult into the bedroom and the boardroom, the political circle and the market square, then perhaps our definition of liturgy is too thin—not high enough to kiss heaven, not deep enough to pressure Hades, not broad enough to touch the world and comfort the poor in it. Liturgy should overflow the sanctuary. Stewardship of creation and care for the poor is not just moral duty, it is a liturgical responsibility. We look upon the poor not with human sympathy but with divine compassion; we look at our enemies with the same urgent desire for reconciliation that God has when he looks upon us sinners; we look at suffering and feel the same willingness to embrace the cross that Christ felt. This is mundane liturgical theology.[3]

In order to think this through, I am going to use the hermeneutic of microcosm, applied on three fronts: first to say human beings are royal priests; second, that cultic liturgy is microcosmic; and third, to flip the idea and see the world as *macro*cosmic liturgy, though this is only accomplished at the cost of asceticism. I will consider these to be examples of *liturgical anthropology*, *liturgical cosmology*, and *liturgical ecology*.

Liturgical Anthropology

Let us first consider a liturgical anthropology that sees the human being as microcosm. You recall that "micro-cosm" means "little house," which does not mean a fraction, it means a miniature. The kitchen is not a microcosm of a house; rather a dollhouse is, because everything in the big house can

---

[1] Joseph Ratzinger, *Spirit of the Liturgy*, trans. John Saward (San Francisco: Ignatius Press, 2000), 175.
[2] Ratzinger, *Spirit of the Liturgy*, 17–18.
[3] David W. Fagerberg, *Consecrating the World: On Mundane Liturgical Theology* (Kettering, OH: Angelico Press, 2016).

be found in the small house. The Church Fathers describe man and woman as a hybrid, a mixture, because both matter and spirit can be found in the human being. Almost any card you are dealt from the patristic deck will include this idea, and I will play my hand with only three cards: two Gregories and a Maximus. Gregory of Nazianzus says:

> The great Architect of the universe conceived and produced a being endowed with both natures, the visible and invisible.... Thus in some way a new universe was born, small and great at one and the same time. God set this "hybrid" worshiper on earth to contemplate the visible world, and to be initiated into the invisible; to reign over earth's creatures, and to obey orders from on high.[4]

His friend Gregory of Nyssa says man was created last because a good host does not bring his guest to the house before the preparation for the feast is finished. God first prepared the *kosmos*—which means "well-disposed, prepared, ordered, and arranged"—and then placed the human being in it to play his particular role:

> For this reason [God] gives him as foundations the instincts of a twofold organization, blending the Divine with the earthy [sic], that by means of both he may be naturally and properly disposed to each enjoyment, enjoying God by means of his more divine nature, and the good things of earth by the sense that is akin to them.[5]

And Maximus the Confessor thinks the human being is last because God intended to unite five extremes in him. Man is, he says, "the laboratory in which everything is concentrated." Andrew Louth explains why:

> Human beings are found on both sides of each division: they belong in paradise but inhabit the uninhabited world; they are earthly and yet destined for heaven; they have both mind and senses; and though created, they are destined to share in the

---

[4] Gregory of Nazianzus, *Oration 45 (Second Oration on Easter)*, 7 (PG 36, 850), cited by Olivier Clément, *The Roots of Christian Mysticism* (New York: New City Press, 1995), 77.

[5] Gregory of Nyssa, *On the Making of Man*, 2.2, in *Nicene and Post-Nicene Fathers*, ed. Philip Schaff and Henry Schaff (Peabody, MA: Hendrickson Publishers, 2004), 5:390.

uncreated nature by deification. All the divisions of the cosmos are reflected in the human being, so the human being is a microcosm.[6]

All three of these passages see the reason for a person's unique, microcosmic makeup as serving the purpose of linking heaven and earth, spirit and matter. Human beings were constructed for the express purpose of serving God's glory by being the tongue of material creation's praise. Thomas Aquinas defined the good as something having the perfection proper to it. A pen is good when it writes, a knife is good when it cuts, a table is good when it holds the weight it is meant to bear. And what is a good person? I submit that the perfection proper to a human being is to join in the life of God. Between the Father, the Son, and the Holy Spirit flows an exchange of love that tradition has called *perichoresis*, and I define liturgy as "perichoresis kenotically extended to invite our synergistic ascent into deification."[7] Liturgy is our perfection, for there we are being filled with the love of God by joining the choreography of his divine love, and performing the work of a cosmic priesthood.

We could reveal the microcosm by calling man and woman "royal priests." As befits their royal status, they were created as the climax of creation and given power and dominion and responsibility. As befits their priestly status, they were given stewardship in order to bring creation into the circulation of *agape* and Eucharist. To deny man and woman's royal vocation or to separate that vocation from their priestly identity equally flunks a full anthropology. On the one hand, man and woman are called to exercise dominion over the environment in which they are placed, which is why the *Catechism* has such a confident description of the human being: man occupies a unique place in creation as the image of God;[8] man is the only visible creature able to know and love his creator;[9] and he possesses the dignity of person with self-knowledge and self-possession.[10] On the other hand, man and woman's royal dominion exists for latreutic purposes. When it comes to humanity, a half-definition is a half-truth: lose either dimension—royalty without priesthood, or priesthood without royalty—and something goes awry. Some secular anthropologies are

---

[6] Andrew Louth, *Maximus the Confessor*, The Early Church Fathers (New York: Routledge, 1996), 73.
[7] My operating definition of liturgy. See David Fagerberg, *On Liturgical Asceticism* (Washington, D.C.: The Catholic University of America Press, 2013), 9.
[8] *CCC*, §355.
[9] *CCC*, §356.
[10] *CCC*, §357.

drawn to the former error and place no Godly limits on man's royalty; some spiritual anthropologies are drawn to the latter error and see man as so heavenly minded that he is of no earthly good. But the *Catechism* locates anthropology within the context of liturgical cult: "God created everything for man, but man in turn was created to serve and love God and to offer all creation back to him."[11] Just as a planet must balance both centrifugal force and gravitational pull, so a human being must find the exact midpoint between heaven and earth so as neither to desert the world nor be marooned on it.

As microcosm, human beings are called to take the world into themselves in order to speak the worship that the universe wordlessly offers. Man and woman are cosmic priests for standing with one foot in the *kosmos noetos* (the intelligible world) and the other in the *kosmos aisthetos* (the sensible world).[12] Cities were founded where traffic crisscrossed along trade routes that connected extreme geographical points; liturgies are found where traffic crisscrosses from extreme ontological points: spirit and matter, heaven and earth, mind and senses, man and beast, man and angel, life and death, justice and mercy, time and eternity, history and *eschaton*, chaos and cosmos, truth and beauty and goodness. Liturgy balances atop these crossbeams because the human liturgist has a foot in each of them. The human being as microcosm is the anthropological possibility for liturgy.

Liturgical Cosmology

Aristotle claimed that for a story plot to be understood, it must be of a length the audience can grasp as it unfolds between beginning and end. He makes his point by comparing a literary grasp to a grasp of beauty. "To be beautiful, a living creature . . . must not only present a certain order in its arrangement of parts, but also be of a certain definite magnitude. Beauty is a matter of size and order" and just as an extremely minute creature could not be discerned as beautiful, neither could "a creature of vast size—one, say, 1,000 miles long—as in that case . . . the unity and wholeness of it is

---

[11] *CCC*, §358.

[12] "Alongside '*kosmos noetos*' (the intelligible world) Holy Tradition sets '*kosmos aisthetos*' (the sensible world). This latter encompasses the whole realm of what belongs to the senses in the sacraments, in the liturgy, in icons, and in the lived experience of God. . . . The beautiful then is as a shining forth, an epiphany, of the mysterious depths of being, of that interiority that is a witness to the intimate relation between the body and the soul" (Paul Evdokimov, *The Art of the Icon: A Theology of Beauty* [Redondo Beach, CA: Oakwood Publications, 1990], 26).

lost to the beholder."[13] His observation inspires the thought in me that we cannot judge history because it is a thousand centuries long and we cannot see the whole thing at once. We cannot understand history's plot because its end and its beginning are beyond the range of our natural eye, which has put some people in a quandary. They do not know if existence is beautiful or not, or if it is true or not, and, sadly, some even wonder whether life is good or not, because they are only seeing a piece of it—their piece, this particular moment. But there is a height from which to see the whole, the plot line of history from start to finish. Liturgy is a microcosmic celebration of the Alpha and the Omega, which provides us with a protological and eschatological vantage point from which we can see why God created, and what God created, and what God hopes for his creation.

"Let us make man in our image, after our likeness," God decreed on the sixth day, and "let them have dominion over the fish of the sea, and over the birds of the air, and over the cattle, and over all the earth, and over every creeping thing that creeps upon the earth" (Gen 1:26). We are stewards, then, of creation, a steward defined as someone who looks after another person's resources. That is the sole basis of our dominion, and we have every bit as much reason to be concerned about our job performance as did the man in Luke 16. "There was a rich man who had a steward, and charges were brought to him that this man was wasting his goods. And he called him and said to him, 'What is this I hear about you? Turn in the account of your stewardship . . .'" (vv. 1–2). One day we will be asked to prepare a full account of our stewardship, and whether we have done the world righteously, prudently, justly. We best sense that obligation when we are kneeling before the true King, because we are otherwise tempted to slip ourselves onto the throne. We can only stand rightly before our neighbour if we are kneeling before God. Worship provides a sort of supernatural ballast to equalize every exercise of our stewardship. When Adam named each animal, he was blessing God for each one; remove that act of worship and we name things for selfish utility. How do we view God, identify our neighbor, and call the world around us? What is our place in the world?

The Lutheran theologian Regin Prenter describes the effects of the Fall upon the ontological location of man and woman this way:

> Man is created by God in his image. That is, he stands before God and is addressed by him; he stands beside his fellow man in a dialogue of love; and he stands over his co-creation in terms of

---

[13] Aristotle, *Poetics*, in *The Basic Works of Aristotle* (New York: Random House, 1966), 1462–63.

knowledge. The fall is man's unexplainable rebellion against his creatureliness through disobedience to God's word.... Sin, understood as rebellious disobedience, is vastly more than an isolated act; it is, then, a destruction of man's very humanity, affecting his relation to the Creator, to his fellow man, and to his co-creation.[14]

That passage took up residence in my memory in this shorthanded version: we were created to stand *under God, beside our neighbor,* and *over creation.* It led me to imagine the Fall in a way that, although upsetting to its natural gravitational symbolism, did justice to the inflationary power of pride: the Fall is the attempt to rise one step higher in the cosmic order than we are supposed to. *Superbia* is the sentiment that makes us want too much elevation. Adam and Eve evacuated the liturgical sweet spot at which they were to exercise their royal priesthood under God, beside their neighbor, and over creation; and when they did, they upset the liturgical orbit of existence. Now pride bristles at being under God and seeks to stand on equal footing with him (thus we neither submit to God, nor render him worship ahead of ourselves); envy bristles at standing beside our neighbor and seeks to stand over him (thus we impose our will and make him our utility); and selfishness reneges at governing creation, and instead we exploit it (thus losing our sympathy for fellow-creatures and abandoning solicitous care for earth and air). By our arrogant self-promotion to deity, we lose our connaturality with both neighbor and world.

Pope Francis's encyclical letter *Laudato Si'* observes the same fact. "[The creation accounts in Genesis] suggest that human life is grounded in three fundamental and closely intertwined relationships: with God, with our neighbour and with the earth itself. According to the Bible, these three vital relationships have been broken, both outwardly and within us. This rupture is sin."[15] That is why the Holy Father concludes that "a true ecological approach *always* becomes a social approach; it must integrate questions of justice in debates on the environment, so as to hear *both the cry of the earth and the cry of the poor.*"[16] Liturgy puts us in our place.

---

[14] Regin Prenter, *Creation and Redemption* (Philadelphia: Fortress Press, 1968), 251.
[15] Pope Francis, Encyclical Letter on Care for Our Common Home *Laudato Si'* (2015), §66.
[16] Pope Francis, *Laudato Si'*, §49.

Liturgical Ecology

Third, we can now flip our perspective and instead of seeing the liturgy as microcosmic world, we can see the world as macrocosmic liturgy. I am led to think of this as a kind of *liturgical ecology*. Ecology means the "study of a house" (*oikos-logos*), and the house we are studying is God's creation. If I had more nerve, I would title my paper "Doing Liturgy in the Big House." Instead, I have based my title on Aidan Kavanagh's oft-repeated line in class that "liturgy is doing the world the way the world was meant to be done." But doing the world the way it was meant to be done carries a cost, because it requires we first be ascetically freed from the passions.

God laid the foundations of this house by wisdom (Prov 3:19), and he tends its good by divine economy (*oikonomia* being "household management"). Toward what end? It behooves us to know this, so that when we tend creation, we will align our dominion with God's tendencies. Toward what does God direct his creation? There are two ways to answer this question. The first is catabatic, meaning creation was constructed in such a way as to expect God's arrival. The second is anabatic, meaning creation was constructed with an upward current carrying man and woman at its apex. And human beings are commissioned to be involved in this economy. They are *oikonomoi*, managers in God's project: they are *liturgical economists* who steward creation toward its eschatological end. That is our job description, and we can do it justly or unjustly.

Justice means giving someone or something its due. When Thomas treated the virtue of religion in the *Summa*, he located it in the section dealing with the cardinal virtue of justice, because religion is giving God the honor he is due. Why would we not? Why would we even think of acting unjustly toward God? Because the honor due God is glory, and we have a preference for self-glory (even if that glory is vain). Giving thanks to the Lord our God is right and just, but we must be reminded of that fact at every Eucharistic dialogue. One way of defining "liturgy" is to understand it as a restored participation in the original created order. Failing this, the signs of creation no longer point to the Creator, and nature quickly becomes opaque, then a substitute, and finally an idol. Injustice and idolatry are bound together. Failing this, our neighbor is no longer seen as a fellow image of God, and he quickly becomes a competitor, then an opponent, and finally an enemy. Uncreated justice and created justice are bound together.

According to some Old Testament commentators, being *imago Dei* means more than possessing reason; it means being a representative of God. The Hebrew word used, *selem*, means a duplicate, like a statue that corresponds to the original. Thus, by erecting his image, a king indicated that he ruled the territory in which his image stood.[17] The Second Council of Nicaea concluded that an icon and its prototype are connected in such a way that the honor paid to the icon is received by the prototype. It would seem, then, that any injustice paid to a living icon would be received by his divine prototype. Consider: If someone gouged the statue of Caesar with a nail, disfiguring it, he would be guilty of treason against the emperor; and if someone defaces, disfigures, or violates an *imago Dei* in some basic way, he is guilty of an act against God. The First Letter of John says, "If any one says, 'I love God,' and hates his brother, he is a liar; for he who does not love his brother whom he has seen, cannot love God whom he has not seen" (1 John 4:20). We can adapt it to say that if anyone thinks he can be just to God but unjust to his brother, he is a liar; for whoever does not give justice to his brother whom he has seen cannot be just toward God whom he has not seen. Justice toward the Uncreated is linked to justice toward the created. Uncreated justice is expressed by worship, adoration, sacrifice, devotion, piety, honor, subordination, and latreutic cult. Created justice is expressed by charity, generosity, self-giving, kindness, magnanimity, benevolence, mercy, and commitment to the common good. That is why the *Catechism* can say, in one breath, "Justice consists in the firm and constant will to give God and neighbour their due."[18] If the secularist unlinks them, ignoring God as he works for goodness on earth, his justice is deficient; if the spiritualist unlinks them, ignoring goodness on earth as he worships God, his justice is deficient.

The sacred liturgy and custody of the profane do not cancel each other out. The sacraments do not evacuate us from the world, they equip

---

[17] "It is precisely in his function as ruler that [man] is God's image. In the ancient East the setting up of the king's statue was the equivalent to the proclamation of his domination over the sphere in which the statue was erected. When in the thirteenth century BC the Pharaoh Ramesses II had his image hewn out of rock at the mouth of the *nahr el-kelb*, on the Mediterranean north of Beirut, the image meant that he was the ruler of this area. Accordingly man is set in the midst of creation as God's statue. He is evidence that God is the Lord of creation; but as God's steward he also exerts his rule, fulfilling his task not in arbitrary despotism but as a responsible agent" (Hans Walter Wolff, *Anthropology of the Old Testament*, trans. Margaret Kohl [Philadelphia: Fortress Press, 1974], 160). "Selem (image) means predominantly an actual plastic work, a duplicate, sometimes an idol.... Just as powerful earthly kings, to indicate their claim to dominion, erect an image of themselves in the provinces of their empire where they do not personally appear, so man is placed upon earth in God's image as God's sovereign emblem. He is really only God's representative, summoned to maintain and enforce God's claim to dominion over the earth" (Gerhard von Rad, *Genesis: A Commentary*, trans. John H. Marks, The Old Testament Library [Philadelphia: Westminster Press, 1972], 60).

[18] *CCC*, §1836.

us to protect it. Sacraments are designed to stimulate the Holy Spirit within us, and what does the Spirit of God want to do? According to his sacrament (Confirmation), he wants to breathe wisdom, understanding, right judgment, courage, knowledge, reverence, and the spirit of wonder and awe over the face of the earth. The life of Christ in us—ecclesiality, as Pavel Florensky calls it—consists in observing the movements of the Spirit of God in our soul, then fortifying these movements with prayer, sacrament, and the practice of virtues. We become conspirators with God: we *con-spire*, breathe together. Liturgical cult stimulates the ministry of justice, mercy, care of the poor, care of the land. Sometimes a shabby reading of the Old Testament pits prophet against priest, profane against sacred, world against temple. But this is a false reading. The prophet does not mind someone going into the temple; the prophet is only bothered if that person does not take the temple with him when he comes back out again! The prophet is criticizing the fact that what has been tilled in the sacred cult (*cult-ivated*) does not take root in the mundane and produce fruit. That is why, in order to cultivate creation and care for the poor, we must first deal with the corruption of sin within, which brings us to liturgical asceticism.

Satan was shrewd. He did not promise Eve something unthinkable to her. To draw her away from God, he bent God's own plan for her deification and dominion. His temptation would only have worked if he were tickling an aspiration placed in Eve's heart by God himself, so he said to her, "You will be like gods." Eve opened her eyes because deification was precisely her *telos*. And Eve opened her ears because dominion was precisely a responsibility she should have exercised as an adult and not as a child. But Satan bent the path to these God-given ends until the arrow missed the mark (sin is *hamartia*) by seizing the gifts prematurely and independently. As a result, and ever since, we have sought a deification that is actually nothing but our own exaltation, which is of no help to my neighbor at all and has serious consequences for the natural world. Now instead of exercising dominion, we sinners domineer. The latter means to rule arbitrarily or arrogantly, the former means to govern and control, directed by legitimate authority—in this case, an authority granted by God himself. The Fall was the forfeiture of our liturgical career and we have lost our balance.

Sin is the cause of injustice, but can we be any more precise? The created environment is God's good gift, over which he exclaimed satisfaction on the sixth day of Genesis, and in which we should find happiness. So why don't we? The mystery of iniquity is that the world can cause worldliness in us; Satan has seduced us into inserting ourselves between the cause and its proper effect. Worldliness is using the world without reference to God. That makes for a contradiction that is reflected in Scripture's own vocabulary. The same gospel that says God so loved the world that he gave his only Son to die for it (John 3:16) also says that Jesus's disciples do not belong to the world (John 17:16), that the world hates them (John 15:19), that they must hate their life in this world (John 12:25), and that Jesus does not pray for the world (John 17:9). Scripture uses the word "world" in both ways—as a good gift and as a source of temptation—and while we do not go into the temple to abandon the world (in the first sense), we do go there in order to escape the world (in the second sense). This is the liturgical paradox: that there is nothing wrong with the world, but we must leave the world and bless the Kingdom of God. Alexander Schmemann wrote, "This exodus from the world is accomplished in the name of the world, for the sake of its salvation.... We separate ourselves from the world in order to bring it, in order to lift it up to the kingdom, to make it once again the way to God and participation in his eternal kingdom."[19]

One chooses between two economies: one obedient and the other disobedient, one worshipful and the other idolatrous, one just and the other unjust, one natural and the other rebellious. Conversion is the act of opting out of the latter for the former. "Do you reject Satan, and all his works and all his empty promises?" The New Testament uses the term *arche* to name the powers or principalities that hold this world captive, a concentrated roster of those malevolent forces being named in Ephesians 6:12: "For we are not contending against flesh and blood, but against the principalities, against the powers, against the world rulers of this present darkness, against the spiritual hosts of wickedness in the heavenly places." But Christ's victory has unleashed a new *arche* into the world, a new power. Not rebellious, but obedient; not selfish, but sacramental; not diabolically dividing, but symbolically uniting. It is a priestly power, a *hiereus arche*. Satan upset creation with *anarchy*, but we join Christ in restoring all creation to liturgical *hierarchy*. And so the Collect for the Solemnity of our Lord Jesus Christ, King of the Universe prays: "Almighty ever-living God, whose will is to restore all things in your beloved Son, the King of the universe, grant, we pray, that the whole creation, set free from slavery,

---

[19] Alexander Schmemann, *The Eucharist: Sacrament of the Kingdom*, trans. Paul Kachur (Crestwood, NY: St. Vladimir's Seminary Press, 1987), 53.

may render your majesty service and ceaselessly proclaim your praise."[20] Liturgy is the activity of Christ, and Christ is king of the world.

I pause only briefly to note that this means "all creation," every creature that God has created, and this includes time. Time was created; it is a creature to be valued, but mastered. We must also approach time ascetically if we are to use it justly. Most of our abuse of the environment comes from wanting too much, too fast, too soon, too eagerly. The disruptive passion seems to be gluttony, which John Climacus defined as "hypocrisy of the stomach,"[21] whose antidote is temperance, which can be trained by fasting. Liturgical fasting has as much to do with patience as it has to do with food. Satan combined gluttony and disobedience by asking, "Can't you have that?" The proper response both in the Garden of Eden and on the fields of our farms today is "We can, but not yet. We must be patient." The environment has an amazing power to renew itself, but our technologies must not push its rhythms beyond its limits. The virtue of prudence is required to read natural law, but the virtue of temperance is required to let that natural law take its course.

So how is it that the good gifts of God (both property and neighbor) cause in us such concupiscence that we abuse them in order to take our own advantage? The ascetical tradition has studied this riddle for a long time and has concluded that there is nothing wrong with the world, but something goes wrong when we put our hand upon it. The passions are our faculties misfiring. Evagrius provides an individuated list that includes gluttony, lust, avarice, sadness, anger, sloth, vainglory, and pride, but Isaac the Syrian groups them under one name, saying, "When we wish to give a collective name to the passions, we call them *world*."[22] Maximus adds, "The one who has self-love has all the passions."[23] The problem is not money, sex, or beer; the problem is avarice, lust, and gluttony. The objects of the world are the matter on which our passions feed. Nature is good, as given, but we do not do nature naturally anymore, and if we wish to clean

---

[20] *The Roman Missal: Renewed by Decree of the Most Holy Second Ecumenical Council of the Vatican, Promulgated by Authority of Pope Paul VI and Revised at the Direction of Pope John Paul II* (Washington, D.C.: USCCB, 2011), 505.

[21] John Climacus, *The Ladder of Divine Ascent*, trans. Colm Luibheid and Norman Russell (Mahwah, NJ: Paulist Press, 1982), 165 (Step 14: On Gluttony).

[22] Isaac the Syrian, Homily 2, in *The Ascetical Homilies of Saint Isaac the Syrian*, trans. Dana Miller (Brookline, MA: Holy Transfiguration Monastery, 1984), 14–15.

[23] Maximus the Confessor, *Four Hundred Chapters on Love*, in *Maximus Confessor: Selected Writings*, trans. George Charles Berthold (Mahwah, NJ: Paulist Press, 1985), 62.

the oceans and the air, we must begin by cleansing our hearts, because the passions have gotten in the way of our peaceful relationship with matter.

We are surrounded by a good creation (we have God's word on that), and it is filled with gifts that will bend submissively under our own hands as sub-creators. Our capacity as royal priests includes a power of creation (*poiesis*) that can make art, found societies, develop science and cities and technology, cooperate with God in civilizing chaos. What good is liturgy without a material on which to exercise it? And what good is chaos without a form that shapes it? But the question still remains whether man's sub-creativity will iconograph God or idolize himself. When the world functions properly, the created serves its sacred function to lift our eyes to heaven, and the created serves its profane function to be material for civilization. But when self-love corrupts our eyesight, then the world fails both functions, though it is not the world's fault.

Strange to say, then, but we cannot do the world rightly until we are indifferent to it. This sounds counterintuitive, but so long as the passions reign, we are slaves to creatures. Indifference must defuse our selfishness. We must find liberty before we can rule. If we are enslaved to the objects of the world, then how can we do the world the way it was meant to be done, and treat our neighbor fairly, and make just distribution of common goods, and tend the environment with true dominion? This is behind Maximus's definition of perfect love: it is equal love toward all, loving all men equally. It is a deceptively simple definition. Think about it: Do you love *all* human beings equally? Or do you give preference to some, have greater attachment to others? In the words of Lars Thunberg's study of Maximus, "He who devotes his loving desire entirely to God, is not affected by any partial attachment to the world and is thus able to love all men equally in imitation of God's own love for all. Resentfulness, on the other hand, is a sign of worldliness and implies a worship of creatures instead of the Creator."[24] The sort of love for our neighbor that is required to bring about justice can only stem from imitation of God's own love for all, freed from favoring parts of the world and parts of the human community.

Liturgical asceticism is required to make the heart supple and train it in divine charity so that we can steward creation and care for all the poor, not just some of them. A crucial practice, the desert monks discovered, was poverty expressed in lifestyle, but I am thinking now of poverty of spirit reigning over the heart in the simple sense of not being attached to any creature. I will not be able to stand aright and offer my holy oblation

---

[24] Lars Thunberg, *Microcosm and Mediator* (Chicago: Open Court Publishing, 1995), 313–14.

in peace so long as I am bent over some paltry pebbles of gold in the undignified posture of someone *incurvatus in se*. I will not be able to treat my neighbour with justice so long as I look at him enviously, or his wife lustfully, or his property avariciously. As long as the passions stop up my ears, I cannot hear either the cry of the poor or the needs of the earth. Until the cataracts of sin are removed by asceticism, I will see both my neighbor and the world falsely, distortedly, as if in a fun house mirror. Pope Francis says his namesake, St. Francis, taught this same integration of truths. "He shows us just how inseparable the bond is between concern for nature, justice for the poor, commitment to society, and interior peace."[25] Liturgical asceticism is the search for that interior peace, called *apatheia*, which is required in order to look upon all things rightly.

The liturgy within the temple is connected to the liturgy outside the temple. John Chrysostom says nothing is better suited to prolonging the effects of the Eucharist than a visit paid to Christ in his little ones. The poor standing in the public square remind the golden-mouthed saint of the majesty of an altar made ready for the sacrifice:

> This altar [of the poor] is composed of the very members of Christ, and the Lord's body becomes an altar for thee. Venerate it; for upon it, in the flesh, thou dost offer sacrifice to the Lord. This altar is greater than the altar in his church.... Do not protest! The *stone* altar is august because of the Victim that rests upon it; but the *altar of almsgiving* is more so because it is made of this very Victim.[26]

What generosity by God! He provides us an altar for sacrifice wherever we are. The poor await us anywhere:

> This altar you can see everywhere, in the streets and in the market place, and at any hour you may offer sacrifice thereon; for it too is a place of sacrifice. And, as the priest standing at the altar brings down the Spirit, so you too bring down the Spirit, like the oil which was poured out in abundance.[27]

---

[25] Pope Francis, *Laudato Si'*, §10.

[26] John Chrysostom, *Homily 20 on II Corinthians*, quoted in Emile Mersch, *The Whole Christ: The Historical Development of the Doctrine of the Mystical Body in Scripture and Tradition*, trans. John R. Kelly (Milwaukee, WI: The Bruce Publishing Company, 1938), 335.

[27] John Chrysostom, *Homily 20 on II Corinthians*, quoted in Mersch, *The Whole Christ*, 335.

Now the narthex becomes truly liminal: a threshold or entrance upon the world. We build up a static charge of *eucharistia* all week long by rubbing shoulders with the world, and discharge it in the glory we give God at the altar; we receive a charge of mercy and grace at that same Mass, and we discharge it throughout the coming week.

Folly is the opposite of wisdom. Folly judges by some temporal good, while wisdom judges by first principle and last end. Liturgy teaches us wisdom, teaches us those first principles and last ends so that we can take the proper measure of all created things, and that's why we go to the temple on a scheduled basis. There, in the sacred space, we learn how the secular should be constructed. There, in the vestibule of heaven, we learn what the earth is for and how to use it prudently. There, in the midst of the community of saints, we learn the eternal value of a single soul and are flooded with love for every one of them, equally, no matter how poor or disreputable. There, before the Cross, we find firm footing so that we are no longer swayed by passing honors and pleasures, natural reputation, praises, comfort, and flattering self-love. Our failure to steward creation and care for the poor comes from placing ourselves at the center, and the only way to solve this problem is to put someone else at the center. This is called conversion. This is called love. And love is liturgy's heart.

A Brief Postscript

That was my conclusion, but I have a postscript in the form of a challenge to liturgical theology, because, after all, this is not a conference on ecology or social justice; it is a conference on the liturgy.

I began with a propaedeutic Thomistic exercise that considered what objections there might be to even including this paper in our conference. I concluded that failure to connect the liturgy with the poor and with stewardship of creation might arise from too thin a definition of liturgy, one that reduced its range. It is my metaphor, but I think Benedict XVI is expressing something similar when he analyzes the liturgical situation across his lifetime. He thinks it was an important step when the *Catechism* placed its treatment of the sacraments within the context of the celebration of divine worship because

> Medieval theology had already detached the theological study of the sacraments to a large extent from their administration in divine worship and treated it separately under the headings of *institution, sign, effect, minister,* and *recipient.* . . . Thus divine

worship and theology diverged more and more; dogmatic theology expounded, not on divine worship itself, but rather on its abstract theological contents ... and liturgy necessarily seemed almost like a collection of ceremonies that clothed the essentials.[28]

But when the pendulum swung, and liturgy edged its way back on stage, he says liturgics became nothing but "the study of prevailing norms in divine worship and thus came close to a sort of juridical positivism." He therefore approves of the Liturgical Movement at its origin when it sought to overcome this dangerous separation. It "strove to understand the essence of a sacrament from the form in divine worship" and to think of liturgy "as the organically developed and suitable expression of the sacrament in the worship celebration." And, in his opinion, *Sacrosanctum Concilium* set forth this synthesis more adequately than had been done in the past, allowing us to understand the Church's divine worship and her sacraments in a new and more profound way. But alas, the professor warns,

> unfortunately very little has been done so far to complete this assignment. Liturgical studies once again have tended to detach themselves from dogmatic theology and to set themselves up as a sort of technique for worship celebrations. Conversely, dogmatic theology has not yet convincingly taken up the subject of its liturgical dimension, either.[29]

In this remark, Benedict XVI is specifically thinking of reconnecting liturgical studies with the dogmatic theology of sacraments, but I would recommend "completing the assignment" by expanding our syllabus a bit further. *Lex orandi* is not only the foundation (*statuat*) of sacramentology; it is also the foundation for the dogmatic understanding of man and matter, time and eschatology, sin and salvation history. I have attempted a small-scale exercise here, in the form of liturgical anthropology, liturgical cosmology, and liturgical ecology, but my next project will be to explore the idea further, and I think to call it "liturgical dogmatics." How can we know what to build with the bricks in our hands if we do not know about temples? How can we know how deep is our connection to the Lazarus on our doorstep if we do not know about the community of heaven? How

---

[28] Joseph Ratzinger, *On the Way to Jesus Christ*, trans. Michael J. Miller (San Francisco: Ignatius Press, 2005), 153–54.
[29] Ratzinger, *On the Way to Jesus Christ*, 153–54.

can we do justice to mortal things without the eternal horizon against which to place them? Exercising stewardship of creation and care for the poor will require doing the world liturgically, whereby our dominion will become *diakonia*, as Jesus on the Cross showed it to be. Liturgical dogmatics should teach us how to do the world as it was meant to be done.

Liturgical Morality
On Liturgical Morality[*]

In the invitation I received to contribute to this issue concerning the new book by Tris Engelhardt, the editors explained that they "were not looking for merely laudatory book reviews, but instead for essays that take seriously the content, arguments, and implications of *After God*." But that, of course, is precisely how academics do laud and honor an author: they take seriously the content, arguments, and implications of what an author says. One praises a pastry chef by sampling his pies, and one pays tribute to an author by responding to his work. So my reactions here should be taken, in defiance of the editors' instruction, as acclamatory and an expression of gratitude to the author for past generosities he has shown me. But it will be a serious treatment of the consequences of his thesis as it impinges on my particular work. I am, in a way, an odd man out. I am a liturgical theologian in the company of moral philosophers and bioethicists, and I am a Roman Catholic in the company of many Orthodox. I do not know which identity makes me the greater oddity, but I will do what I can as a Catholic to examine a liturgical base for bioethics. Engelhardt has invited this very effort by beginning to clear the brush down a new path. My own work has explored how two particular individuals have understood the concept of liturgical theology. They were the Orthodox theologian Alexander Schmemann and the Catholic theologian Aidan Kavanagh, and insofar as I have furthered their view, I am honored to sometimes be mentioned with them in what is called the Schmemann-Kavanagh-Fagerberg school of thought. This understanding of "liturgical theology" differs from the more common treatment given to a "theology of the liturgy," and if the reader will be patient with a momentary backward glance to explain the difference, I can then take my forward look grounded on the trajectory established in this context. It points us toward the idea of "liturgical morality."

---

[*] David W. Fagerberg, "On Liturgical Morality," in *Christian Bioethics: Non-Ecumenical Studies in Medical Morality* 23, no. 2 (August 2017): 119–36.

The common treatment given to a theology of liturgy begins with the assumption that theology is a discipline conducted in the university, and liturgy is a nontheological activity of believers. An academic theologian looks down from his ivory tower upon a great variety of subjects, such as ancient creeds, or the doctrine of the Trinity, or the writings of Augustine or John Damascene. In similar fashion, they think, an academic theologian might look down from his ivory tower upon a survey of liturgical practices, or the development of sacramentaries, or a comparison of lectionaries, and then, from the raw material he examined, he constructs theological propositions. Practicing believers cannot be called theologians, because theologians dwell in the academy and believers dwell in the nave, therefore the liturgical life is only raw material for real theology, as the straw was raw material for Rumpelstiltskin. The academic theologian might personally believe that theology should have a doxological spin put on it; the academic theologian might be happy when liturgy can smile and wave at him from across the street; but since theology is exclusively a university discipline, it has a different origin and purpose than liturgical practice.

To the contrary, the idea of liturgical theology that I learned, and which I propose, understands liturgy itself to be theological. Liturgy is a theological matrix. Liturgical theology is the Church in motion. Liturgy gives birth to theology because "prayer is seen in the Fathers to be, as it were, the amniotic fluid in which our knowledge of God takes form,"[1] in the arresting image of Andrew Louth. Such knowledge of God as takes form in us from prayerful liturgy is theology, and available to every person of prayer who is formed by the grammar of liturgy, even if they have not been to university to learn the academic jargon. This does not deny that liturgy can be treated by a whole range of academic disciplines (history, ritual studies, anthropology, textual analysis, sacramentology, architecture, musicology, etc.), but liturgical theology is interested in discovering a deeper and more profound unity between liturgy and theology. At these depths, *lex orandi* is recognized as the foundation for *lex credendi* because it takes seriously the word that stands in the middle of the original phrase: *lex orandi statuat lex credendi*. The law of prayer is the foundation, substance, basis, establishment, footing for the law of belief. Liturgy is primary theology (*theologia prima*)[2] that can be subsequently studied (*theologia secunda*). But the primacy of liturgical theology means that we

---

[1] Andrew Louth, *Discerning the Mystery: An Essay on the Nature of Theology* (New York: Oxford University Press, 1983), 65.

[2] David W. Fagerberg, *Theologia Prima: What Is Liturgical Theology?* (Chicago: Hillenbrand Books, 2003).

derive doctrine and dogma, piety and ethics, from the life of the Church at liturgy, not from out of our own scholarly heads. A mother gives birth to the child, not the other way around; a house rests upon the foundation, not the other way round; the law of belief comes from the law of prayer, not the other way around. This requires a definition of theology that is grander, and simultaneously more available, than the definition that treats theology as simply one of the university disciplines. In the words of Tomáš Špidlík, "The ancient Christian East understood the practice of theology only as a personal communion with *Theos*, the Father, through the *Logos*, Christ, in the Holy Spirit—an experience lived in a state of prayer."[3] To properly understand this requires taking the *lex* with as much force as the *orandi*. The appeal to *lex orandi* is an appeal to tradition, law, revelation, the grammar of Church doctrine, the application of the commandments of God, and acceptance of the Church's rule of faith—all of which can be experienced as a living basis within the liturgical life of the Church. Theology is experiential union with God.

To grasp this understanding of liturgical theology I had to turn to the ascetical tradition, because it provided a thicker definition of theology.[4] At the fountainhead stands Evagrius of Pontus, who learned from the desert monks a threefold staging of life: first a person must engage in a battle with the passions in order to become clearheaded again, called *praktike* because it is a very practical discipline. (*Askesis* means discipline.) Second, a person can turn to contemplation of God when the passions have been gotten somewhat under control. Initially this is contemplation of God as disclosed in the cosmos, and therefore *physike* because one is alert to see the Creator in the creation. But the third and final and ultimate goal is to contemplate God directly, which can only be done by entering into union with God, and to the surprise of modern ears this final stage was called *theologia*. An ordinary, ascetical, liturgical Christian can be called a theologian insofar as he has been formed by the liturgy wherein he has experiential union with God. The exercise of liturgy into which we are thrown upon our baptismal day has formative power upon our persons, however, in order to be formed by the liturgy's *lex orandi*, a person must be capacitated for liturgy by an ascetical struggle with the passions, passions

---

[3] Tomáš Špidlík, *The Spirituality of the Christian East*, trans. Anthony P. Gythiel (Collegeville, MN: Cistercian Press, 1986), 1.

[4] Though the origins were already present in Kavanagh's book *On Liturgical Theology*, in my first chapter of *On Liturgical Asceticism*, I trace those references (Washington, D.C.: The Catholic University of America Press, 2013).

whose egocentric effect prevents a person from worshiping God because he self-glorifies instead of doxologizes.

If theology means union with God through the life of Christ, and if in liturgy we have sacramental connection to that life of Christ (we are washed in his Resurrection, we eat his body), and if *askesis* means discipline (in the sense of forming), then liturgical asceticism is the discipline required to become an icon of Christ and make his image visible on our faces and in our lives. The union of liturgy and asceticism and theology can be seen in the definition of theology by someone like Archimandrite Vasileios: "True theology is always living, a form of hierurgy, something that changes our life and 'assumes' us into itself: we are to become theology. Understood in this way, theology is not a matter for specialists but a universal vocation; each is called to become a 'theologian soul.'"[5]

Asceticism is expired (breathed out) by the liturgy, because in the liturgy we con-spire (breathe with) the Holy Spirit as he oxygenates our souls and bodies. And I do definitely mean to include the latter. Bodies might be overlooked by the academic definition of theology, but they are not overlooked by the ascetical definition of theology. John Climacus says, "The soul indeed is molded by the doings of the body, conforming to and taking shape from what it does,"[6] which is why the ascetic begins his ascent to heaven by exercising control over the body (*praktike*). The kingdom of God means the spiritualization of all things, including our bodies. Theology has corporeal, full-life effects.

The reader might just be beginning to suspect, then, that theology has bioethical consequences, and this is precisely the challenge Engelhardt has laid at my feet. If I already suppose *liturgical theology* to view liturgy as a pneumatic exercise that makes theologian souls, and suppose *liturgical asceticism* understands such theologian souls to be molded by the doings of the body, then am I driven to think in terms of *liturgical morality*?

Engelhardt's thesis is that bioethics finds itself lost without a divine teleology that also concerns our corporeal behavior. There must be a God's-eye view that has an eye on our anthropological end. We get one sort of bioethics if we disenchant matter, and I think nearly all the authors he examines are simple materialists for whom the body is confined to the physical world, with no spiritual or transcendental relevance. But we

---

[5] Archimandrite Vasileios, *Hymn of Entry: Liturgy and Life in the Orthodox Church* (Crestwood, NY: St. Vladimir's Seminary Press, 1984), 27.

[6] John Climacus, *The Ladder of Divine Ascent*, trans. Colm Luibheid and Norman Russell (Mahwah, MJ: Paulist Press, 1982), 227. Another translation is by Holy Transfiguration Monastery, 2001.

get a totally different sort of bioethics if world, matter, and bodies are transfigurable, sacramental, iconic, and liturgical. He therefore presents the argument thus:

> The works of the law in one's heart will not be distorted only if one lives a morally and liturgically rightly-ordered life. Only then will one's knowing not be misguided. Given one's nature as a being called to be a god by grace, one can by this nature begin to know what one ought to do, but only through right worship and right acting, which maintains the rightly-ordered character of that nature, for we are beings that by nature are called to worship God and be united with him.[7]

In exploring the idea of liturgical morality, I shall intend a connection between liturgy and morality in the same profound sense communicated by that term *statuat*: liturgical *lex orandi* is the foundation, substance, basis, establishment, and footing, not only for the law of Christian *belief* (*credendi*) but also for the law of Christian *behavior* (*moralis*). Liturgical morality will parallel liturgical theology in its assertion that the event of liturgy is the matrix out of which morality arises.

If this were not the case, then the liturgical theologian would be part of the problem and not part of the solution: his preoccupation with liturgy would isolate God from questions of morality by confining God to the sacred and making him irrelevant to the profane. In that case, the liturgical theologian would not permit God past the threshold of the narthex, into the world, where moral questions confront a person. I do not deny that some people talk about the liturgy in such terms, but we will not do so here. The emphasis upon liturgy would do harm if it cleaved reality, detaching liturgy from life, sacred from profane, priestly temple from political throne, worship from work, faith from reason, piety from practice, the spiritual from the corporeal, and theology from morality. Instead, liturgical morality would seek to heal those divisions that the serpent has caused. It is a healing that must happen in the marrow of our daily lives, not just in conceptual schemes, although we call upon those conceptual schemes to take the union in more than a shallow way. (The most shallow example I have read was an author once pointing out that we are polite in the communion line: that was how he connected liturgy

---

[7] H. Tristram Engelhardt, *After God: Morality and Bioethics in the Secular Age* (Crestwood, NY: St. Vladimir's Seminary Press, 2017), 219.

and social justice.) I want liturgical morality to mean more than that. I want to go to a depth where the ordinary Christian would find liturgy to be the *statuat* of morality and serve as a guide to bioethical questions that professional ethicists confront.

Moralis is ex-pired (breathed out) by the liturgical lungs of the Church because the Holy Spirit in-spires (breathes life into) the behavior of the person as that person leaves the temple's liturgy. The pneumatic respiration we do in the liturgy oxygenates our political body. We then conduct a "liturgy after the liturgy," in the words of Ion Bria. He quotes Bishop Anastasios Yannoulatos, saying, "The liturgy is not an escape from life, but a continuous transformation of life according to the prototype Jesus Christ, through the power of the Spirit.... The liturgy has to be continued in personal, everyday situations. Each of the faithful is called upon to continue a personal 'liturgy' on the sacred altar of his own heart, to realize a living proclamation of the good news 'for the sake of the whole world.'"[8] Bria extrapolates by saying that although the Divine Liturgy of the Eucharist is certainly the climax of the Church's life; it is also a service for the building up of the one Body of Christ. There is therefore a double movement in the Liturgy: the assembling of the people of God to perform the memorial of the death and Resurrection of Jesus, and the members of the Church being sent out as authentic testimony to Jesus in the world. Such a "liturgy after the Liturgy" requires four things, he says: (1) an ongoing reaffirming of the true Christian identity, constantly renewed by the Eucharistic Communion; (2) enlarging the witness by creating a new Christian milieu, each in his own environment (family, society, office, factory, etc.); (3) the liturgical life nourishing the Christian life not only in its private sphere but also in its public and political realm; and (4) since liturgy means public and collective action, therefore there is a sense in which the Christian is a creator of community, and this Christian charisma is important in order for the Christian "to be a continual builder of a true *koinonia* of love and peace even if he is politically marginal and lives in a hostile surrounding."[9]

In order to make proper judgements about the social and personal challenges that confront us, we must take the measure of man's eternal horizon, which liturgy displays. We can track our way through the

---

[8] Ion Bria, "The Liturgy after the Liturgy," *International Review of Mission* 67, no. 265 (1978), 87.

[9] Bria, "The Liturgy after the Liturgy," 88–90. Bria then also presented this theme in a book: *The Liturgy after the Liturgy: Mission and Witness from an Orthodox Perspective* (Geneva: World Council of Churches, 1996).

bioethical landscape around us only by looking upward at the North Star that liturgy delivers. Engelhardt's book provides ample analysis of what happens if we lose this North Star, this eternal horizon, what he calls a "God's-eye perspective"—there is no need for me to rehearse his material here, as the reader would be better served to see them firsthand in the book. But I will suggest that this reigning metaphor of the book functions in two ways, at two levels, and purposely so.

First, the God's-eye perspective names a perspective that is objective and universal, instead of relativistic and idiosyncratic. The God's-eye perspective has the following characteristics, Engelhardt says: it transcends the limited meaning we grasp ("this book examines the roots and conditions of this full immanentization of all meaning . . ."); it is fundamental ("an experience of ultimate meaning"), single ("One needs a moral perspective that is not one among the multiplicity of socio-historically constituted perspectives"), objective ("The secular morality thus presupposes what it cannot have: the objectivity of a God's-eye perspective"), transcendent ("the dominant secular culture positively eschews any grounding in the transcendent"), metaphysical ("traditional morality claimed a metaphysical anchor"), ontological ("our experience of reality is shaped by our commitments regarding the deep ontology of things), independent ("God provides a meaning and final perspective outside of . . ."); a standard ("to make a moral judgment, one needs a standard") that also enforces ("the priority of the moral point of view requires God, Who enforces, not just defines, His moral point of view") and judges ("the final and eternal self-conscious point of view to give a final judgment"); serves as a common source ("those who do not share a common vision of the right, the good, and the virtuous" resort to procedures that will not establish moral rightness); is authoritative ("the authority of the more-than-minimal state is therefore a great puzzle"), transcendent, and commanding ("recognize a fully transcendent God Who commands"); and functions independently (without this perspective "there is no socio-historically independence tendered of reality and morality").[10]

All this is a play, of course, on the common expression "to have a bird's-eye view." When we are lost in the thicket, when we wonder if this path is the right one, when we are curious about what lies ahead or at the end of the trail, then we wish that we could have a view from a high angle, an overall look at something, a glance at the total picture. For a while—a long while—natural law provided this objective bird's-eye view,

---

[10] Engelhardt, *After God*, 11, 32, 38, 58, 60, 70, 74, 85, 87, 187, 191, 219, 416.

and Engelhardt has some positive things to say about the medical moral manualist tradition before a paradigm change set it aside. "The traditional morality claimed a metaphysical anchor in natural law, in being as it is in itself."[11] The bird's-eye view was a perspective on a fuller reality, not just my own perspective; it was a viewpoint above my own head's reasoning; it implied objectivity. But as God faded into the background, and natural law grew wispier, this objectivity was lost. The role that natural law had once played was turned over to rational argument to provide, but Engelhardt provides a detailed description of why rational argument, on its own, failed to provide this altitudinal viewpoint. Reason was unable to function as an ersatz natural law because it was fractured by pluralism. The wreckage of reason's breakup on the shoals of relativism is traced in this book, which is filled with examples of people who claim that reason alone can provide this higher perspective, and then fail to deliver on their claim. Objectivity was once the whole point; but it has now been abandoned in favor of multiple viewpoints, multiple rationalities, multiple moralities. We have given up trying to find our home base and settled for living anywhere. As Chesterton wrote, "In the bleak and blinding hail of skepticism to which [man] has been now so long subjected, he has begun for the first time to be chilled, not merely in his hopes, but in his desires. For the first time in history he begins really to doubt the object of his wanderings on the earth. He has always lost his way; but now he has lost his address."[12]

The theologian can give an account as to why this happened because the theologian knows the doctrine of creation and the doctrine of sin. Once upon a time, natural law was understood to be a window upon God, because God was understood to be the author of natural law. Natural law is a reflection of Divine Wisdom. Natural law was not understood as a philosophical deduction from nature, it was understood as the law of God as written into our natures. Thomas Aquinas says that "all things partake somewhat of the eternal law, in so far as, namely, from its being imprinted on them, they derive their respective inclinations to their proper acts and ends."[13] Animals are directed by instinct, but rational men and

---

[11] Engelhardt, *After God*, 60.

[12] G. K. Chesterton, *What's Wrong with the World*, in *The Collected Works of G. K. Chesterton* (San Francisco: Ignatius, 1987), 4:77.

[13] Thomas Aquinas, *Summa Theologica*, trans. Fathers of the English Dominican Province (Westminster, MD: Christian Classics, 1981), I-II, q. 91, a. 2.

women have something over and above instinct: they receive laws spoken to their reason:

> Now among all others, the rational creature is subject to Divine providence in the most excellent way, in so far as it partakes of a share of providence, by being provident both for itself and for others. Wherefore it has a share of the Eternal Reason, whereby it has a natural inclination to its proper act and end: and this participation of the eternal law in the rational creature is called the natural law.[14]

When the eternal law directs the sun in its orbit, it is called a law of nature; when the eternal law directs a rational creature, it is called natural law. Therefore, natural law does not mean a law derived from the workings of nature on its own, and it does not mean a law we derive from our minds apart from God. "The light of natural reason, whereby we discern what is good and what is evil, which is the function of the natural law, is nothing else than an imprint on us of the Divine Light. It is therefore evident that the natural law is nothing else than the rational creature's participation of the eternal law."[15] Rational man was made with the capacity to detect the law of God in natural law, and detecting it, he should obey it, and when he does, it is God's law he is obeying—not nature's, not his own.

Alas, sin. The light of natural reason has not gone out, since the image of God cannot be destroyed. But the light has been sufficiently dimmed that we do not see the connection behind created law to the Uncreated lawgiver. We have therefore come today to use the word "natural" in a distorted way. We take it to mean "whatever we happen to find." That is how we take it on the anthropological level: the wilderness is natural for being as it is, as we happen to find it, free from human influence. That is how we take it on the theological level: nature is the absence of supernature, natural law is whatever we happen to find, it is autonomy, unrelated to God. But surely this can't do when it comes to morality, since we happen to find people doing all sorts of things, not all of them good. Divine providence extends to all things, including man and woman, which means that men and women, like all other creatures, have acts and ends that are proper to them. We should struggle to deduce what acts are improper to men and women, or which of their acts are directed toward improper ends. But the

---

[14] Thomas Aquinas, *Summa Theologica*, I-II, q. 91, a. 2.
[15] Thomas Aquinas, *Summa Theologica*, I-II, q. 91, a. 2.

light in our eye —even our bird's eye—has dimmed, like Jacob's was when he confused Esau with Isaac. We grope with our fingers, nearly blindly, and our senses are deceived by goat skins. Natural law needs revealed law, and revealed law needs a heart restored to flesh.

It is not enough to see with reason's bird's-eye, therefore, and this is the second move Engelhardt makes. In places in his book, he sounds as if it would be sufficient to see with a bird's-eye perspective, one that has the qualities listed in the paragraph above: transcending our human mind, fundamental, objective, metaphysical, ontological, independent, common, authoritative, commanding, a standard. Such a viewpoint might be sufficient—if, but only if, we could attain it. But fallen reason can now only produce an ersatz natural law, because once we separate natural law from the Law Giver, then no objectivity or truth is guaranteed. Engelhardt describes in detail the demoralization and deflation of morality and bioethics due to the fact that the de-godded, secular moral perspective cannot produce a sufficient canon from reason alone to lay a foundation for ethics. Reason has failed to provide this God's-eye perspective.

In other words (mine), something more is required than a birds-eye perspective. We require the "eye of the Dove," which is how the Church Fathers spoke of the Holy Spirit's presence in a person. Engelhardt first describes the necessity of some bird's-eye view to point out the failings of unmoored pluralism, and then he specifies that it must be the view of this particular bird's eye. Once our *nomos* has been separated from the *Logos*, our *nous* is in need of resurrection, not just a pair of new spectacles crafted by Kant and company. Engelhardt began by arguing for a universal perspective; he ends up arguing for the particular truth of Christian revelation. Such revelation will appeal to our reason, and it will activate our reason, but it will not be attained by our reason alone, because the Fall has put us in need of regeneration. Henri de Lubac offers a metaphor for this healed reason when he writes, "If it can be said that, in climbing up the ladder that leads from reason to faith, we face insurmountable distances between certain rungs, the same is not true when coming down the ladder from faith to reason."[16]

After creation, the Fall; after the Fall, a new act by God. Spiritual gifts. A holy eye. Our eye "catches" the light Mt. Tabor. It sees the world with God's eye, the eye of the Dove. Engelhardt explains the two-step process

---

[16] Henri de Lubac, "Apologetics and Theology," in *Theological Fragments* (San Francisco: Ignatius Press, 1989), 103.

in summary statements contained on the same page. First, he has brought the reader to the point of admitting that a God's-eye view is needed:

> The non-Orthodox are not here invited to concede the truth of orthodoxy's claims, but only to examine whether, if the claims are true, they would show a way beyond our intractable moral and bioethical pluralism.... The claim is not just that one can envisage a God's-eye perspective as Kant did for morality, but that one can experience the existence of that God's-eye perspective with a compelling force of truth distantly like what occurs in first-person reports such as "I see blue." The claim is that humans have a *nous*, a capacity non-empirically to see reality.[17]

And there is a way to brighten our eye, to enable it to see again after having been dimmed, a way to empower it to see something that even the law alone (natural or revealed) did not show it. And when that is attained, the dominoes fall in sequence:

> What is at stake are three claims. The first claim is that there is a God's-eye view. The second claim is that this perspective can be experienced. The third claim is that if one knows experientially that there is a God's-eye perspective, as well as what this perspective requires, then one can avoid bioethical and moral pluralism as well as the demoralization of morality and bioethics.[18]

The first domino is a revealed starting point. Even if the reader does not share this already from the standpoint of faith, Engelhardt is asking him to admit that it would get us past the intractable pluralism that plagues us. The second domino is liturgical theology: this perspective can be experienced—not deduced, not inferred, not supposed, not analyzed, but experienced—as *theologia prima*. The third domino is liturgical morality: the liturgical foundation of bioethics comes from the experiential theology of that holy eye.

Liturgical life is lived neither in isolation from the world, nor as disregard for the world, nor in disdain toward the world. Rather, liturgy is, in the oft-repeated words of Aidan Kavanagh in class, "doing the world the way the world was meant to be done." The eye of the Dove is not a

---

[17] Engelhardt, *After God*, 368.
[18] Engelhardt, *After God*, 368.

gift to only see God haunting the temple; it is a gift to see God's power and rule in the world. The laws that govern bioethics are not laws that are intended for Christians alone; they are intended for every son of Adam and daughter of Eve. What we learn within the walls of the temple is intended to enlighten the world to which we return. In the liturgy we discern the Alpha and Omega of creation; we discover our human place under God, beside our neighbor, and over creation; we experience a true vision of the community of human beings when we contemplate Mary and the saints; we rehearse a choreography that should be our way of walking through the world, especially in its moral demands.

Maximus the Confessor worked with a temple topography that saw the Church building as an image of the whole world, not just the spiritual part of it. He says that the Church is distinguished as sanctuary (symbolizing the invisible and spiritual world), and nave (symbolizing the visible, sensible world). Despite this distinction, the Church, just like the cosmos, "is one in its basic reality without being divided into its parts by reason of the differences between them, but rather by their relationship to the unity it frees these parts from the difference arising from their names. It shows to each other that they are both the same thing, and reveals that one is to the other in turn what each one is for itself."[19] What does the sanctuary reveal about the nave? What does the nave reveal about the sanctuary? What is the basic reality that is shown by difference but not dualistically divided? "The nave is *the sanctuary in potency* by being consecrated by the relationship of the sacrament toward its end, and in turn the sanctuary is *the nave in act* by possessing the principle of its own sacrament."[20] When the potential of the world is actualized, we will be in eternal liturgy, just as John of the eagle eye witnessed in his apocalyptic vision (Rev 21:1–2). The world is heaven in potency; heaven is the world enacted at its truest depths. The world exists to be transfigured into the kingdom, and the heavenly Jerusalem in its entirety will become God's dwelling place. Temple and polis will be coterminous. The eye of the Dove sees this potency, and especially when it looks at any human person, which is why that person must be treated with such care. That's why certain ethics (principles of right behaviors) and morals (judgments about goodness) follow.

---

[19] Maximus the Confessor, "The Church's Mystagogy," in *Maximus Confessor: Selected Writings* (Mahwah, NJ: Paulist Press, 1985), 188, italics added.

[20] Maximus the Confessor, "The Church's Mystagogy," 188.

Such a suggestion would sound impossible for a human being, even arrogant in a Promethean sort of way, if a man had not already existed whose life was precisely an example of this condition, and unless that man could share that life with others. The theandric state of Jesus is our hope. He is the union of the created and uncreated, the hypostatic union of divine and human natures. And what he is by nature, we are to become by grace. That's why we approach the sacraments. The supreme vocation of created beings is to have by grace what God has by nature. Vladimir Lossky therefore concludes this destiny has already been reached in the divine person of Christ, risen and ascended. But there is more. There are others who will participate in this life. First in line is Mary.

If the Mother of God could truly realize, in her human and created person, the sanctity which corresponds to her unique role, then she cannot have failed to attain here below by grace all that her Son had by his divine nature. But, if it be so, then the destiny of the Church and the world has already been reached, not only in the uncreated person of the Son of God but also in the created person of his Mother. That is why St. Gregory Palamas calls the Mother of God "the boundary between the created and the uncreated." Beside the incarnate divine hypostasis there is a deified human hypostasis.[21]

The theandric Christ invites disciples, but disciples who, with Mary, cross the boundary. By assuming a liturgical posture toward Christ, we are made co-sons, we share in his filial relationship, we are raised by grace to his theandric life. Vladimir Solovyof called this "godmanhood."

I think of Solovyof because the dead-ending moralists whom Engelhardt analyzes all operate with variations on materialism, and Solovyof combated a materialist anthropology throughout his lifetime. In the lectures he delivered between 1877 and 1884, published now as *Lectures on Godmanhood*, he says:

> If man is only a fact, if he is inevitably limited by the mechanism of the external reality, then let him seek not anything greater than natural reality, let him "eat, drink, and be merry";

---

[21] Vladimir Lossky, "Panagia," in *The Mother of God: A Symposium*, ed. E. L. Mascall (Westminster, MD: Dacre Press, 1959), 34.

> ... A man, however, does not wish to be a mere fact, to be only a phenomenon; in this unwillingness is already a hint that actually he is not a mere fact, that he is not a phenomenon only, but something greater.[22]

A man does not wish to be a mere fact; he is something greater. Materialism is a mechanistic view that says everything consists of mere force and matter, and all that occurs, occurs of necessity according to immutable laws. The one with the most force can therefore do with man as he wishes; the power of the will trumps the logos of the ethos. We have seen this played out numerous times in the last century. However, "as soon as we admit that the life of the world and of humanity is not an accident without any meaning or purpose ... but represents a definite and integrated process, we are forced at once to give recognition to the content realized by that process."[23] The spiritual forces of will and intellect and senses demand a definite object of desire, perception, and feeling, Solovyof believes. "It is obvious that man cannot wish only for the sake of wishing, think for the sake of thinking, or feel for the sake of feeling."[24] Therefore man has to wish *something*, think *something* or about something, feel *something*. From this Solovyof concludes that man's experience is an experience of an interior demand for objectivity:

> He demands that the object of his will would have its own dignity in order that it may be desired by him or, to use school language, in order that it would be *objectively-desirable*, that it would be an object of good; in the same way he demands that the object and the content of his thought to be *objectively true*, and the object of his feeling be *objectively-beautiful*, i.e., [true and beautiful] not for him only but for everyone unconditionally."[25]

In his other classic work *The Justification of the Good: An Essay on Moral Philosophy*, Solovyof explores the objective foundation for morality by recognizing a tripartite anthropology. "However convincing or authoritative a moral teaching may be, it will remain fruitless and devoid of power unless it finds a secure foundation in the moral nature of man.... There

---

[22] Vladimir Solovyev, *Lectures on Godmanhood* (London: Dennis Dobson Publishers, 1948), 81.
[23] Vladimir Solovyof, *The Justification of the Good: An Essay on Moral Philosophy* (London: Constable and Company, 1918), 88.
[24] Solovyof, *The Justification of the Good*, 89.
[25] Solovyof, *The Justification of the Good*, 89.

exists an ultimate basis of universal human morality, and upon it all that is of importance in ethics must rest."[26] The good is a way of realizing the world's purpose, which confirms its objectivity, and human work is required to bring about the world's purpose because "this participation of man must necessarily be included in the very purpose of God's activity in the world."[27] The inner forms of the good are threefold, based on man's relation to his objective place in the world. We can summarize the tripartite goods, and their moral form, by repeated summaries of Solovyof across the pages as he describes shame, pity, and piety as the foundations of morality, altruism, and religion:

- Man stands in three relations: to material animality, to other people, and to a higher principle (experienced as "below, par, and above").
- Toward his material animality he experiences shame, toward other people he experiences pity, and toward the higher principle he experiences piety (or reverence).
- "The fundamental feelings of shame, pity, and reverence exhaust the sphere of man's possible moral relations to that which is below him, that which is on a level with him, and that which is above him."[28]
- These experiences summon reactions, which can be called mastery, solidarity, and submission.
- Solovyof's chapter titles are "The Ascetic Principle in Morality," "Pity and Altruism," and "The Religious Principle in Morality."
- A sinful expression of each of these exists: they are materialism, egoism, and atheism.
- Such a distortion must be fought. For general humanity they are combatted in the forms of asceticism, altruism, and religious morality. In religious practice they are combatted in the forms of fasting, almsgiving, and prayer.
- Here you can see the three, working backward from top to bottom: "The first concentrated active expression of the religious feeling or piety—its chief work—is prayer; in the same way, the work of

---

[26] Solovyof, *The Justification of the Good*, 25.
[27] Solovyof, *The Justification of the Good*, 172.
[28] Solovyof, *The Justification of the Good*, 35.

pity is almsgiving, and the work of shame is abstinence or fasting. These three works condition the beginning and the development of the new life of grace in man."[29]

- The perfection of the good finally shows itself as the organization of a threefold love: a *descending* love upon material nature that brings it into the fullness of absolute good; and *equalizing* love wherein moral and political pity for men becomes a spiritual love for them; and an *ascending* love which is all-embracing and boundless.

Does the reader notice how these three integrate and overlap? That is crucial to the thesis. If it is evident, I can present Solovyof's explanation of each in more detail. Regarding the first, he says man is the animal capable of *shame*; though the feeling serves no social purpose, and is not found in animals, and cannot be accounted for by evolution alone, man does definitely feel it: he is ashamed of being dominated or ruled by animality. This distinguishes him from all lower nature, and it determines his ethical relation to his material nature. It proves that he is not merely a material being; materialist anthropology is in error. Shame is a sensation, and when it passes into the medium of abstract thought, it is conscience, but both of them say, "This is not good, this is wrong, this is unworthy." Regarding the second, he says *pity* experiences solidarity with others because its essence lies in the fact of a given subject being conscious in a corresponding manner of the suffering or the want of others. Darwin thought he could see a rudimentary form of solidarity among animals, leading Solovyof to say that a pitiless man falls even lower than the animal level. Regarding the third, he discerns a feeling of *reverence* that is not reducible to either of the first two feelings. Reverence does not determine man's moral attitude to his lower nature or his attitude toward beings similar to him. This higher thing is something that he can be neither ashamed of nor feel pity for, but which he must revere. Such reverence or awe (*reverential, pietas*) forms in man the moral basis of religion.

Solovyof thinks he has found the tripartite foundation of moral life. "Mastery over the material senses, solidarity with other living beings, and inward voluntary submission to the superhuman principle—these are the eternal and permanent foundations of the moral life of humanity."[30] And he thinks this is true for all human beings, and not just for Christians. Even without a knowledge of *imago Dei* and the body as a temple, a

---

[29] Solovyof, *The Justification of the Good*, 440.
[30] Solovyof, *The Justification of the Good*, 35.

person is ashamed of being ruled by animality; even without knowledge of Trinitarian koinonia reflected in the spiritual communion of saints, a person feels rudimentary solidarity with his neighbor; and even without knowledge of the creator and triune God, a person recognizes something higher, something to revere, and this is the first touch of religion. Solovyof has been examining the human experience as contained in human sensations, and from that basis has moved into morality: "Reason develops psychological experience into principles called moral philosophy."[31]

My interest in invoking Solovyof is to underscore the interconnectedness of the three. One cannot to do the second stage alone (altruism) without situating it between mastery of the self (asceticism) and submission to God (liturgical piety). Ethics and asceticism and piety are interlinked. This means that liturgical morality requires both a God's-eye view (experienced and instilled by liturgy) and liberation from slavery to the passions (liturgical asceticism). The forms of the good must be freed. "The moral meaning of life is originally and ultimately determined by the good itself, inwardly accessible to us through our reason and conscience in so far as these inner forms of the good are freed by moral practice from slavery to passions and from the limitations of personal and collective selfishness."[32] The situation into which we have backed ourselves, as Engelhardt demonstrates, is that we think we can manufacture the good instead of being determined by it. But Solovyof has confidence that morality is based on a principle that is unconditional. "Rational faith in the absolute good is based upon inner experience. . . . Having justified the good as such in moral philosophy, we must, in theoretical philosophy, justify the good *as Truth*."[33] (The last line of the book.)

This means that liturgical morality is not doing a different world; it is doing the world rightly. If I were on a pilgrimage and wanted to know how to behave on the journey, as well as at the destination, I would be wise to heed those who have been informed about the purpose and end of the journey. "The unconditional principle of morality can therefore be expressed as follows: In complete inner harmony with the higher will and recognising the absolute worth or significance of all other persons, since they too are in the image and likeness of God, participate, as fully as in thee lies, in the work of making thyself and every one more perfect, so that the Kingdom of God may be finally revealed in the world."[34] The

---

[31] Solovyof, *The Justification of the Good*, 173.
[32] Solovyof, *The Justification of the Good*, xxxi.
[33] Solovyof, *The Justification of the Good*, 474–75.
[34] Solovyof, *The Justification of the Good*, 174.

kingdom of God is the unconditional principle of morality, which implies the perfection of a human being.

This is not a task the Christian sets down and leaves behind when he departs the temple. Liturgical morality means that our *latreia* accompanies us out into the world as *pietas* (a virtue meaning duty, or conscientiousness, or fulfillment of a vow). Engelhardt cites numerous authors who argue that although a Christian in the health field may be personally religious, he must be professionally secular, i.e., he must never allow duty to God to interfere with secular professional obligations. When the dominant culture bans sin from the conversation, it is banning God from the conversation, which is an even more effective "death of God" movement than the one the philosophers prattled about in the 1960s. They were only saying the concept of God is threadbare, now we are saying the presence of God is no more. Such authors are happy with the divide between the sacred and the profane; such authors are happy with a liturgy that is so otherworldly that it has no impact on this world; Christians never are. The idea of liturgical morality rejects any conclusion that God is not present in the world because he is confined to the tabernacle. The God who knew his way out of the grave also knows his way out of the Church building, where secularism has tried to embalm him.

Alexander Schmemann addressed this already fifty years ago when he analyzed the concept of secularism. Having emigrated from the actively atheistic Soviet government, he was sensitive to those milder passive forms of atheism that took root under the category of "secularism." What is secularism?

> [It is] a worldview and consequently a way of life in which the basic aspects of human existence—such as family, education, science, profession, art, etc.—not only are not rooted in or related to religious faith, but in which the very necessity or possibility of such a connection is denied. The secular areas of life are thought of as autonomous, i.e., governed by their own values, principles, and motivations, different from the religious ones.[35]

Translated to our topic: secular moralism is autonomously governed by its own values, principles, and motivations. This does not deny God's existence, it denies God's relevance.

---

[35] Alexander Schmemann, "Problems of Orthodoxy in America: The Spiritual Problem," *St. Vladimir's Seminary Quarterly* 9, no. 4 (1965): 173.

But Schmemann goes on. American secularism is not anti-religious. "It is a characteristic feature of American secularism that it both *accepts* religion as essential to man and at the same time denies it is an integrated world-view permeating and shaping the whole life of man."[36] An American secularist can be a religious person, attend services, be punctual in prayer, have his marriage solemnized and his home blessed, and yet throughout it all his understanding of religion is rooted in his secularist worldview and not vice versa. The life he lives in this age (this *seculum*), says Schmemann, derives from its own philosophy of life, and not from the creed he confesses in Church. That is how secularism can approve of religion. "In secularism, when it 'approves' of religion and even declares it necessary, it does so only inasmuch as religion is ready to become a part of the secularistic world-view, a sanction of its values and a help in the process of attaining them. No other word indeed is used more often by secularism in reference to religion than the word 'help.'"[37]

As Engelhardt seems to have demonstrated, the culture of the day accepts Christianity so long as it helps its agenda. Christianity is given a seat at the table of moral discussion so long as it does not disrupt the commands being received from the gods of the day. I refer to the secular "philosophies of life" as false gods in order to say that the conflict must occur on Mt. Carmel, as it did for Elijah. This is about the charge of idolatry: Who is your God? The morality is liturgical because it is about true gods and false gods, true worship and false worship. Indeed, Schmemann concludes elsewhere, "Secularism, I submit, is above all a *negation of worship*. I stress:—not of God's existence, not of some kind of transcendence and therefore of some kind of religion. If secularism in theological terms is a heresy, it is primarily a heresy about man. It is the negation of man as a worshiping being, as *homo adorans*: the one for whom worship is the essential act which both 'posits' his humanity and fulfills it."[38]

Liturgical morality asks, What would it mean to worship the true God? What would it mean to believe that the true God is our creator? What would it mean to believe that we are made in the image of God and are destined for resurrection? What more force is brought by calling something a sin instead of a lifestyle choice? For what are we designed? About what should we be ashamed? With whom should I feel sympathy? How would the higher degree of reverence affect my lower degrees of

---

[36] Schmemann, "Problems of Orthodoxy in America: The Spiritual Problem," 173.
[37] Schmemann, "Problems of Orthodoxy in America: The Spiritual Problem," 174.
[38] Alexander Schmemann, "Worship in a Secular Age," in *For the Life of the World* (Crestwood, NY: St. Vladimir's Seminary Press, 1973), 118.

altruism and asceticism? What we have lost is not so much a God in the sky; he will do no harm to the dominant culture there, and the dominant culture will not mind if Christians absent themselves once a week to worship him on those empyrean heights. What we have lost is a God on the ground—a theological anthropology—the belief that there is a place we ought to be going. If we are made for godmanhood, then there is a way we ought to be developing. And the grammar of morality is contained in that "ought." If I am just wandering around, no one can say I ought to turn left or right, but if it is a matter of reaching a destination, someone might say I ought to take the righthand fork in the road. What good is a morality that never contradicts my desires or impulses!

Engelhardt writes, "The Liturgy provides the privileged epistemic standpoint that unites,"[39] and then he quotes Archbishop Hilarion: "The *lex credendi* grows out of the *lex orandi*, and dogmas are considered divinely revealed because they are born in the life of prayer and revealed to the Church through its divine services."[40] The law of belief and the law of behavior both grow out of the *lex orandi*. The amniotic prayer fluid forms ascetics within the womb of the Church who become both theologians and moralists. And if we abandon that God in favor of our own gods, the resultant idolatry makes our moral heads spin. There have been plenty of instances throughout history when this has happened; we seem to be living through another instance of it now. And since I write from the campus of the University of Notre Dame, I will close with a condemnation of the upset France experienced in the eighteenth century, as described by the founder of Notre Dame's community of Holy Cross, Blessed Basil Moreau. He lived through his own country's dispute about idolatry, when the false goddess of reason opposed the true God, and both worship and morality were affected:

> In these present days of anarchy, we have made a god of our own reason; we have usurped the sanctuaries of divinity for the caprices of our mind and heart. No Christian Frenchmen will ever forget the goddess of reason, exalted to the opprobrium of our ancestors and the shame of a beautiful country. To overthrow the established order, this goddess had to be surrounded with bloody hatchets, savage bodyguards, and mad leaders. Under the rule of

---

[39] Engelhardt, *After God*, 377.
[40] Found in Bishop Hilarion, "Theological education in the 21st century" (lecture, Wycliffe College, Toronto, October 22, 2008), http://www.interfax-religion.com/?act=documents&div=134.

the sovereign, France had made its god. There was no law except arrests, no rule except death, no ministers except executioners. For it is true that whenever human beings try to steal divine authority under pretext of securing greater liberty, their vainglory makes them the slave of disorder and sin, and yet we go madly on trying to realize the promise, "You will be as gods."

We would go so far as to rule God entirely from our creation. God can no longer command the nations to adore him alone in the way he prescribes. Governments claim the right to choose a divinity of their own making and to trace the rules of their religious worship, if they do not altogether deny divinity. God must be content with whatever homage they deem to give him. He must not presume to teach them what is good and what is evil, what is permitted and what is forbidden. Philosophers have the right to fix limits and write moral laws. And what a morality this is! God could surely apply to them the cutting irony spoken against the same disorder of the human mind and heart at the beginning of the world: "Behold, Adam has become as one of us" (Genesis 3:22). Pride thus leads us so far that we wish to withdraw from our Creator and the light of revealed religion, to find truth for ourselves and invent our own worship and rules of conduct.[41]

---

[41] Basil Moreau, *Essential Writings* (Notre Dame, IN: Christian Classics, 2014), 85–86.

Liturgical and Pastoral Theology
The Church as Pastoral Icon of the Mercy of the Good Shepherd[*]

These unworthy comments rest upon an image I am bringing to a passage in Scripture.[1] I confess to committing an act of eisegesis. I agree that a *scientific* reading of Scripture should use exegesis, whereby a meaning is "drawn out" of the text, but I also propose that a *spiritual* reading of Scripture is sometimes of equal value, whereby we are "drawn into" the text. How else do we fuse our horizon with the eternal Word but by laying ourselves upon the sacred page? I wish to draw us into an image contained in Hebrews 11:1, where we find the word "hypostasis." The component parts of the word are easy enough to see: *hypo* means "under or beneath"; and *stasis* means "a position or standing." Hypostasis refers to that which stands under something, giving it actual existence and real being. This is evident in its Latin translation, *sub-stantia*. Thus Hebrews 11:1 is rendered in both the King James and Douay-Rheims translation as follows: "Now faith is the *substance* of things hoped for, the evidence of things not seen." But the word *hypostasis* was also used in the legal world to describe documents that gave evidence of ownership to a property, so The Amplified Bible translation says, "Faith is the title deed of things hoped for." The word indicates an emphasis on confidence and firm trust, which can be detected in several other translations: "Faith is the realization of what is hoped for" (New American Bible), or "the confidence in what we hope for" (New International Version), or "the assurance of things hoped for" (Revised Standard Version). I do not dispute any of these translations, nor am I trying to exegete a better one. They all work from the bottom upward:

---

[*] David W. Fagerberg, "The Church as Pastoral Icon of the Mercy of the Good Shepherd," *Nova et Vetera* 16, no. 1 (2018): 21–38.

[1] This paper was delivered September 2016 at the Pontifical University of the Holy Cross in Rome as part of the Extraordinary Jubilee of Mercy called by Pope Francis. The XIII International Symposium of University Professors was on the topic of "Knowledge and Mercy: The Third Mission of the University" in "Celebration of the Jubilee of Mercy of Universities, Research Centres, and Institutions for Artistic Higher Education." The theme at Holy Cross was "The Merciful Face of the Father." This paper was one of three presented there. I am grateful to them for permission to print it here.

faith is the foundation on which is built the assurance, confidence, and substantial hope we have in the covenants and promises of God.

But there is a different image that comes from an etymology of the word "hypostasis," an image that works from the top downward. I am going to apply this difference twice, once to faith and hope, and then to love and mercy.

G. L. Prestige contributed to a lexicon of patristic Greek terms, and at the end of his research he wrote a book titled *God in Patristic Thought* that explains the theology of the Church Fathers by looking at specific words they used. When he comes to the word *hypostasis*, he notes that "the historian, Socrates, quotes Irenaeus Grammaticus for the application of the term hypostasis to the dregs of wine in the cask. There is nothing new in this usage, since Aristotle and Hippocrates are both quoted by Liddell and Scott as using the term to denote sediment. However, it also occurs in a wider sense to denote the underneath or hidden part of any object."[2] In a wine barrel, some sediment settles (*stasis*) at the bottom (*hypo*), though most of the cask is liquid. Winemakers still today speak of red wines "throwing sediment" when they age. Something hypostasizes at the bottom: the free-floating sediment substantializes at the bottom. Prestige also finds this sense in the Clementine Homilies, which discussed the legend of Kronos and said the primordial substance "sank downwards" when it was devoured by the titan.[3] And Hippocrates used the term to mean "a deposit," leading the medical world to still use hypostasis to refer to "the settling or accumulation of blood in the lower part of an organ."

Now let us turn back to Hebrews 11:1 and hear the verse with this wine barrel in mind: "Faith is the *hypostasis* of things hoped for." Faith is the sediment of hope; the liquid hope solidifies at the bottom of the cask as faith; when hope hypostasizes, faith results; faith stands under our hope; faith is the substance of things hoped for. From the bottom up, faith is the ground upon which one builds a hope, but from the top down, hope is being given substantial form when it hypostasizes as faith. Hope settles at the base of our hearts and exists there as faith. Hypostasized hope is no vague sentiment; it is a substantial confidence. And the whole chapter of Hebrews 11 gives a lengthy rendition about people who had not just a general, liquid optimism about God but a particular, faithful certainty in

---

[2] G. L. Prestige, *God in Patristic Thought* (London: SPCK, 1985), 163.
[3] Homily of Clement 6.7. "When, then, they say that this primordial substance, although most filthy and rough, was devoured by Kronos, that is, time, this is to be understood in a physical sense, as meaning that it sank downwards. And the water which flowed together after this first sediment, and floated on the surface of the first substance, they called Poseidon."

God: Abel's sacrifice; Enoch's translation; Noah's shipbuilding; Abraham's departure; Sarah's maternity; Jacob's blessing; Joseph's protection; Moses's exodus; and the judges and prophets who conquered kingdoms, wrought justice, obtained promise, and stopped the mouths of lions. These were substantial forms of hope. In *Spe Salvi* Ratzinger comments about the history of this translation. Thomas Aquinas used the terminology of his philosophical tradition to say that faith is a *habitus*, i.e., "a stable disposition of the spirit, through which eternal life takes root in us and reason is led to consent to what it does not see."[4] Ratzinger thinks this modifies "substance" insofar as it is describing faith in embryo: there are already present in us the things that are hoped for, and that creates certainty. Luther and other Protestants took it in a subjective way to mean faith as an expression of an interior attitude, but scholarship today generally moves toward an agreement that Hebrews does not just mean a personal reaching out toward something absent; rather, Hebrews means to say that faith gives us something. So Ratzinger concludes, "Faith draws the future into the present, so that it is no longer simply a 'not yet.' The fact that this future exists changes the present; the present is touched by the future reality."[5]

And here, at last, is my parallel application of this image to our topic at hand. As *faith* is the hypostasis of *hope*, I want to suggest that *mercy* is the hypostasis of *love*. When love solidifies at the bottom of the wine barrel, it is mercy. Love hypostasizes as mercy. Or, mercy is the substance of love. Mercy is how the general virtue of love is realized (made real, given being). Mercy is not a general love; it is a hypostasized love, having settled down with specificity to serve a particular person, a particular situation, and apply the love of God to a particular circumstance. Mercy is love concretized, instantiated, made real, substantialized. This is the understanding I see in Pope Francis's Bull calling for this Extraordinary Jubilee of Mercy. He writes, "In short, the mercy of God is not an abstract idea, but a concrete reality.... It is hardly an exaggeration to say that this is a 'visceral' love. It gushes forth from the depths naturally, full of tenderness and compassion, indulgence and mercy."[6] Mercy gushes forth from the bottom of the wine barrel as hypostasized, concrete love.

---

[4] Pope Benedict XVI, Encyclical Letter *Spe Salvi* (2007), §7.
[5] Benedict XVI, *Spe Salvi*, §7.
[6] Pope Francis, Bull of Indiction of the Extraordinary Jubilee of Mercy *Misericordiae Vultus* (2015), §6.

Pastoral Theology

I further suggest that hypostatic love, i.e., mercy, gives us a description of the pastoral work of the Church. Pastoral theology is theology that occurs on the hypostatic level. Remembering that wine makers talk about "throwing sediment," I imagine pastoral theology as "thrown doctrine," doctrine thrown from our creeds and our libraries into daily life. It is theology under the domain of prudence. There is a false impression that when the adjective "pastoral" is attached to the discipline of theology, the former waters down the latter, or plays loose with orthodoxy, or becomes less rigorous. But this is not the case at all. Pastoral theology is hypostasized theology: it is substantialized theology united to mercy, moving from the generic to the specific question at hand. It is theology that shepherds (pastors) souls to eternal life. The pastoral task is aimed at priceless human souls and their communion with God. Jesus is the pastoral icon of the face of the Father, because as supreme pastor of his Church, he fulfills the two merciful tasks of a shepherd: protecting his sheep and leading them to pasture. The Church, his mystical body, is called to do the same. The Church's ministry proclaims the Kingdom of God in real life, i.e., it proclaims the Kingdom pastorally when, through preaching and sacrament, she leads humanity to the pasture of eternal life. Faith and doctrine and theology are no less rigorous for being pastoral; in fact, they may be all the more muscular if they are to conduct daily battle with sin and selfishness. The love that circulates between the persons of the Trinity is hypostasized in the Church, making her an icon of mercy. Both the *totus Christus* and the individual person whom the Church penetrates sacramentally are called to be an icon of him who is an icon of the Father. Each individual Christian receives grace in order to become mercy.

But this category of hypostasis does not only apply to our love becoming concrete; it was a term with Christological history and so applied to the merciful face of the Father taking human form. The word had picked up more precise meaning in the controversies concerning the Trinity and the Incarnation. After the grammar had settled, the Church could say that Jesus is one hypostasis with two natures, and that there is one God in three hypostases, and with this clarification the word could be used in the defense of icons, where it distinguished nature from a particularly existing thing.

Iconoclasts had three main reasons for thinking that icons were being used idolatrously. First, if the icon represented the divine nature alone, it would be a violation of the biblical prohibition about making idols; second, if the icon represented both the human and divine natures of Christ, then the natures were being confused, as the Monophysites did; third, if the icon represented only the human Christ, then the natures were being separated, as the Nestorians did. They thought iconographers were depicting the nature of God, or one of the two natures of Jesus. Here is where the term "hypostasis" could help, because it named the distinct member of some group that shared the same nature. Maximus the Confessor said, "An angel is distinct from another angel, a man from another man, an ox from another ox, a dog from another dog, by reason of their hypostasis, not their nature and essence."[7] This can be applied to the Trinity: the Father and Son and Holy Spirit are distinct by reason of their hypostasis, not by reason of being different natures or essences. One God, three persons. And this can be applied to Jesus, as Theodore the Studite did:

> When I say "man," I mean the common essence [ousia]. When I add "a" I mean the hypostasis: that is, the self-subsisting existence of that which is signified....
>
> "Man" in general is a common noun; but the particular name, such as "Peter" or "Paul" is a proper noun.... If, therefore, Christ were called simply "God" and "man" in the Scriptures, then He would have assumed simply our nature in general. However, Gabriel said to the Virgin "Behold, you shall conceive in your womb and bear a son, and you shall call His name Jesus." So Christ is called not only by a common noun but also by a proper name: this separates Him by his hypostatic properties from the rest of men, and because of this He is circumscribable.[8]

All human beings have a common nature, but at that level we could not distinguish one of us from another. The human nature we have is the same. But when that nature hypostasizes, it settles into something particular, concrete, individual, delineated—it becomes personal. That fellow over there may be called "man" or "*a* man," and if the latter he could be named "Paul." That carpenter over there, the one from Nazareth, may be called "man" and he may be called "God," but at the level of hypostasis he is "*a* man with human and divine natures," and as such, he is named "Jesus." The divine and human natures are in union at the level of person in a way that

---

[7] Maximus the Confessor, quoted in Christoph Schönborn, *God's Human Face: The Christ-Icon* (San Francisco: Ignatius Press, 1994), 104.
[8] Theodore the Studite, *On the Holy Icons* (Crestwood, NY: St. Vladimir's Seminary Press, 1981), 83–84.

does not confuse the natures, or change them, or divide them, or separate them, as the Council of Chalcedon said.

Applied to our case, when love hypostasizes, it becomes personal. It is no longer general love, but personal love. Mercy is love hypostasized into something particular, concrete, individual, delineated. If I can walk past the beggar and not give him what he needs at the moment, my love has not hypostasized, even if I feel general pity for his state. That is the whole point of the parable of the good Samaritan. Jesus tells of a priest and a Levite who both see a man who has been beaten, and we have no reason to doubt that they were sorry about his condition. But Jesus says it was the Samaritan traveler who, "when he saw him, . . . had compassion," and found his love hypostasizing from theory to praxis. This was clearly understood by the scholar who started the whole conversation, because when Jesus asked him which of the three was neighbor to the victim, he answered, "The one who showed *mercy* on him" (Luke 10:29–37). I can love humanity in general, in the abstract, but I am only a neighbor if that love treats an individual man with mercy.

Theodore says that a hypostasis is the circumscription of a general nature until it consists of certain properties. I say that mercy is the circumscription of generic love until it consists of certain properties appropriate to the moment, to the neighbor, to the need encountered. Mercy is prudential love, and the skill required to identify what circumscription is required is a skill called pastoral theology. In fact, this seems built into our understanding of charity. On the one hand, even those who have not studied scholastic terminology know that *caritas* means love, friendship with God, the third of the theological virtues. On the other hand, the meaning more often carried by the word "charity" is almsgiving, giving to those in need, concrete acts that alleviate suffering and distress. The word "charity" has come to reflect both the liquid and the sediment! *Caritas* is both the virtue that takes hold of us as a second nature (*habitus*), and it is the charitable act done personally. *Caritas* does not just remain a virtue; it becomes an enacted virtue. *Caritas* becomes charity by passing through pastoral theology, like light passing through a prism becomes color. And at the end, we will be judged on whether the two facets of *caritas* connect in us: Does our love bear fruit? So Benedict XVI says love itself will be our judge: "*Caritas* does not stand opposed to the law; it is itself a law court; it alone and in particular is the divine court of law: it discriminates between left and right (Mt 25!). Whoever loves stands 'on the right,' and whoever does not love is turned to the left. Without it, nothing 'good' is good."[9]

For a Christian, this charity is of a special character. It is not human charity, it is graced charity. Whenever we treat our neighbor with mercy, we are doing so as sacraments of love ourselves. It comes from the new *habitus* the person receives in baptismal grace. The *Catechism* says, "Grace is a *participation in the life of God*. It introduces us into the intimacy of Trinitarian life: by Baptism the Christian participates in the grace of Christ, the Head of his Body. As an 'adopted son' he can henceforth call God 'Father,' in union with the only Son. He receives the life of the Spirit who breathes charity into him and who forms the Church."[10] At the bottom of the baptismal barrel the sinner can find a substantially new life, if he will dive for it. At these depths, the power of the sacramental water corrodes the shackles of original sin that bind us in mortality and selfishness, and regenerates us to new life. Jesus is the mercy of the Father, a hypostasized love who walks among us, and in baptism we are given his love and life and pastoral charity as our new *habitus*. It's not just that we hypostasize our love; the point is that God has hypostasized himself: the Son, eternally begotten of him, became mercy in the flesh. The Church is God's love hypostasizing. Once our soul has been healed of sin, then sanctified and deified, this new nature disposes us to certain modes of activity. Theodore went so far as to say that Christ and his painted icon have the same hypostasis; I will follow his lead and say that Christ and his living icons, the Christians, have the same hypostasis. We form one mystical person with Christ.[11]

Pastoral theology treats the sacraments on this personal level, not on their metaphysical level. Pastoral theology understands the hypostatic quality each sacrament owns. Marriage is personalized love, because a man does not love all women, but this one woman; penance is personalized confession, because a person is not admitting general sinfulness, but is asked to name particular sins; anointing of the sick is personal in application, because although we are on a constant slope toward death, this sacrament anoints at the particular moment when we begin to be in danger of it. All the sacraments are given personally and received personally, but I would like to focus on four of them. Three give a character, and the fourth concerns a substantial change. The former will help me make

---

[9] Benedict XVI, *Pilgrim Fellowship of Faith: The Church as Communion* (San Francisco: Ignatius Press, 2005), 50.
[10] *CCC*, §1997.
[11] Pope Pius XII, Encyclical Letter *Mystici Corporis* (1943), §67.

a connection between hypostatic mercy and the iconic nature of pastoral theology. This same word, "character," was used both in three sacraments and in iconography.

A *kharax* meant a pointed stick that could inscribe a mark upon wax. Such an etching tool was used to transfer the outline of an image onto a board prepared with gesso by cutting the image into the board's coating. The *kharax* produced an engraved mark, an imprint that was called a *charakter*. Therefore, term "character" was used interchangeably with the term "icon" and "image" to mean the defining quality or face of the one depicted in the icon. We may similarly say that the three sacraments that etch the character of Christ upon us do so because they incise Christ's Cross upon our hearts; they imprint the face of Christ upon our faces, he who is the hypostasized merciful face of the Father. That's going to leave a mark. A *kharax* leaves a character, which the *Catechism* says "remains for ever in the Christian as a positive disposition for grace, a promise and guarantee of divine protection, and as a vocation to divine worship and to the service of the Church."[12] Baptism, Confirmation, and Ordination are pastoral sacraments of ministry, which promise protection in the vocation to worship and service. A Christian is someone who has been "Christoformed" by the third person of the Trinity at the directive of the Father. The Christian character—the face with which a Christian looks upon the world—is Christ's own face, who is the merciful face of his Father. The Church must be merciful in order to be God's image.

Spiritual Warfare

It sounds easy enough; we certainly desire it, if we are people of faith. But hypostasizing our love requires overcoming some hurdles called vices, or passions. Baptism begins an interior battle with the passions, and all the sacraments aid that battle, but that battle (which I have called "liturgical asceticism") will occupy our entire life. Passions distort our vision. First, they distort the perception we have of God. Like heat waves rising from desert sand will distort our vision of a distant object, so the rising waves of passion will obscure our vision of the Father's face. We fail to read God's merciful face, and instead read resentment and judgment and hostility in it. This spiritual darkening causes us to miss the merciful glances the Father constantly directs our way. And second, these passions also distort

---

[12] *CCC*, §1121.

the perception we have of our neighbor. We cannot see our neighbor with mercy when we envy him; we cannot see him with love when we are enraged.

Evagrius of Pontus was the first to give a systematic articulation of the primary passions from which the others flow. His thought subsequently entered the West to stimulate its thinking about capital vices and deadly sins, but let us use his list of eight for our brief consideration: "First is [the passion] of gluttony, then impurity, avarice, sadness, anger, acedia, vainglory, and last of all, pride."[13] I want to ask, Which of these passions cripple mercy? The answer is: All of them! That is the worst thing about the passions. All of them cause the twin effect of refusing to receive mercy from God and refusing to give mercy to our neighbor.

- Evagrius says *gluttony* is not so much overeating as it is lack of trust in providence. This temptation pushes concern for oneself to the forefront, so we do not fully trust God's mercy to meet our needs. And our neighbor angers us by preventing us from attaining something on which we have set our appetites. Nervous acquisitiveness prevents us from merciful sharing with our neighbor. We are always building bigger barns so that we can lay up good things for many years, and can eat, drink, and be merry (Luke 12:19), not knowing that this very night our life may be demanded of us.
- *Impurity* is the failure to observe moderation in soul, and is an impediment to chastity. Impurity turns us in upon ourselves, stokes our lust, and fuels our self-pleasure, and this adulterates our natural love. Impurity is countered by chastity, which is why St. John Paul II called chastity "a spiritual energy capable of defending love from the perils of selfishness."[14] Chastity makes for purity, which is why Paul Evdokimov connects it to the sacrament of marriage. "Chastity signifies that one belongs totally to Christ, undividedly. For monks it is an engagement of the soul in unmediated relationship, and for the spouses, engagement through the *hypostasis* of matrimony."[15] Blessed are the pure in

---

[13] Evagrius, *The Praktikos and Chapters on Prayer*, trans. John Bamberger (Collegeville, MN: Cistercian Publications, 1981), no. 6.

[14] Pope John Paul II, Apostolic Exhortation Following the Synod of 1980 *Familiaris Consortio* (1981), §33.

[15] Paul Evdokimov, *The Sacrament of Love* (Crestwood, NY: St. Vladimir's Seminary Press, 1985), 67, italics added.

heart, for they shall see God's eros; also blessed are those who possess such a heart, for they shall be able to give pure love.

- *Avarice* is an irregular love of money or rank or knowledge. It desires something more than befits its value. The avaricious man will always feel a lack, an insatiability, no matter how many gifts he receives from God. Therefore the avaricious man never thinks he has enough in order to practice almsgiving. If we cannot practice mercy out of our ten talents, having a thousand talents will not make it any easier. John Climacus writes, "Avarice is said to be the root of all evil, and so it is, because it causes hatred, theft, envy, separations, hostility, stormy blasts, [and] remembrance of past wrongs."[16] Avarice sterilizes the soil, and no mercy will ever grow there.

- *Sadness or dejection* is described by Evagrius as regret for having started upon the spiritual path. For the monk, this may mean cherishing memories of his former life; for the secular Christian, this means doing our piety with regret and reticence. Then we act like a slave instead of a son. Modern psychology might call it a passive aggressive behavior: I will obey God, but you will find me grumbling as I do so. Only if we are freed from this passion can we serve the Lord with gladness (Ps 100:2), and, having put our hand to the plow, not look back with regret (Luke 9:62). If a person were conscious of the amount of mercy God had shown him, he would not be downcast. When he fasted, he would not look gloomy like the hypocrites; when he prayed, he would not be like the hypocrites who pray on the street corner; when he gave alms, he would not blow a trumpet before him, as the hypocrites do (Matt 6). It is hypocritical to be sad or dejected at the thought of giving piety and mercy.

- *Anger* is the fiercest passion of all, and it affects our relationship with both our God and our neighbor. First, before God, this passion sulks and refuses to accept mercy, as did the elder brother when he thought his father was stealing from him to make a feast for his prodigal brother. Second, before our neighbor, this passion sulks and refuses to give mercy, as did the elder brother when he thought his younger brother had trespassed against him in some way. The prodigal's sin was against his father, yet the elder brother nursed his own grudge. Any anger—be it indignation, or wrath, or

---

[16] John Climacus, *The Ladder of Divine Ascent*, trans. Colm Luibheid and Norman Russell (Mahwah, NJ: Paulist Press, 1982), 190.

vengeance—neutralizes mercy because, Evagrius says, this boiling and stirring up of wrath constantly irritates the soul. It is a desire to get vengeance and never to have pity. Pity, which is one of the first daughters of mercy, only tastes bitter in the angry mouth.

- Evagrius calls a sixth passion *acedia*, which is perhaps best translated as despondency. We might also translate it as sloth, but something more than laziness is meant. *Acedia* means a lethargy in one's spiritual duties. Mercy will not rise up from such a state of torpor; listlessness does not put mercy into action. The man who suffers *acedia* will find arduous the command to feed and water and welcome and clothe and visit his neighbor. Thomas Aquinas identified *acedia* with the "sorrow of the world" described by Paul in 2 Corinthians 7:10.[17] It is the very opposite of the spiritual joy that accompanies mercy. The person who suffers *acedia* does not show joy on his face. Evagrius's list does not mention the passion of *envy*, but the Western list of vices does so here, and the medieval preacher's manual *Fasciculus Morum* defines envy as "sadness about someone else's happiness and glee about someone else's ruin and adversity."[18] Envy will leave the Pharisee unsure whether he is more angry at Zacchaeus for inviting Jesus or at Jesus for accepting.

- *Vainglory* and *pride* are the seventh and eighth passions in Evagrius's list. The modern world thinks of these as almost synonymous, but Evagrius has a difference in mind. Vainglorious people "desire to make their struggles known publicly, to hunt after the praise of men."[19] It is the desire to boast of one's achievements. When that achievement is salvation, then we are talking about pride. "It induces [the person] to deny that God is his helper and to consider that he himself is the cause of virtuous actions."[20] Together, vainglory and pride lay the foundation for considering oneself a self-made man who neither needs mercy nor will give mercy. The Pharisee spurns the mercy offered by God and locks the gates of his hell from inside his heart. The proud Pharisee boasts that he is not like the rest of humanity—greedy,

---

[17] "For godly grief produces a repentance that leads to salvation and brings no regret, but worldly grief produces death" (2 Cor 7:10). Thomas, *ST*, II-II, q. 35, a. 4.
[18] Siegfried Wenzel, trans., *Fasciculus Morum: A 14th-Century Preacher's Handbook* (University Park, PA: Penn State University Press, 1989), 148.
[19] Evagrius, *The Praktikos and Chapters on Prayer*, 19.
[20] Evagrius, *The Praktikos and Chapters on Prayer*, 20.

dishonest, or like that tax collector who, unbeknownst to the Pharisee, is uttering the first instance of the Jesus Prayer: "God, be merciful to me a sinner" (see Luke 18:13). Believing that he relies on justice, not mercy, the Pharisee does not extend mercy to his own creditors. But eventually the king will call in the man he had forgiven and say, "You wicked servant! I forgave you all that debt because you pleaded with me; and should not you have had mercy on your fellow servant, as I had mercy on you?" (Matt 18:32–33).

This is our sad situation. This is our inheritance after the corruption caused by the devil in Eden. Isaac the Syrian says, "When we wish to give a collective name to the passions, we call them *world*. And when we wish to designate them specifically according to their names, we call them *passions*."[21] The world is the passions collectively, and worldliness is a corrupted heart that has been drained of mercy. The whole purpose of liturgical asceticism is the therapeutic purpose of recreating a heart of mercy. Isaac records the answer given by an elder to the question "What is the merciful heart?":

> It is the heart's burning for the sake of the entire creation, for men, for birds, for animals, for demons, and for every created thing; and by the recollection and sight of them the eyes of a merciful man pour forth abundant tears. From the strong and vehement mercy which grips his heart and from his great compassion, his heart is humbled and he cannot bear to hear or to see any injury or slight sorrow in creation. For this reason he offers up tearful prayer continually even for irrational beasts, for the enemies of the truth, and for those who harm him, that they be protected and receive mercy. And in like manner he even prays for the family of reptiles because of the great compassion that burns without measure in his heart in the likeness of God.[22]

How shall a merciful heart be restored to man and woman? At every Easter Vigil the Church reads aloud the scriptural marking posts leading to the Cross that the catechumen will encounter in his hypostatic plunge to the bottom of the baptismal font. Rising up a new human being, his

---

[21] Isaac the Syrian, Homily 2, in *The Ascetical Homilies of Saint Isaac the Syrian*, trans. Dana Miller (Brookline, MA: Holy Transfiguration Monastery, 1984), 14–15.

[22] Isaac the Syrian, Homily 71, in Miller, *The Ascetical Homilies*, 344–45.

worldly heart of stone will be replaced by a merciful heart of flesh. Then the catechumen goes to the altar to imbibe Christ's blood flowing from his merciful heart, to eat his own body, which he makes present along with his soul and divinity in the Eucharist. This is the fourth sacrament I want to look at.

The change to our person in this sacrament is deep and true, for it unites us with Christ. Nicholas Cabasilas speaks about it this way:

> What a thing it is for Christ's mind to be mingled with ours, our will to be blended with His, our body with His Body and our blood with His Blood! . . . It is clear, then, that Christ infuses Himself into us and mingles Himself with us. He changes and transforms us into Himself, as a small drop of water is changed by being poured into an immense sea of ointment.[23] . . . What, then, is greater than that the Father of the only-begotten Son Himself recognizes in us His members and finds the very form of the Son in our faces?[24]

St. Paul was right when he told the Church in Rome that God had predestined them to be conformed to the image of his Son (Rom 8:29). We are to become an icon of the incarnate icon of God. The unseen kingdom of God is seen first in the incarnate Christ, and then in the baptized Christian who dwells in the faith, hope, and love that are infused from his life-giving Spirit. The result of this inheritance is new eyes. We receive the eye of the Dove in the sacraments and tutor it in liturgy, and pastoral theology trains its eyebeam upon the world, and that involves the whole of Catholic education.

Theology in the University

I was invited to speak about the theological discipline, specifically liturgical and pastoral theology, but I am aware that this workshop occurs within a larger agenda. The letter of invitation said, "The organization of this event will involve all Universities, Research Centres and Advanced Professional Training Schools present in Rome," and it can be "an opportunity to respond to the attention that the whole Church pays to the

---

[23] Nicholas Cabasilas, *The Life in Christ* (Crestwood, NY: St. Vladimir's Seminary Press, 1974), 123.
[24] Cabasilas, *The Life in Christ*, 127.

world of universities." Thus, concurrent with this session are sessions about environment, architecture, bioethics, philosophy, communications, law, economics, social and economic development, management, medicine, psychology, education, natural sciences, social sciences, philology, history, sport, history of Christianity, and technology. What has theology to do with them? Does theology have anything to say to these other branches of human sciences, or does it stand isolated, in some remote sacred sphere lacking contact with the other profane sciences of the university? In closing, I'd like to venture a thought about this, again using the concept of hypostasis, or person.

We are asking about the relationship between *gnosis* and *eleos*, knowledge and mercy, comprehension and compassion, expertise and empathy. A one-sided and superficial understanding might think we have to choose between them, either forsaking mercy in order to increase our stock of knowledge, or forsaking science and technology in order to act more mercifully. But neither Pope Francis nor St. John Paul II seem comfortable with such a conclusion. In the words of the latter, whom the former quotes in his Bull of Indiction:

> The word and the concept of "mercy" seem to cause uneasiness in man, who, thanks to the enormous development of science and technology, never before known in history, has become the master of the earth and has subdued and dominated it. This dominion over the earth, sometimes understood in a one-sided and superficial way, seems to have no room for mercy.[25]

Mercy does not require us to be simpletons, and science does not require us to be merciless. The dominion over the earth made possible by the university sciences does have room for mercy, and I will suggest that pastoral theology can aid the other sciences because it provides a liturgical anthropology under this category of hypostasis.

There are three possible ways to consider human beings when we train our eyes on humanity: we might focus *en masse*, on the individual, or on the person. First, we could regard mankind in general. Many ideologies have done so when they wanted to manipulate the masses, and advances in science and technology, psychology and education, have made possible a political and social engineering of the multitude such as we have not seen before. Second, we could regard individuals. An individual is a part

---

[25] Pope Francis, *Misericordiae Vultus*, §11.

of the whole, a cell in the organ, a splinter off the stick. Individuals are distinguished according to the function they play in the group, or the contribution they make to the colony, and they are only considered as a means to that end. Vladimir Lossky says the individual comes about by splitting and apportioning, by dividing and parceling out, by excluding and contrasting himself with others, which means an individual must compete with other individuals, and is in perpetual conflict with other members. But third, we could regard persons, who are different from individuals in precisely the fact that they do not establish their identity by splitting and dividing and conflicting. Lossky writes, "A person can be fully personal only in so far as he has nothing that he seeks to possess for himself, to the exclusion of others, i.e., when he has a common nature with others."[26]

Where do we find such personhood? The supreme case is God, Lossky says. "The Hypostases are not three parts of a whole, of the one nature, but each includes in Himself the whole divine nature."[27] There is no conflict, no fractioning of the divine essence, no splitting and apportioning. Each Person of the Trinity is fully God, and gives himself in mutual, personal relationship to the other Persons. Where else do we find personhood? In those created beings who are icons of this Triune God: creatures who, as *imago Dei*, are persons in the true theological sense. "A human being is not limited by his individual nature. He is not only a part of the whole, but potentially includes the whole, having in himself the whole of the earthly cosmos, of which he is the hypostasis. Thus each person is an absolutely original and unique aspect of the nature common to all."[28] Here is unity but not uniformity; here is uniqueness but not isolation; here is community but not at the expense of identity. This is our human nature perfected in the Church. By the sacraments of the mystical body of Christ, the Holy Spirit is at work in our person. We con-spire with him—we "breathe together." The Church is a conspiracy of mercy. And the result is that the human person—the human hypostasis—becomes deified. The theological discipline tells all other university sciences what man and woman are destined for, namely, full personhood. Paul Evdokimov summarizes it in this way:

> In every human being conformed to Christ the human person is the place of communion . . . and, by virtue of that communion, becomes a hypostasis. . . . *The hypostasis, it becomes clear, is thus:*

---

[26] Vladimir Lossky, *In the Image and Likeness of God* (Crestwood, NY: St. Vladimir's Seminary Press, 1974), 106.

[27] Lossky, *In the Image and Likeness of God*, 106.

[28] Lossky, *In the Image and Likeness of God*, 107.

the person of a deified being. In Christ deified human nature is enhypostasized in a divine person. In the deified human being the created person, by its very deification, is united to the deifying divine energy, which is then enhypostasized in that person. The hypostasis is the personal presence, unique and incomparable, of the theandric life of each Christian.[29]

Masses are grouped, individuals are numbered, but persons are named. The person does not want to exist simply as an individual. The personhood we desire is not an arithmetical concept, and no person should be used as a means to another end. Thus John Zizioulas concludes:

> Outside the communion of love, the person loses its uniqueness and becomes a being like other beings, a thing without absolute "identity" and "name," without a face.... Life for the person means the survival of the uniqueness of its hypostasis, which is affirmed and maintained by love.... The goal of salvation is that personal life which is realized in God should also be realized on the level of human existence. Consequently, salvation is identified with the realization of personhood in man.[30]

If we apply the distinction between masses, individuals, and persons, we can conclude that Catholic university professors, whatever their discipline, should always align their studies with the revealed fact that man and woman were created as persons to grow into a theandric life. None of our disciplines should ever consider the human being as destined for anything less. Mercy must deal with one person at a time. Pastoral liturgy is not different from general liturgy for being vaguer, more ethereal, more practical; it is different for being personal. There may not be room for mercy at the level of the genus that operates as a blind life force; there may not be room for mercy at the level of the individual if we think he can be sacrificed for the greater good of the hive; but persons will always deserve merciful treatment. The merciful eye sees past the generic, past the unit, to the person.

When that knowledge is coupled with mercy, it yields Catholic humanism. Étienne Gilson defined the medieval concept of science by calling it a virtue, because a virtue, he says, is "the power to act." It comes

---

[29] Paul Evdokimov, *Orthodoxy* (New York: New City Press, 2011), 78–79, italics added.
[30] Evdokimov, *Orthodoxy*, 49–50.

from *vir*, which means strength or power. (I imagine the medieval university professor encouraging his modern university counterparts to become virile scientists!) Gilson says science is a power that "puts reason into a state in which it can judge certain objects of knowledge soundly."[31] In other words, educators want to create a power of knowing—*a virtue of knowledge*—in their students so that those growing minds can simultaneously accommodate knowledge about earth and heaven, nature and supernature, the empirical and the spiritual, the historical and the eschatological, efficient causes and the final one, natural law and revealed law, knowledge and wisdom, knowledge and mercy, what human wisdom has discovered about beings and what divine Sophia has revealed about the *logoi* of those beings. One can hardly call such an education narrow-minded. Catholic education has a greater horizon in its curriculum than secular education does, because liturgy has drawn back the veil of the hidden holy place, and liturgical theology has learned the teleological purpose of each person, and pastoral theology has the commitment to coordinate mercy and technology toward this one end.

Conclusion

I should not end what I hope was a respectable paper by closing with a personal anecdote that may make you look at me suspiciously, but I'm going to do so anyway. Not too long after I accepted Fr. Giovanni's invitation, he asked me for an abstract that could go into the general publicity. As you know, writing an abstract is basically writing the paper in advance of actually writing it, because although an author leaves wiggle room for himself, he must determine the vision. And my vision of this talk came to me in a dream. An actual, nighttime dream. I am not prone to them, and do not receive them with the rate of frequency described in Scripture, and would not base my life on them, but you might find this one interesting.

I was in Rome in my dream, which makes sense. I was in a Roman plaza with a large pool in the middle, which is a common sight. But the pool had a life-sized crucifix lying horizontally upon the water. It was a pool in a public square, but also seemed to be a baptismal font. And Jesus was alive on the Cross, lifting his head the way you might lift yours in bed if you wanted to see your toes. And he had freed one arm, like in Murillo's painting of Jesus embracing St. Francis of Assisi. We could psychoanalyze

---

[31] Étienne Gilson, *The Christian Philosophy of St. Thomas Aquinas* (Notre Dame, IN: University of Notre Dame Press, 1956), 262.

the components of my dream, but I think the real meaning of dreams is found in the feelings that a dream image creates, and the feeling I was given was that this Christ was not dead weight on a vertical cross; he was alive and resisting and struggling to get up from a horizontal cross. He was attempting to sit up—a slight adaptation of the Greek word for resurrection: *anastasis*, "to stand up again." Jesus was sitting up again. And the first conscious thought I had as I came out of the dream was "Romans raised up criminals on a cross so they could watch them die, but the Church is where Christ is raised up so the world can watch him live." The Church is where the world can see the first effects of resurrection.

The Mystical Body of Christ, with its liturgical and sacramental and pious disciplines, is like a great contraption of transformation: knowledge turns into love, grace turns into works, self overcomes self to become *caritas*, doctrine yields mysticism, the passions become a merciful heart, hope is hypostasized as faith, and love is hypostasized as mercy. A sacrament is an efficacious sign of life overcoming death, a moment when Christ infuses his life into us. The Church militant is the struggle of the merciful Christ to rise up in us in order to enlist us into his struggle. The Good Shepherd rose up from Hades, where he took on the smell of his sheep, and leads them up a sacramental path whereby they are spiritually trained to follow their Pastor in search of other souls, i.e., to do pastoral theology. Each Christian receives grace for the purpose of becoming personal, hypostatic mercy.

Liturgical Persons

Icon as Image of the Deified Person
Icon as Image of Asceticism and Deification[*]

The subtitle, or alternative title, for this paper could be "Ascetic Aesthetics." Besides affording the pleasure of trying to say it rapidly several times in succession, this phrase affords another advantage: it connects the good with beauty as constituent of truth. That is what the icon images through the coordination of asceticism and deification. Let me first state my thesis as concisely as possible, and then we will unpack the idea more slowly.

The ascetical struggles for the good, which is beautiful, and the aesthetic manifests this truth. Plato said beauty is the splendor of truth (from *splendere*, "to shine"). When truth shines, there is beauty. But Paul Evdokimov cautions that splendor such as this "is inherent in truth which does not exist in the abstract. In its fullness, truth requires a personalization and seeks to be enhypostazied [sic], that is, rooted and grounded in a person."[1] Truth will be fully splendored only when it is manifested at the highest created level, which is personhood. In other words, the highest truth, the fullest beauty, the greatest good must shine forth from a person, an *imago Dei*, because the God of which the person is an image is tri-personal himself. Now, iconography deals with personal images. Icons are images of persons become light by participation in the life of the Trinity. Abstract truth is splendored in the person. But, alas, before we even begin to attain this, we must deal with the fact that our personhood is wounded. Our humanity must be healed first, then find its completion, and then, when its goodness is recovered, beauty will be revealed. Something is called good, says Thomas Aquinas, when "it has the perfection proper to it." For example, sharp vision is the good of the eye. So what is a good person? What is the perfection proper to a human being? It is to be deified: to grow from the image of God into the likeness of God. This growth in goodness, by which a human being attains his end, is an ascetical process.

---

[*] David W. Fagerberg, "Icon as Image of Asceticism and Deification," in *Sacred Imagination*, ed. Charles Gordon, C.S.C., and Margaret Hogan (Portland, OR: University of Portland, 2009), 137–49.

[1] Paul Evdokimov, *The Art of the Icon: A Theology of Beauty* (Redondo Beach: Oakwood Publications, 1990), 24.

Asceticism is the personalization of truth, by the pursuit of goodness, which results in a true person, and iconography is an aesthetic which displays this human splendor. Ascetic aesthetics is the splendor of truth in a deified person.

That is the thesis of this talk in the most condensed language I could manage. We have only to unpack it. To start with, we can be helped with a marvelous illustration that comes from Pavel Florensky's remarkable book *Iconostasis*. Here is the passage in its entirety, with a couple of interruptions by me:

> Consider. If an artist in depicting a magnet were to be satisfied with showing merely the visible aspect (I mean, here, visible and invisible in the common way of speaking), then he would be depicting not a magnet but merely a piece of steel; the real essence of the magnet—that is, its force-field—would go not only unrepresented but also unindicated (though undoubtedly we would simply imagine it into the representation). Furthermore, when we speak of a magnet, we *mean* the force-field along with the piece of steel—but we don't mean the opposite: a piece of steel and, secondarily, a force-field.[2]

In other words, suppose I told you to draw a picture of a bar of steel in the corner of your notebook right now. Those of you who can remember how to make two overlapping rectangles connected by an angle line at the corner points will produce a pretty good-looking three-dimensional bar of steel. "But have you drawn a magnet?" Florensky asks. The essence of a magnet is its force field; that is what distinguishes a magnet from an ordinary bar of steel. But how do we draw magnetism? On the one hand, we cannot leave out drawing the force field, because that is what makes the magnet a magnet. But on the other hand, we would be "fashioning a visual lie" were we to draw the force field.

> Now consider the other approach. If an artist were to use some physics textbook in depicting the force-field as something visually equal to the steel of the magnet, he would thereby be mingling thing and force, visible and invisible, in his representation, and in doing so he would be fashioning a visual lie about the thing as well as misrepresenting the definitive characteristics of the field

---

[2] Pavel Florensky, *Iconostasis* (Crestwood, NY: St. Vladimir's Seminary Press, 1996), 127.

(i.e., its invisibility and its activating power); hence, he would be showing two untruths about the magnet in his depiction, none of which is the magnet.³

I can draw a bar of steel because it is a visible thing, but how can I draw "magnetism"? This is an aesthetical problem. The word comes from *aisthetikos*, meaning "sensitive," from *aisthanesthai*, meaning "to perceive, to feel." Something aesthetic is something perceptible. A melody can exist in my head, but it is not aesthetical music until I am humming it aloud; the form of a sculpture can exist in my head, but it is not aesthetical until I cast that idea in bronze and you can perceive it with both your eyes and your fingertips. The problem here is how an invisible force could be given aesthetic, perceptible expression. To make the force visual would be a falsehood. So Florensky concludes:

> Clearly, in depicting a magnet both the field and the steel must be shown; but their depictions must also be incommensurate, showing that the magnet's two dimensions belong to two different planes. . . . I dare not try to instruct the artist in how actually to represent this unmingled mingling of two planes of existence; but I am entirely certain that figurative art has the capacity to do it.⁴

Since I lack that artistic capacity, I would have to ignore Florensky's caution and go ahead and add some squiggly lines on each end of the steel to indicate an invisible force. But it would have to be clear that the lines drawing the bar and the squiggly lines representing an energy are incommensurate lines; they are different kinds of lines; the straight lines are drawing an object, the squiggly lines are representing something.

Now, Florensky's point in all this is that an iconographer faces the same—if not an even greater—challenge. The artist was faced with the dilemma of drawing neither steel nor magnetism, but magnetized steel. The iconographer is faced with the challenge of drawing neither a person nor divinity, but a deified person. As Leonid Ouspensky says, "The icon indicates holiness in such a way that it need not be inferred by our thought but is visible to our physical eyes."⁵ But how can one draw "holiness" any

---

³ Florensky, *Iconostasis*, 127.
⁴ Florensky, *Iconostasis*, 127.
⁵ Leonid Ouspensky, *Theology of the Icon* (Crestwood, NY: St. Vladimir's Seminary Press, 1992), 1:162. The tenth chapter, "The Meaning and Content of the Icon," is one of the finest things written on the correlation between the theological basis and the artistic canons of iconography.

more than one could draw "magnetism?" The latter is at least a physical force, a created energy, while the former is a supernatural energy, an uncreated light. This brings Florensky to conclude that we seek

> the representation of the invisible dimension of the visible, the invisible understood now in the highest and ultimate meaning of the word as the divine energy that penetrates into the visible so that we can see it.... Analogically, then, we can say this: the form of the visible is created by these invisible lines and paths of divine light.[6]

The form of something makes it what it is. The icon is what it is because divine light has made it so. An icon is neither the natural image of a person nor an abstract representation of glory; an icon is an image of glorified nature. This is what causes the unusual look that an icon has: the iconographer is dipping the bristles of his brush in divine light, not in paint, in order to write the face of a person who has been illuminated by the light of Mt. Tabor, not by the light of the sun.

Hypostasis is the Greek word for person, and the totality of Christian doctrine is summarized in two statements about persons. First, the doctrine of the Trinity states that God is one nature and three persons—one *ousia*, three *hypostases*. Second, the doctrine of the Incarnation states that Jesus is one person and two natures—he is a *hypostatic* union, a union at the level of person. The two natures, says the Council of Chalcedon, remain without confusion, without separation, without change, and without division, and the two natures are united at the level of the hypostatic, the person. The entire battle with the iconoclasts was a matter of getting this straight (which is why the restoration of icons is called "the triumph of Orthodoxy" to this day).

The iconoclasts thought that icons were being used idolatrously, and thought so for one of several reasons. If the icon represented the divine nature alone, it was in violation of the biblical prohibition of idolatry. If the icon represented both the human and divine natures of Christ, it was because the natures were confused, as the Monophysites did when they said the divine nature absorbed or supplanted the human Jesus. If the icon represented only the human Christ, then the two natures were separated, as the Nestorians did when they would call Mary the mother of Jesus but not the mother of God. What was at stake in the controversy with the

---

[6] Florensky, *Iconostasis*, 128.

iconoclasts was the correct understanding of the Incarnation, on which depends the correct understanding of our salvation. Did God become truly man, or not? Was Jesus truly God, or not? The question about what can be written in an icon pressed for a clarification about nature and person.

Ouspensky very helpfully points out that the two sides never could reach agreement because they started with different premises. The iconoclasts understood an image to be of the *same nature* as the thing it represents. They thought the image should be the same as its prototype, and therefore sought to overcome any essential difference between them. By this definition, the only proper icon of Christ is the Eucharist. To the complete contrary, the Orthodox iconodules started from the assumption that the icon is different from the prototype. The iconoclasts thought the Eucharist is an icon because the transubstantiated bread is Christ; the Orthodox thought the Eucharist is *not* an icon because it is truly and substantially Christ, and not an image. If an icon is different from its prototype, then an icon is the painted image of the person of Christ who exists in two natures. "This is why the Orthodox and the iconoclasts could come to no mutual agreement; they spoke different languages and all the arguments of the iconoclasts missed the mark."[7]

Two theologians arose to address the errors of the iconoclasts. First, Theodore the Studite gave a reply to the charge that iconography is idolatry. He totally agrees that the Bible forbids images of God, the ineffable and invisible One, but says things have changed after the Incarnation. Theodore writes:

> Insofar as Christ proceeded from a Father who could not be represented, Christ, not being representable, cannot have an image made by art. In fact, what image could correspond to the Divinity, the representation of which is absolutely forbidden in divinely-inspired Scripture? But from the moment when Christ was born of a representable Mother, he clearly has a representation which corresponds with the image of his Mother. And if He had no image made by art, that would mean that He was not born of a representable Mother, that He was born only of the Father; but this contradicts His whole economy.[8]

---

[7] Ouspensky, *Theology of the Icon*, 32.
[8] Theodore the Studite, Refutation 3, ch. 2, sec. 3. This translation is from Leonid Ouspensky's article "The Meaning and Language of Icons," in Leonid and Ouspensky and Vladimir Lossky, *The Meaning of Icons*, trans. G. E. H. Palmer and E. Kadloubovsky (New York: St. Vladimir's Seminary Press, 1983), 31.

The uncircumscribable God became circumscribable. Iconography was not possible until after Christmas:

> For He who is uncontainable was contained in the Virgin's womb; He who is measureless became three cubits tall; He who has no quality was formed in a certain quality; He who has no position stood, sat, and lay down; He who is timeless became twelve years old by increasing in age; He who is formless appeared in the form of a man; He who is bodiless, when he had assumed a body, said to His disciples, "Take, eat, this is my body." Therefore, the same one is circumscribed and uncircumscribable, the latter in his Divinity and the former in his humanity—even if the impious iconoclasts do not like it.[9]

Iconography is the profession of a true incarnation. And in the Incarnation the Son of God became a human being, while losing nothing of his divinity. "When anyone is portrayed, it is not the nature but the hypostasis which is portrayed. For how could a nature be portrayed unless it were contemplated in a hypostasis?"[10]

The second theologian to weigh in was John of Damascus, to whom it fell to give a more adequate definition of image. He says simply, "An image is a likeness of the original with a certain difference, for it is not an exact reproduction of the original."[11] An image is neither an exact reproduction (it is not a clone or a photocopy), nor is it an abstract representation such that no likeness between the image and prototype adheres. Rather, an image is a likeness . . . but with a difference.

To make his point, John points to a series of six examples of images. The first is most surprising, so we will go in reverse order, and begin with the last. "The sixth kind of image is made for a remembrance of past events" either for honor or shame, and "these images are of two kinds: either they are words written in books . . . or else they are material images."[12] The words in Scripture which tell the story of Aaron's rod that blossomed are a verbal remembrance of a past event, and the rod itself inside the ark of the covenant is an object remembering the same events. (This is a concession to the human mind, which perceives immaterial things clothed in analogical material form, so it would be an interesting thought

---

[9] Theodore the Studite, *On the Holy Icons* (New York: St. Vladimir's Seminary Press, 1981), 82.
[10] Theodore the Studite, *On the Holy Icons*, 90.
[11] John of Damascus, *On the Divine Images* (New York: St. Vladimir's Seminary Press, 1980), 73.
[12] John of Damascus, *On the Divine Images*, 77–78.

experiment to consider analogical theology as an iconic activity.) The idea of icon in Scripture is also behind the fifth and fourth kinds of image that John mentions. "The fifth kind of image is said to prefigure what is yet to happen, such as the burning bush or the fleece wet with dew, which are foreshadowings of the Virgin Theotokos."[13] Biblical typology that examines the similitude between the Old and New Testaments is iconology in action. And, "The fourth kind of image consists of the shadows and forms and types of invisible and bodiless things which are described by the Scriptures in physical terms. These give us a faint apprehension of God and the angels where otherwise we would have none."[14] (The relationship between testaments is iconic, so it would be an interesting thought experiment to read Scripture iconically, instead of didactically or inspirationally or historically.)

The next kind of image John mentions is known in the West by a Latin phrase: *imago Dei*. "The third kind of image is made by God as an imitation of Himself: namely, man. How can what is created share the nature of Him who is uncreated, except by imitation?"[15] Recall that an image is a likeness of the original but with a difference. A person has a created human nature, not an uncreated divine nature, yet a person is an image of God by imitation. Then, the second kind of image gets us into the very mind of God. An artist has an image of the statue in his head before he goes to the marble. In a similar way, "The second kind of image is God's foreknowledge of things which have yet to happen, His changeless purpose from before all ages."[16] God is immutable, and his counsel has been determined from all eternity. He carries out his plans at the time preordained by him, and we can call the figures of what he is going to do in the future, as well as the distinct determination of each of us, images. (It would be an interesting thought experiment to think of theological anthropology in iconic terms, and to iconically think about providence, predestination, and the ordinances of God.)

But the fullest image—the likeness with the least difference from the original—concerns the hypostatic persons of the Trinity. It is different from the other, instituted images, because this is a natural image:

> There are different kinds of images. First there is the natural image. In every case it is necessary for a natural image to come

---

[13] John of Damascus, *On the Divine Images*, 77.
[14] John of Damascus, *On the Divine Images*, 76.
[15] John of Damascus, *On the Divine Images*, 76.
[16] John of Damascus, *On the Divine Images*, 74.

first, and only later those images which are made by words or artistic representation. First we have a human being; only then can we have words or pictures. The Son of the Father is the first natural and precisely similar image of the invisible God, for He reveals the Father in His own person. "No one has ever seen God" (Jn 1.18), and again, "... not that any one has seen the Father" (Jn 6.46). The apostle says that the Son is the image of the Father: "He is the image of the invisible God" (Col 1.15). . . . When Philip says to Him, "Lord, show us the Father and it is enough for us," Jesus said to him, "Have I been so long a time with you, and you have not known Me? Philip, he who sees Me sees also the Father" (Jn 14.8–9). The Son is the natural image of the Father, precisely similar to the Father in every way, except that He is begotten by the Father, who is not begotten. For the Father begets, but Himself is unbegotten, while the Son is begotten, and is not the Father, and the Holy Spirit the image of the Son for no one can say "Jesus is Lord," except by the Holy Spirit (I Cor 12.3). Through the Holy Spirit we know Christ, who is God and the Son of God, and in the Son we see the Father. The Word is the messenger who makes the divine nature perceptible to us, and the Spirit is the interpreter of the Word.[17]

The Son is the image of God the Father, and we can be made into images of the image of God. Iconography is not based upon an artistic theory of representing the transcendent, it is based on a soteriological therapy whereby we become Christoform. When the saint is conformed to the image of the Son of God, it is something more than the third kind of image (the created *imago Dei*). We do have a human, created, religious relationship to God, true; but now we are to receive the Son's own filial relationship to the Father. This is *theosis*, or deification. A block of marble is carved by the artist according to the image the artist has in his mind; that is one kind of image, John of Damascus said, and God had that image in his eternal mind when he created us. But what if the statue were to come alive? What if the created *imago Dei* were now to come alive in full likeness of God? Asceticism is that growth from image into likeness.

The fathers saw this economy slowly unfold across the history of humanity, as well as across individual lives, as a progression from slave to servant to son. Humankind was once obedient in the way a slave is, then

---

[17] John of Damascus, *On the Divine Images*, 74–75.

dutiful the way a servant is, but now we are invited to the relationship with the Father that the Son has with the Father. It is a movement from the pagan light of conscience, through Mosaic revealed law, to John 15:15: "No longer do I call you servants, for the servant does not know what his master is doing; but I have called you friends, for all that I have heard from my Father I have made known to you," and Romans 8:15–17: "For you did not receive the spirit of slavery to fall back into fear, but you have received the spirit of sonship. When we cry, 'Abba! Father!' it is the Spirit himself bearing witness with our spirit that we are children of God, and if children, then heirs, heirs of God and fellow heirs with Christ." This is not the perfection of a natural human capacity, it is a supernatural gift of grace accomplished through the mediation of Christ, in whose hypostatic union God and mankind are unified. The agent who communicates this to us is the Holy Spirit, which is why the Christian life is called "spiritual." Both the Son's Incarnation and humanity's deification are accomplished by the Holy Spirit, as the Nicene Creed professes: the Son was "incarnate by the Holy Spirit" and the Spirit is the "Lord and Giver of Life." This is not religion, it is liturgy.

Now, asceticism is nothing else but the hand of God writing the Son's countenance on our face by the Holy Spirit, so I have taken to calling this process *liturgical asceticism.* "If liturgy means sharing the life of Christ (washed in his Resurrection, chrismated with his anointing, eating his body), and if *askesis* means discipline (in the sense of forming), then liturgical asceticism is the discipline required to become an icon of Christ. His image is made visible in our faces."[18] Asceticism is cooperation with grace's intent for each person. We commonly associate the word "asceticism" with struggle, and there is struggle involved, true, but it is a struggle with sin in order to attain life, and more life. Asceticism is a struggle to dismantle whatever would hamper the Holy Spirit in us, who is life. Asceticism should not be primarily associated with discomfort but with growth, in the same way that athletic exercise is not primarily about pain but about strengthening. Indeed, that is the root of the word itself. It comes from *askein*, which means "work," in the sense of exercise and practice, and *askesis* came to mean "training," aptly illustrated by the sort

---

[18] David W. Fagerberg, *Theologia Prima: What Is Liturgical Theology?* (Chicago: Hillenbrand Books, 2004), 233–34.

of discipline that an athlete undergoes to prepare for a competition. Hence the monks in the desert were called "spiritual athletes."

In his *Conferences*, Cassian records a conversation with Abba Moses, who patiently explains that "all arts and sciences have some immediate goal or destination (*scopos*); and also an ultimate aim, a *telos*."[19] The farmer's immediate goal is to dig out the weeds, but it is toward the *telos* of having fertile crops and living well; merchants purchase stock and risk storms at sea in the hope of profit; the soldier withstands hardships of training, but with the ultimate end of winning glory. So it also is with asceticism, Abba Moses explains:

> The ultimate goal of our way of life is, as I said, the kingdom of God, or kingdom of heaven. The immediate aim is purity of heart. For without purity of heart none can enter into that kingdom. We should fix our gaze on this target, and walk towards it in as straight a line as possible.[20]

Paul uses the very term in Philippians 3:

> In Greek the words for "press forward to the mark" are *kata scopon dioko*. . . . It is as if [Paul] said: "With this aim, whereby I forget what is behind—the sins of the old man—I strive to attain to the prize of heaven." . . . Then whatever can guide us towards purity of heart is to be followed with all our power: whatever draws us away from it is to be avoided as hurtful and worse. It is for this end—to keep our hearts continually pure—that we do and endure everything.[21]

Asceticism is pressing forward to this mark. Every baptized Christian is placed under this ascetical discipline—it is part of their discipleship—but some Christians live that asceticism in an intensified way (just as all persons should exercise for health but the athlete exercises in an intensified way). My point is that asceticism is not a masochistic term, it is a term for the negative cost of our positive sanctification.

Why is there a cost at all? Because the vices hinder the spiritual life. A person is unresponsive to the Holy Spirit's movement if the vices have

---

[19] Cassian, *The First Conference of Abba Moses*, in *Western Asceticism*, ed. Owen Chadwick (Philadelphia: Westminster Press, 1958), 195.

[20] Cassian, *The First Conference of Abba Moses*, 197.

[21] Cassian, *The First Conference of Abba Moses*, 197.

deadened that person, as a dead body is unresponsive to the movement of a soul. The vices obstruct spiritual life by misdirecting a person's faculties. These faculties were understood in the ancient world to be three in number. A human being is able to think—this is the intellective faculty; a human being can be moved to action by having his ire stirred up—this is the irascible faculty; and a person has appetites that generate desire—this is the concupiscible faculty. These faculties were created good, as all creation is good, but they are capable of corruption if they break out of the order that comes from God. When these faculties are directed to incorrect ends, or operate with improper measure, or are bent (as C. S. Lewis calls our fallen state), then they do not operate in a healthy manner, and the Eastern Christian tradition called them "passions." Evagrius of Pontus summed up the wisdom of the desert by identifying eight evil passions and organizing them around the three faculties. The concupiscible passions are gluttony, lust, and avarice; the irascible passions are dejection, anger, and despondency; and the intellective vices are vainglory and pride. Like a cough is a symptom of tuberculosis, these passions are each a symptom of sinful estrangement from God. St. Isaac the Syrian says that when we say "the world," we simply mean the passions in total. "When we wish to give a collective name to the passions, we call them *world*. And when we wish to designate them specifically according to their names, we call them *passions*."[22] Asceticism is the name of the struggle that Scripture talks about as overcoming the world—not in its good sense of cosmos but its fallen sense of rebellion. The struggle is made possible by God's grace, but it is conducted conjointly with a human will that wishes to break free of anything that alienates us from God. The Holy Spirit moves with initiating energy, and asceticism is the person's cooperation. Asceticism comes of the Spirit's energy and our synergy.

If one thinks of each of the passions as a poison, then the opposite virtue can be thought of as an antidote. Puffed up vainglory is deflated by humility; anger thrashing about is restrained by still stronger meekness; the swamp of avarice is drained by poverty and compassion for the poor; and so on. I shall not consider each of these pairings—although the Middle Ages found great profit in correlating the vices and virtues—but I would like to give a few examples. The *Sayings of the Desert Fathers* (which include women, like Abbess Syncletica or Abbess Sarah) read like a physician's

---

[22] Isaac the Syrian, Homily 2, in *The Ascetical Homilies of Saint Isaac the Syrian*, trans. Dana Miller (Brookline, MA: Holy Transfiguration Monastery Publications, 1984), 14.

prescription pad about what antidote will cure what passion. For example, avarice is desiring something more than befits its value:

> Abba Macarius, when in Egypt, found a man who had brought a beast to his cell and was stealing his possessions. As though he was a traveler, who did not live there, he went up to the thief and helped him to load the beast, and peaceably led him on his way, saying to himself: "We brought nothing into this world; but the Lord gave: as he willed, so it is done; blessed be the Lord in all things."[23]

Take despondency, as another example. It is described by Evagrius as "the noonday demon" because

> he presses his attack upon the monk about the fourth hour and besieges the soul until the eighth hour. First of all he makes it seem that sun barely moves, if at all, and that the day is fifty hours long.... Then too he instills in the heart of the monk a hatred for the place, hatred for this very life itself, hatred for manual labor.[24]

The cure requires stability, one of the vows of Benedict. As Saint Syncletica admonished:

> If you live in a monastic community, do not wander from place to place; if you do, it will harm you. If a hen stops sitting on the eggs she will hatch no chickens: and the monk or nun who moves from place to place grows cold and dead in faith.[25]

And when a new monk says he cannot find peace as a hermit, or in community, Abba Theodore encourages him with patience:

> "Tell me, how many years have you been a monk?" And he said: "Eight." And the old man said: "Believe me, I have been a monk

---

[23] *Sayings of the Desert Fathers*, in *Western Asceticism*, ed. Owen Chadwick (Philadelphia: Westminster Press, 1958), 177.

[24] Evagrius, *Praktikos* 6, in *The Praktikos and Chapters on Prayer*, trans. John Bamberger (Collegeville, MN: Cistercian Publications, 1981), 18.

[25] *Sayings of the Desert Fathers*, 85.

for seventy years, and I have not been able to get a single day's peace. And do you want to have peace after eight years?"[26]

Take gluttony, as a final example. John Climacus calls it "hypocrisy of the stomach" and recommends that you "control your belly before it controls you":[27]

> An old man said: "One man eats a lot and is still hungry. Another eats a little and has had enough. The man who eats a lot and is still hungry has more merit than the man who eats a little but enough for him."[28]

Most of the stories are about the struggle, because most of the time we are struggling. But sometimes a story is included about the successful controlling of a passion. That is a state called *apatheia*. The passions are called *pathein* and dispassion is *apatheia*. Here is a story presented in simple, charming form by Helen Waddell's translation, which I think describes a state of calm *apatheia* in the face of avarice and vanity:

> There were two old men living together in one cell, and never had there risen even the paltriest contention between them. So the one said to the other, "Let us have one quarrel the way other men do." But the other said, "I do not know how one makes a quarrel." The first said, "Look, I set a tile between us and say, 'That is mine,' and do thou say, 'It is not thine, it is mine.' And thence arises contention and squabble." So they set the tile between them, and the first one said, "That is mine," and the second made reply: "I hope that it is mine." And the first said, "It is not thine: it is mine." To which the second made answer, "If it is thine, take it." After which they could find no way of quarreling.[29]

The Desert Fathers portray the joyful ascetical struggle for purity of heart, understood to mean "to will one thing." And blessed are the pure in heart, for they shall see God. These ascetics went into the desert to perform an

---

[26] *Sayings of the Desert Fathers*, 83.
[27] John Climacus, *The Ladder of Divine Ascent*, trans. Colm Luibheid and Norman Russell (Mahwah, NJ: Paulist Press, The Classics of Western Spirituality, 1982), 165.
[28] *Sayings of the Desert Fathers*, 128.
[29] Helen Waddell, trans., *The Desert Fathers* (Ann Arbor, MI: University of Michigan Press, 1972), 142.

experiment upon the human heart and find out the cost of *apatheia*, and they share their discovery with us.

One ministry of the monk is to be a human sacrament of the eschatological truth that runs through world history, like a current runs through the center of the river, moving all the water forward. The monk is a walking billboard for this eschatological dimension; that is why monasticism is essential to the Church. The monk's drastic resignation from temporal things witnesses to those of us who have obligations in the temporal order so that we will not forget the eternal. John Climacus says, "The poverty of a monk is resignation from care." The resignation that the spiritual athlete makes in the desert is more dramatic, but the secular Christian has more cares to resign from, since he or she has been entrusted with responsibilities from God and must carry them out without being sidetracked from the Kingdom. We are charmed in fairy tales by the idea of a mirror by which we could see into the future: the monk is a mirror of the eschaton, and when we look at the face of a saint in an icon, we are looking into our future.

This involves a lifetime because persons are a *homo viator*: a being-on-the-way. There is an unfinished quality to each person, an infinite potential. By God's design we are incomplete so that we can cooperate with God in our own self-development. The power to do this is called the virtue—coming from "virtu," meaning "power." As we write our lives, we either color our character with the virtues, or smear our character with the vices. We are created with the power to cooperate in our growth into the likeness of God. Patristic theologians expressed this with an interesting metaphor. An artist painting a portrait of the king will usually sketch an outline in charcoal first. When you look at this charcoal silhouette, you will be able to tell it is the king, but the portrait will exhibit a much greater resemblance when the colors are painted in. Gregory of Nyssa describes the painters transferring "human forms to their pictures by the means of certain colors, laying on their copy the proper and corresponding tints, so that the beauty of the original may be accurately transferred to the likeness." Now, a person is said to be created in the image of God insofar as he is a charcoal sketch, but our Maker wants "the portrait to resemble

His own beauty, by the addition of virtues, as it were with colours."[30] Here is how Methodius speaks of it:

> Man had indeed been brought forth "after the image" of God, but he still had not yet achieved such "likeness" itself. In order to complete this task, the Word was sent into the world. First he assumed our human form, a form marred by the scars of many sins, so that we, for whom he took this form, would be enabled on our part to receive his divine form. For it is possible to achieve a perfect likeness of God only if we, like talented and accomplished painters, depict in ourselves those traits that characterized his human existence, and if we preserve them in us uncorrupted, by becoming his disciples, walking the path he has revealed to us. He who was God chose to appear in our human flesh so that we could behold, as we do in a painting, a divine model of life, and thus we were made able to imitate the one who painted this picture.[31]

This "filling in" by the life of the virtues is goodness coming to be. Remember that Thomas defined the good as being when something has the perfection proper to it. A pen is good when it writes, a knife is good when it cuts, a table is good when it is sturdy and holds the weight it is meant to bear. So what is a good person? I submit that the perfection proper to a human is to join in the life of God. Between the Father, the Son, and the Holy Spirit flows an exchange of love that tradition has called perichoresis. It is a composite Greek word: *peri* and *choreia*, which means to dance around. The Holy Trinity is a divine movement in which each person of the Holy Trinity exists in a mutual, loving indwelling with the other two. Deification involves being taken up into the perichoresis of the Trinity and becoming a participant in that personal communion of love. (To write out the prescriptions of the moves would be a *choreia-graphe*: asceticism is the choreography of agape.)

This perichoresis has been extended to invite our participation. This has been my operating definition of liturgy, of late: *Liturgy is the Trinity's perichoresis kenotically extended to invite our synergistic ascent into*

---

[30] Gregory of Nyssa, *On the Making of Man*, 5.1.
[31] Quoted in Christoph Schönborn, *God's Human Face: The Christ-Icon* (San Francisco: Ignatius Press, 1994), 56.

deification. It is the prolongation of the Son's agapic descent to simultaneously enable humanity's Eucharistic ascent.

This is a liturgical anthropology, and its aesthetic depiction is the icon. An icon is liturgical art—not meaning in this case that icons are only found inside a church building, or carried in processions, or painted by pious people. An icon is liturgical art because it is the aesthetic expression of a human being's liturgical end, namely sanctification, holiness, sainthood. There is only one sorrow, and that is not becoming a saint. There is only one good for a human being, and that is being filled with the love of God and joining in the choreography of love. Then we become true persons. Our true humanity is a liturgical posture in which the Son's love of the Father becomes ours, and the Trinity's love for every creature becomes ours as well. Then we look upon the poor not with human sympathy but with divine compassion; we look at our enemies with the same urgent desire for reconciliation that God has when he looks upon us sinners; we look at suffering and feel the same willingness to embrace the cross that Christ felt. That is when a true personhood will shine forth, and then that one will be a beautiful person. His truth, rooted in this good, will splendor in beauty. When Dostoevsky said, "The world will be saved by beauty," he did not mean that humanity will be distracted from its sorrows by pretty things, the way Marx thought religion would distract the masses as an opiate. Dostoevsky meant that the liturgical beauty of a living icon will tell the world the truth about what a good human being is: he is someone who is finished, completed, and has found perfection.

But now we are back to Florensky's problem. How is this ascetical holiness rendered aesthetically visible? C. S. Lewis dealt with a similar question, though not concerning icons, in his essay on "Transposition." It is written as an apologetic reply to critics who say that religion merely arises out of our animal nature: from a projection of our primitive fears, from dreams about the dead, from a Freudian sexual complex, from our animal wonder at the force of life in an ear of corn. The critics say that the mystical sensations religious people claim are the same kind of sensations we have for ordinary feelings. Lewis replies: Of course. "The resources are far more limited, the possible variations of sense far fewer, than those of emotions. The senses compensate for this by using the same sensations to express more than one emotion."[32] The same feeling may express more than one emotion, because feelings are a lower system and emotions are higher system. "Transposition occurs whenever the higher reproduces itself

---

[32] C. S. Lewis, "Transposition," in *The Weight of Glory* (New York: Macmillan, 1980), 63.

in the lower."³³ For example, the same bodily sensation of butterflies in the stomach, or the hair standing up on the neck, might accompany the higher emotion of either joy or fear. There is no one-to-one correspondence. Transposition is when a richer system is represented in a poorer system, and the only way this is possible is by giving each element in the poorer system more than one meaning. It is like transposing a full orchestral score to be played with only ten fingers on only one instrument, the piano. So we see how the skeptic reaches his conclusion, and where he has made his mistake:

> We now see that if the spiritual is richer than the natural . . . then this is exactly what we should expect. And the sceptic's conclusion that the so-called spiritual is really derived from the natural, that it is a mirage or projection or imaginary extension of the natural, is also exactly what we should expect, for, as we have seen, this is the mistake that an observer who knew only the lower medium would be bound to make in every case of Transposition. The brutal man can never by analysis find anything but lust in love; . . . the physiology never can find anything in thought except twitching of the grey matter.³⁴

To make his point Lewis offers an imaginative illustration. Suppose there was a woman thrown into a dungeon who there bears and rears a son. The son grows up seeing nothing but the dungeon, and perhaps a bit of blue sky through the slant of the window. The mother does not give up hope, so she constantly teaches her son about the outer world which he has never seen. She does so by drawing pictures. "With her pencil she attempts to show him what fields, rivers, mountains, cities, and waves on a beach are like." The son listens carefully, and nods at his lessons, until one day he says something that gives his mother pause:

> Finally it dawns on her that he has, all these years, lived under a misconception. "But," she gasps, "You didn't think that the real world was fully of lines drawn in lead pencil?" "What?" says the boy. "No pencil marks there?" And instantly his whole notion of the outer world becomes a blank. . . . He has no idea of that which will exclude and dispense with the lines, that of which the lines

---

³³ Lewis, "Transposition," 63.
³⁴ Lewis, "Transposition," 64.

were merely a transposition.... The child will get the idea that the real world is somehow less visible than his mother's pictures. In reality it lacks lines because it is incomparably more visible.[35]

So also with us, Lewis concludes. "If flesh and blood cannot inherit the Kingdom, that is not because they are too solid, too gross, too distinct, too 'illustrious with being.' They are too flimsy, too transitory, too phantasmal."[36]

The mother's challenge was to use two-dimensional pencil lines to draw a three-dimensional real world. The iconographer's challenge is to use two-dimensional brush strokes to draw an infinitely more real world. How can we make the infinitely more real world perceptible on the board of the icon? What technique is required to transpose the higher spiritual reality into a lower artistic medium? What will make ascetical holiness aesthetically perceptible? The tradition has standardized a canon of aesthetic symbols to operate like the squiggly lines around a magnet. We know that the two types of lines are incommensurate: the straight lines depicting the steel represent a visible object, and the squiggly lines depicting a force represent an invisible force. Artistic conventions enable us to perceive of what cannot be seen, can only be felt. Similarly, the iconographic aesthetic canons enable us to perceive what cannot be seen, can only be felt in the company of a saint. The lines on the icon are also incommensurate to the representational art. Some brush strokes are supposed to depict a real person, but some brush strokes are symbolic of a divine energy in that person. There is a large palette of iconic convention to choose from: color selection, a layering from dark to light, geometric circles and triangles and rectangles, proportionality from nose to head to body, facial features of thin lips and large foreheads, a frontal face, halos, architectural convention of buildings, unusual folds in robes that defy gravity, inverse perspectival vanishing points, gold leaf, light that casts no shadows, and always those penetrating, inviting eyes. It is not my place to speak about these aesthetics, for one who comes after me will be able to give you much better insight.

My purpose has only been to suggest that these canons of iconography are the aesthetics of the divine energies. My purpose has been to say that before the iconographer can write the image of the saint on the board, the Holy Spirit must write the countenance of Christ upon the saint. God is the first iconographer. *Graphe* means "to write," as you know from

---

[35] Lewis, "Transposition," 68–69.
[36] Lewis, "Transposition," 68–69.

"biography." Biographers write down the life (*bios*) of a person. With every moral act we make, or fail to make, we are each of us writing our own lives (an *auto bios graphe*). But God is the first iconographer, and the God who wrote the law upon two tablets of stone with his finger of fire can write a new life upon hearts of stone with the finger of his Holy Spirit. Then the saint becomes, himself, an autograph of God: *auto-graphe*, written with God's own hand. Liturgical asceticism is *theography*: God writing himself upon us. Before the aesthetical must come the ascetical.

Mary
Mary as Liturgical Person[*]

I hope to offer some stammering words about Mary, and I am grateful to do so for a personal reason. It is a small repayment toward a debt I owe to Our Lady. When I want to puzzle my friends as to why I became Catholic, I give them a pop quiz on the liturgical calendar and say, "Because my birthday is August 15 and Jesus still can't refuse his mother anything." The medieval person knew he had refuge to Mary because though he was a sinner, he was *her* sinner (*son pecheor*).[1]

I want to speak about "Mary as liturgical person." The reader will notice that I've used neither a definite nor an indefinite article in this title, for although I do think Mary is *a* liturgical person, and I do think she is *the* archetypal liturgical person, what I want to focus on here is how Mary exemplifies liturgical personhood itself.[2] Mary is the paradigm of Christian liturgical life in the cult of the New Adam. Ask what it means to live as liturgical person, and Mary reveals that. Ask what is Mary's place in the history of salvation, and liturgy reveals that. Seeing how Mary is liturgical person brings her nearer to every Christian who is also in formation as

---

[*] David W. Fagerberg, "Mary as Liturgical Person," *Logos: A Journal of Eastern Christian Studies* 53, nos. 3–4 (2012): 299–315.

[1] See Eileen Power, introduction to Johannes Herolt, *Miracles of the Blessed Virgin Mary* (New York: Harcourt, Brace and Company, 1928), xxvii: "The point is not that the man is a sinner, but that he is *her* sinner, 'son pecheor,' as Gautier de Coincy puts it." And also Henry Adams, *Mont-Saint-Michel and Chartres* (New York: G. P. Putnam's Sons, 1980), 144:
"*Mais cele ou sort tote pities*
Tote douceurs tote amisties
Et qui les siens onques n'oublie
SON PECHEOR n'oblia mie.
'HER sinner!' Mary would not have been a true queen unless she had protected her own."

[2] Canon 96 of the Code of Canon Law says, "By baptism one is incorporated into the Church of Christ and is constituted a person in it with duties and rights." The commentary explains that this canon is using a classic definition of person, namely, "a subject of rights and duties." A liturgical person is someone with duties and rights in the cult of the New Adam. *The Code of Canon Law: A Text and Commentary*, ed. James A. Coriden, Thomas J. Green, and Donald E. Heintschell (Mahwah, NJ: Paulist Press, 1985), 70.

liturgical person. She is for us the model of liturgical life, and as such, she is the icon of humanity in its fullness.

Jean Corbon writes, "The Virgin Mary is the Church as it dawns in a single person."[3] In so saying, he must be using a thicker grammar about the Church than is used in ordinary conversation. He must mean something like what St. Clement of Rome meant when he said, "If we do the will of God our Father, we shall be of the first Church, which is spiritual, which was created before the sun and moon."[4] This is the protological and eschatological Church, which is both the reason for creation's start, as well as the transfiguring power to bring creation to its proper end. This Church is something like a dynamism within history, as Olivier Clément suggests when he writes, "The Church is nothing other than the world in the course of transfiguration."[5] This Church is salvation-in-motion, as Charles Journet suggests when he writes, "The Church is the world being reconciled to God,"[6] and pointedly adds, "Thus the frontier of the Church passes through each one of those who call themselves her members, enclosing within her bounds all that is pure and holy, leaving outside all that is sin and stain."[7] This Church is a divine artifact, as Pope Benedict XVI suggests when he writes, "The Church is not a manufactured item; she is, rather, the living seed of God that must be allowed to grow and ripen. This is why the Church needs the Marian mystery; this is why the Church herself is a Marian mystery."[8] This living seed has been at work underneath the whole cosmic history until it broke surface in the Incarnation to become visible, as the General Introduction to *Collection of Masses of the Blessed Virgin Mary* says:

> Through its sacred signs the liturgy celebrates the work of salvation that God the Father accomplished through Christ in the Holy Spirit. This salvation is a work that God the Father has carried on through the ages. This is the salvation announced by the patriarchs and prophets.... This is the salvation that was fully

---

[3] Jean Corbon, *The Wellspring of Worship* (Mahwah, NJ: Paulist Press, 1988), 173.
[4] 2 Clement 14:1. Something that is created, not Uncreated, but which existed before matter (i.e., sun and moon) is a motivating component of Sophiology. Consider Sergius Bulgakov, *The Bride of the Lamb*, trans. Boris Jakim (Grand Rapids, MI: Eerdman's, 2002).
[5] Olivier Clément, *The Roots of Christian Mysticism* (New York: New City Press, 1995), 95.
[6] Charles Journet, *The Theology of the Church* (San Francisco: Ignatius Press, 2004), 38.
[7] Charles Journet, *The Church of the Word Incarnate* (New York: Sheed and Ward, 1955), xxvii.
[8] Joseph Cardinal Ratzinger, "'My Word Shall Not Return to Me Empty!'" in Hans Urs von Balthasar and Joseph Cardinal Ratzinger, *Mary: The Church at the Source* (Ignatius: San Francisco, 1997), 16–17.

revealed in Christ Jesus.... This is the salvation that comes to pass in the "age of the Church."... This is the salvation that will reach its consummation in Christ's glorious Second Coming.[9]

This is the Church that Ambrose saw in his neophytes at his mystagogy. In the Song of Songs, he hears Christ speaking to a newly baptized. "Christ, beholding His Church,... seeing, that is, a soul pure and washed in the laver of regeneration, says: 'Behold, you are fair, My love, behold you are fair, your eyes are like a dove's.'"[10] The baptized are beautiful for having the Holy Spirit now living in them, looking out from their eyes, so to speak; they are beautiful for being transparent to the light of the indwelling Spirit and showing forth the beauty of what the Church really is, as it is intended by God.[11] Therefore, Ambrose concludes, "The Church is beautiful in them."[12] He reverses our ordinary grammar. He doesn't speak about the Church we go into, but the Church that comes into us; he doesn't speak about us being in the Church, but the Church being in us.

This Church-in-motion is the liturgy. Liturgy is the life of Christ soaking into us ever since our dip in the baptismal font to moisten these dry mortal bones for resurrection. Liturgy is a Eucharistic transfusion of Christ's blood into our veins, like an intravenous drip, so that his life animates our hands for his work. Christ has brought liturgy to earth. So *Mediator Dei*'s two-part definition of liturgy begins with the activity of Christ, and then includes us.

> The sacred liturgy is, consequently, the public worship which our Redeemer as Head of the Church renders to the Father, as well as the worship which the community of the faithful renders to its Founder, and through Him to the heavenly Father. It is, in short, the worship rendered by the Mystical Body of Christ in the entirety of its Head and members.[13]

Liturgy is the activity of the Mystical Body, and since Christ is head of that Body, in some way the Incarnation is continued. Emile Mersch puts it, "The hypostatic union does not affect our Lord alone, but is somehow

---

[9] General Introduction to *Collection of Masses of the Blessed Virgin Mary* (New York: Catholic Book Publishing Co., 1988), no. 4.
[10] Ambrose, *On the Mysteries*, 7:37.
[11] Gratitude to my colleague Pamela Jackson for phrasing it this way in a conversation.
[12] Ambrose, *On the Mysteries*, 7:39.
[13] Pope Pius XII, Encyclical Letter on the Sacred Liturgy *Mediator Dei* (1947), §20.

prolonged in us, the members; we are the prolongation of the head..... The same hypostatic union causes to flow into our human nature the life that it imparts to the humanity of Christ."[14] Liturgy, as I am speaking of it here, is no more a human ritual construct than the Church is a human organizational construct. They are both divine artifacts. Liturgy is the perichoresis of the holy Trinity descended far enough toward us in kenosis so as to invite our ascension into deification. Liturgy is the life of Christ within us pressing to get out—*ex-pressing* itself as Church. And about this, von Balthasar notices, "In Mary, the Church is embodied even before being organized in Peter."[15]

To summarize: whereas Mary is the Church as it dawns in a single person, and whereas liturgical activity is the life of the Church in motion, therefore understanding Mary as liturgical person will reveal not only her identity, but ours, too, for she is the archetype of what we are called to become. So reminds John Paul II in *Redemptoris Mater*: "Strengthened by the presence of Christ (cf. Mt. 28:20), the Church journeys through time towards the consummation of the ages and goes to meet the Lord who comes. But on this journey—and I wish to make this point straightaway—she proceeds along the path already trodden by the Virgin Mary."[16] This is Mary's eschatological quality, if we understand eschatology as the new age already dawned but whose fullness we still await. "She is the Queen who is the sign of the Church in its future glory, because what has been accomplished in her as a member surpassing all others will be accomplished in all the members of Christ's Mystical Body."[17]

This leaves me with the dilemma of deciding which of Mary's liturgical traits I shall focus upon. Mary is *doxological* as she offers glory to God with her whole being; she is *Eucharistic* as she embodies Israel's praise and creation's thanksgiving; she is *spiritual* for having enjoyed a personal Pentecost in anticipation of the corporate Pentecost on the disciples (in both cases, the Spirit came down where Mary was); she is *theological* insofar as she enjoys a mystical union with God; she is *ascetical* insofar as her will was conformed to Christ's; she is entrusted with *intercessory*

---

[14] Emile Mersch, *The Whole Christ: The Historical Development of the Doctrine of the Mystical Body in Scripture and Tradition*, trans. John R. Kelly (Milwaukee, WI: The Bruce Publishing Co., 1938), 283 and 356.

[15] Hans Urs von Balthasar, "The Marian Mold of the Church," in Hans Urs von Balthasar and Joseph Ratzinger, *Mary: The Church at the Source* (San Francisco: Ignatius, 2005), 140.

[16] Pope John Paul II, Encyclical Letter *Redemptoris Mater* (1987), §2.

[17] Explanatory note before Mass of "The Blessed Virgin Mary, Queen of all Creation," in *Collection of Masses of the Blessed Virgin Mary*, 43.

prayer; she is an *eschatological* person for being the last of the former age and the first of the final age; and so forth. All of these are facets of the liturgical person, and they are facets that Mary embodies. But they are too many to deal with here.

Paul VI offers me some aid in *Marialis Cultus* by shortening and organizing my list when he examines "the relationship between Mary and the liturgy," offering Mary "as a model of the spiritual attitude with which the Church celebrates and lives the divine mysteries."[18] He identifies four spiritual attitudes which belong to both Mary and the Church. First, Mary is the *attentive Virgin*, who receives the word of God with faith; "the Church also acts in this way, especially in the liturgy, when with faith she listens, accepts, proclaims and venerates the word of God."[19] Second, Mary is the *Virgin in prayer*; "the title ... also fits the Church, which day by day presents to the Father the needs of her children."[20] Third, Mary is the *Virgin-Mother*; "the Church prolongs in the sacrament of Baptism the virginal motherhood of Mary."[21] And, fourth, Mary is the *Virgin presenting offerings*—of her son in the Temple, and of her son on the Cross; "this the Church does in union with the saints in heaven and in particular with the Blessed Virgin, whose burning charity and unshakeable faith she imitates."[22]

I am going to make one final reduction and restrict myself here to two liturgical traits in Mary. I do so with the hope that as these two identities are unified in Mary, we can then see their unity in their corresponding liturgical form. Mary is virgin and mother—an apparent contradiction that fascinated the tradition. Somehow, these two opposites, virgin-motherhood, come together by the grace of God in one person. Corresponding to this, I suggest that Mary's liturgical personhood is sacrificial and sacramental. She is a sacrificial person in her virginity and a sacramental person in her motherhood, and together they make up the totality of her liturgical personhood. As virginity and motherhood are united in her, so we should find sacrament and sacrifice united in our liturgy, for liturgy is the trysting point where heaven, bending down, kisses earth, and earth, yearning upward, kisses heaven. Mary stands at that liturgical center point, herself mother and virgin. She is God's way down to man, and man's way up to God. She is the liturgical matrix personified,

---

[18] Pope Paul VI, Apostolic Exhortation *Marialis Cultus* (1974), §16.
[19] Paul VI, *Marialis Cultus*, §17.
[20] Paul VI, *Marialis Cultus*, §18.
[21] Paul VI, *Marialis Cultus*, §19.
[22] Paul VI, *Marialis Cultus*, §20.

because the purpose of liturgy is to unite the created and uncreated. In the words of Vladimir Lossky:

> "To have by grace what God has by nature": that is the supreme vocation of created beings.... This destiny is already reached in the divine person of Christ, the Head of the Church, risen and ascended. If the Mother of God could truly realize, in her human and created person, the sanctity which corresponds to her unique role, then she cannot have failed to attain here below by grace all that her Son had by his divine nature. But, if it be so, then the destiny of the Church and the world has already been reached, not only in the uncreated person of the Son of God but also in the created person of his Mother. That is why St. Gregory Palamas calls the Mother of God "the boundary between the created and the uncreated." Beside the incarnate divine hypostasis there is a deified human hypostasis.[23]

Not all numbers are the same distance apart. The biggest distance between any two numbers is between zero and one, for that is an ontological gap between nothing and being. But the next biggest distance is between one and two, for that means the unique thing is not alone. Christ was unique, but did not wish to be alone. In her witness as a deified human hypostasis, Mary shows the possibility of the Church's existence. "In receiving everything for the first time in faith for our sake, Mary was able to pass everything on to us."[24]

So let us first consider Mary as sacramental person, the new Eve and the mother of renewed life. All the fecund and feminine imagery seems fitting here: she is the Mother of the Lord and the Mother of the Church, *Mater Christi* and *Mater Ecclesia*;[25] she is the new daughter of Zion, the new Ark of the Covenant who bears the Word of God within her and conducts that Word of God to others. Mary is the source of the source of the sacraments. In his sermon on the Nativity of the Theotokos, Gregory Palamas says, "Today a new world and a mysterious paradise have been revealed, in which and from which a New Adam came into being,

---

[23] Vladimir Lossky, "Panagia," in *The Mother of God: A Symposium*, ed. E. L. Mascall (Westminster, MD: Dacre Press, 1959), 34.

[24] Edward Schillebeeckx, *Mary: Mother of the Redemption* (New York: Sheed and Ward, 1964), 97.

[25] This is the point made throughout Hugo Rahner's study *Our Lady and the Church* (Bethesda, MD: Zaccheus Press, 2004).

re-making the Old Adam and renewing the universe."[26] The hypostatic union takes place within the womb of Mary, and with flesh borrowed from her, as Symeon the New Theologian summarizes:

> Just as then, at the creation of our ancestor Eve, God took the rib of Adam and made the woman from it, in the same way now also our Maker and Creator God took flesh from the Mother of God and Ever-Virgin Mary, as a kind of leaven and a certain beginning from the dough of our nature, and united it with His Divinity, which is unattainable and unapproachable—or, to say it better, He united His whole Divine Hypostasis essentially with our nature.... For just as from the rib of Adam He made woman, so from the daughter of Adam, the Ever-Virgin Mother of God, Mary, he borrowed the virginal flesh without seed, and being clothed in it, became man like unto the first-created Adam.[27]

Lumen Gentium observes that Mary cooperated "in the work of the Saviour in giving back supernatural life to souls. Wherefore she is our mother in the order of grace."[28] In the Christian Church, the order of grace is sacramental because all matter is pliable in the hands of God and can be restored to its original symbolic function. All it takes is human petition and divine concession. (This is called *epiclesis*.) Benedict XVI sees a connection between sacrament and Mary's intercession at the wedding of Cana, when she "moves Christ to perform a sign that already anticipates his coming hour—as continues to happen, again and again, in the Church's signs, that is, in her sacraments."[29] Mary's maternal intercessions prod God to hone his sacramental skill. The poet Paul Claudel writes, "That Word which begets you, O Mary, is ever with you in order that you may whisper in the Father's ear the names of all who are capable of being his sons. And if he pretends not to see, your skill insures that his groping fingers will find his lamb."[30] The Church's sacramental presence in the world is a maternal

---

[26] Gregory Palamas, *Mary the Mother of God: Sermons by Saint Gregory Palamas*, ed. Christopher Veniamin (South Canaan, PA: Mount Thabor Publishing, 2005), 2.
[27] Symeon the New Theologian, *The First-Created Man: Seven Homilies* (Platina, CA: St. Herman of Alaska Brotherhood, 1994), 96.
[28] Second Vatican Council, Dogmatic Constitution on the Church *Lumen Gentium* (1964), §61.
[29] Joseph Cardinal Ratzinger, "The Sign of the Woman," in *Mary: The Church at the Source*, 55
[30] Paul Claudel, *I Believe in God: A Meditation on the Apostles' Creed* (Chicago: Holt, Rinehart and Winston, 1963), 91. He further dares, "There are things that Christ himself does not understand unless His mother whispers them in his ear."

tenacity and tenderness, as A.-M. Roguet pictures it: "No matter; the Church is not a great lady, careful above all for her reputation, nor a pedant who will deliver a lecture to a child who has fallen into the well: She is a Mother who cares nothing for what people will say, or for her outward dignity, so long as she saves the children who are in her charge. She does not think it is a breach of the Savior's orders to practice mercy."[31]

This sacramental ministry is served by the ordained ministry that derives from the apostolic succession, true, but Mary is in the midst of the Apostles in both the icon of the Ascension and the icon of the Dormition. Concerning the latter, John of Thessalonica places on her lips these grateful words when the Apostles are miraculously transported to Jerusalem for her death: "Behold, they are gathered together, and I am in the midst of them, like a vine bearing fruit."[32] As Mother of the Church, she is the vine which bears apostolic fruit. The relationship of sacramental grace and the episcopal canals through which it flows has also been worked out by reflecting upon the relationship of Mary with Joseph. Benedict XVI writes:

> For her part, Mary is the living Church. It is upon her that the Holy Spirit descends, thereby making her the new Temple. Joseph, the just man, is appointed to be the steward of the mysteries of God, the paterfamilias and guardian of the sanctuary, which is Mary the bride and the Logos in her. He thus becomes the icon of the bishop, to whom the bride is betrothed; she is not at his disposal but under his protection.[33]

So it is in every birth of faith—every one of them is a work of the Holy Spirit, a virgin birth conceived in the womb of mother Church, and the priest stands by, dumbfounded at the miracle, like Joseph, both looking at something that is not their own handiwork.

This Marian explanation of our sacramental rebirth in baptism is frequently explored. Augustine spoke of the baptismal font as the uterus of mother Church,[34] and in his sermons to the catechumens he enjoins them to remain patient and hopeful: "Look, mother Church is in labor, see, she is groaning in travail to give birth to you, to bring you forth into

---

[31] A.-M. Roguet, *Christ Acts through the Sacraments* (Collegeville, MN: Liturgical Press, 1954), 111.

[32] Brian Daley, trans., *On the Dormition of Mary: Early Patristic Homilies* (Crestwood, NY: St. Vladimir's Seminary Press, 1998), 57.

[33] Joseph Ratzinger, "Et Incarnatus Est de Spiritu Sancto," in *Mary: The Church at the Source*, 88.

[34] Henri de Lubac, *The Motherhood of the Church* (San Francisco: Ignatius Press, 1982), 52.

the light of faith. Do not agitate her maternal womb with your impatience, and thus constrict the passage to your delivery.... [The Lord] too accepted this slow business of coming to birth in time."[35] Olivier Clément quotes a passage from Gregory of Nyssa, when the saint writes, "What came about in bodily form in Mary ... takes place in a similar way in every soul that has been made pure. The Lord does not come in bodily form, for 'we no longer know Christ according to the flesh,' but he dwells in us spiritually and the Father takes up his abode with him, the Gospel tells us. In this way the child Jesus is born in each one of us."[36] Commenting on this, Olivier Clément adds:

> Union with God may also be expressed in terms of inward birth. The soul corresponds to the Blessed Virgin. It recalls the mystery of the incarnation. And the incarnation is spiritually extended to holy souls who are thereby preparing for Christ's return. All the mysteries of the Gospel are not only performed in the liturgy but take possession of us in the spiritual life. The Word is continually being born in the stable of our heart.... To ensure this birth of Christ in us is the true function of liturgical times and seasons, interpreted inwardly by ascesis, prayer and contemplation.[37]

The true end of liturgy is to arrive where Mary did.

Sacramental life is maternal. Fr. Alexander Schmemann somewhere reminds us that the Church is not an institution with sacraments; she is a sacrament with institutions. The Church is structure, but more importantly she is life, and the latter is the reason for the former. Christ did not come that we might have rubrics and have them abundantly; he came that we might have life, and since he, himself, is this life, he abundantly gives us himself in the sacraments. What is the Church? asks Schmemann.

> On the one hand the Church is certainly structure and institution, order and hierarchy, canons and chanceries. Yet this is only the visible structure. What is its content? Is it not also, and primarily, that which is to change and to transfigure life itself? Is it not the anticipation, the "Sacrament" of the kingdom of God? Yes, the Church is structure, but the unique purpose of that structure

---

[35] St. Augustine, Sermon 216:7, 8, in *The Works of Saint Augustine: Sermons*, vol. III/6 (New York: New City Press, 1993), 167–68.

[36] Gregory of Nyssa, *On Virginity*, ch. 2, quoted in Clément, *The Roots of Christian Mysticism*, 251.

[37] Clément, *The Roots of Christian Mysticism*, 251.

> is to be an "epiphany," to manifest and to fulfill the Church as expectation and fulfillment....
>
> It is, of course, in worship that this experience of the Church is given. It is in her *leitourgia* that the Church transcends herself as institution and structure and becomes "that which she is": response, adoration, encounter, presence, glory, and, ultimately, a mystical marriage between God and his new creation. It is precisely here that Mary stands at the center—as the personification, as the very expression, icon, and content of that response, as the very depth of man's "yes" to God in Christ.[38]

With this, Schmemann has led us to our second point, Mary as virgin and the sacrificial nature of the Church. When the Church transcends herself and takes flight with the wings of the dove, then the Church becomes that which she is: she becomes "all eye," as Ezekiel describes the cherubim. The first Church, of which the angels were members, was spiritual; but now she who is more honorable than the cherubim, more glorious beyond compare than the seraphim, has become mother of God in the flesh. The eternal plan for the protological Church to stretch itself forward to the eschatological Church unfolded a new chapter when it was laid forth in a manger for all to see. That Church-made-visible is the visible Church.

This, again, is why the iconographic tradition places Mary in the midst of the Apostles in the other icon we mentioned, the icon of the Ascension:

> There is no "icon" of the Church except the human person that has become totally transparent to the Holy Spirit, to the "joy and peace" of the Kingdom." If Christ is the "icon" of the Father, Mary is the "icon" of the new creation, the new Eve responding to the new Adam, fulfilling the mystery of love.... Thus, being the "icon" of the Church, Mary is the image and the personification of the world. When God looks at his creation, the "face" of the world is feminine, not masculine.[39]

The Theotokos is the icon of the Church. She is the personification of the Church's sacrificial *orans*. She is the personal image of response, adoration,

---

[38] Alexander Schmemann, *Celebration of Faith*, vol 3, *The Virgin Mary* (Crestwood, NY: St. Vladimir's Seminary Press, 1995), 64–65.

[39] Schmemann, *The Virgin Mary*, 65. Chesterton, as usual, puts it succinctly: "Men are men, but Man is a woman" (*Napoleon of Notting Hill*, in *The Collected Works of G. K. Chesterton* [San Francisco: Ignatius Press, 1991], 6:220).

encounter, presence, glory, and ultimately a mystical marriage. Mary is sacrificial person, the purest offering by the human race. God is depicted as one searching, yearning for, cultivating a point at which he could enter human history. This was revealed throughout Israel's history, so Benedict XVI observes that the New Testament images of Mary are grounded in Old Testament acts of redemption through women, and mentions Eve, the mothers in Israel's history, prophetesses and judges, Israel as covenant partner bride, and Sophia.[40] The plan of salvation was a plan for a habitat for divinity. The *Catechism of the Catholic Church* says, "For the first time in the plan of salvation and because his Spirit had prepared her, the Father found the dwelling place where his Son and his Spirit could dwell among men."[41] Nicholas Cabasilas went so far as to say that God created humanity in order to find a mother.[42]

The place where God dwells is a temple, the place of sacrificial encounter. Hence the natural assumption by tradition that the only place Mary, herself a temple for God, could live would be in the temple of Jerusalem. "Where else could be better for God's tent to be pitched?" exclaims Gregory Palamas. "Surely it was absolutely necessary for the actual Tabernacle to be set up in the same place as the figurative one?"[43] The Protoevangelium of James records that at age three Mary was brought by her parents to the temple of the Lord, and "she danced with her feet, and all the house of Israel loved her."[44] The Orthodox vespers liturgy for the feast sings, "Today the Theotokos, the Temple that is to contain God, is being escorted into the temple of the Lord."[45] (This additionally highlights the doctrine of the Assumption. The ark will be translated from the temple in Jerusalem to the temple in the heavenly Jerusalem. As the true ark, "this sacred vessel must needs be taken to its proper resting-place in heaven, following the risen Lord."[46]) The holiest would dwell in her, so she

---

[40] Joseph Cardinal Ratzinger, *Daughter Zion: Meditations on the Church's Marian Belief* (San Francisco: Ignatius Press, 1983), 13–29.

[41] *CCC*, §721.

[42] Clément, *The Roots of Christian Mysticism*, 293.

[43] Gregory Palamas, "On the Entry into the Holy of Holies II," in *Mary the Mother of God*, 25.

[44] Protoevangelium of James, 7. One also remembers David dancing before the ark of the Lord. The task given to the young Mary is sewing the veil for the holy of holies. "And there was a council of the priests, saying: Let us make a veil for the temple" (v. 10). When the priest emerged from the holy of holies, it was a theophany of God's appearance. Mary, the holy of holies from whom God-in-the-flesh will appear, sews the veil which she is in her person.

[45] Orthodox Vespers for the Entrance of the Mother of God into the Temple, in *Festal Menaion* (Uniontown, PA: The Sisters of St. Basil the Great, 1985), 123.

[46] Rahner, *Our Lady and the Church*, 127.

would dwell in the holy of holies. Fed by the hand of an angel, she was a daughter of the sanctuary because she would become sanctuary for the only begotten Son. The ark of the covenant had long since been lost, but this child is the True Ark. It is as if this small piece of temple real estate was a fenced reserve of Eden, where one last chance for the human race to get it right could be had, and this time, by preemptive grace, the New Eve did. In St. Irenaeus's words, "The knot of Eve's disobedience was untied by Mary's obedience; what the virgin Eve bound through her disbelief, Mary loosened by her faith."[47] She lived the sacrificial life humanity should have preserved. Adam and Eve were created as cosmic priests in earth's liturgy, and the Fall was the forfeiture of their liturgical career. Mary, a deified human hypostasis, is the throne of a restored liturgical humanity.

Mary is how God comes to man, and how man goes to God. Christmas is certainly the Uncreated's kenosis, but the Christmas liturgy simultaneously rejoices over creation's ascent. In Schmemann's words:

> In Christ's birth, therefore, poetry and faith see not only that He comes into the world, but that the world goes out to meet Him: the star, the wilderness, the cave, the manger, the angels, the shepherds, the wise men. And at the radiant heart of this procession, as its center and fulfillment, stands Mary, the very best and most beautiful fruit of creation.... Gazing at this image and rejoicing in it, we behold the only authentic image of the true world, of true life, of the true human being.[48]

So at the Orthodox Vespers for Christmas, the liturgy exclaims:

> Each of the creatures you have made
> Brings you thanks:
> the angels, song;
> the heavens a star;
> the Magi, gifts;
> the shepherds, wonder;
> the earth, a cave;
> the desert, a manger;
> while we bring a Virgin Mother.[49]

---

[47] Irenaeus, Adv. Haereses, 3:22.
[48] Schmemann, *The Virgin Mary*, 34–35.
[49] Hugh Wybrew, Vespers for Birth of Jesus, 25 December, in *Orthodox Feasts of Jesus Christ and the Virgin Mary* (Crestwood, NY: St. Vladimir's Seminary Press, 1997), 53.

Mariology is "thus the 'locus theologicus' *par excellence* of Christian anthropology."[50] Standing in this liturgical posture, she reveals humanity's *raison d'être*. In Paul Evdokimov's arresting words, "The maternity of the Virgin presents itself as the human figure of the paternity of God." He means that

> if fatherhood is the category of divine life, motherhood is the religious category of the human life.... To the divine fatherhood as qualifying the being of God corresponds directly the motherhood of woman as the distinctive religious quality of human nature, its capacity to receive the divine. The aim of Christian life is to make of every human being a mother, predestined for the mystery of birth, "in order that Christ be formed in you." Sanctification is the action of the Spirit who brings about the miraculous birth of Christ in the depth of the soul.[51]

The true end of liturgy, again, is to arrive where Mary did.

St. Augustine made this virgin-motherhood a theme in his preaching. Jesus said whoever does the will of his Father is his brother and sister and mother. Therefore Augustine concludes, "It was more important for Mary to have been a disciple of Christ than to have been the mother of Christ, and she was happier to be his disciple than to be his mother." The "truth-Christ" was in her mind, and the "flesh-Christ" was in her womb, and "What is in the mind is more important than what is carried in the womb." Augustine is playing off 2 Corinthians 11, where Paul says he has betrothed the Corinthians to one husband in order to present them as a chaste virgin to Christ, and so Augustine reminds his listeners (and us) that the Church is both virgin and mother. The virginity of the mind is the integrity of the Catholic faith. "Therefore let the members of Christ give him birth in their minds, just as the virgin Mary gave him birth in her womb. In this way you will be mothers of Christ."[52]

> You have been sons and daughters—now be mothers, too! Children of your mother, you were born as members of Christ when you were baptized. Now bring all whom you can to the bath of baptism, so that as you became sons and daughters when

---

[50] Schmemann, *The Virgin Mary*, 53.
[51] Paul Evdokimov, *The Sacrament of Love* (Crestwood, NY: St. Vladimir's Seminary Press, 1985), 34–35.
[52] Augustine, "Sermon on the Words of the Gospel: A Greater Than Jonah Is Here," nos. 7, 8. Gratitude to Fr. Brian Daley for kindly providing me with his unpublished translation.

you were born, you may be able to become mothers of Christ by bringing others to their birth.[53]

Mary's virginal motherhood is an icon and a prototype for each liturgical person. These two qualities do not conflict in the order of grace. Raised a virgin in the temple, she prepared to be the mother of God: Mary was a hesychast before she was the Theotokos. Only by her virgin-sacrificial posture does she have maternal-sacramental agency.

Mary's liturgical personhood and ours are intimately connected. Louis Bouyer says, "Mary was not an unheard of exception, she is the masterpiece of grace."[54] "She is, as it were, the living Image, present within time, of what will be brought about in us all only at the end of time. Though unique and pre-eminent, she is yet the image of what we have to become."[55] Union with God is participation in the life of the Trinity. Such participation in the perichoresis of love that flows between the persons of the Trinity is the reason for creation, and this is the Church, beautiful in her transfigured ones. The world in its course of transfiguration has yielded up Mary. Commenting on the passage "My word shall not return to me empty," Pope Benedict observed:

> When the text says that the word, or the seed, bears fruit, it means that, unlike a ball that hits the ground and bounces back up, the seed actually sinks into the earth, assimilates the earth's energies, and changes them into itself. It thus brings about something truly new, for now *it* carries the earth in itself and turns the earth into fruit. The grain of wheat does not remain alone, for it includes the maternal mystery of the soil—Mary, the holy soil of the Church, as the Fathers so wonderfully call her, is an essential part of Christ.... To be soil for the Word means that the soil must allow itself to be absorbed by the seed, to be assimilated by the seed, to surrender itself for the sake of transforming the seed into life. Mary's maternity means that she willingly places her own substance, body and soul, into the seed so that new life can grow.[56]

---

[53] Augustine, "Sermon on the Words of the Gospel: A Greater Than Jonah Is Here," no. 8.
[54] Louis Bouyer, *The Spirit and Forms of Protestantism* (Westminster, MD: Newman Press, 1957), 207.
[55] Louis Bouyer, *The Seat of Wisdom: An Essay on the Place of the Virgin Mary in Christian Theology* (New York: Pantheon Books, 1960), 129.
[56] Joseph Cardinal Ratzinger, "'My Word Shall not Return to me Empty!,'" in *Mary: The Church at the Source*, 14–15.

In her fiat, the destiny of the world has already been reached, so she is the model of a humanity fully alive. She set no hindrance to grace's work, there was in her no opaqueness to obscure the divine light streaming into her. Virginity is precisely this transparency to God, and it was this very virginity that opened her to motherhood.

Mary thus experienced her virginity and motherhood in one single, personal motion. It should be the same for the Church, which should experience descending sacrament and ascending sacrifice in one single, liturgical motion. The synergy between the two is essential to liturgical personhood. The Church is called to participate in the grace she sacramentally distributes; the sacraments she distributes demand holiness of her; her holiness breaks forth in sacrificial love; such love is directed to the purpose of restoring supernatural life to souls; the aim of liturgical life is to engender this virgin-motherhood in each Christian. The Holy Spirit which came upon Mary, the virgin mother, is intent on overshadowing us, as well, and to the same effect.

Conclusion

Draw a liturgical circle. Draw a circle around the liturgy to single out an object of study. We want to study *this* (and point to the circle). Fine. Creating taxonomies is what academic theology does. But please notice that there is an outside of the circle, too. Liturgy has an inside and an outside. Liturgy viewed microcosmically is small, sacramental, and takes place in the Church; liturgy viewed macrocosmically is great, universal, and takes place in the world. But they are connected. The little liturgy directs the great liturgy; the great liturgy puts the little liturgy into practice. It's like taking the back off a watch and finding the teeth of a small cog turning a number of larger cogs. We both *celebrate* liturgy and *live* liturgy.

I said in the Introduction that "The liturgical microcosm includes temple, priesthood, sacrament, and icon; the liturgical macrocosm includes time and cosmos, asceticism and deification, icons and beauty, sacrifice and social renewal, death and resurrection, Scripture and spirituality." I will propose in the Conclusion an image for connecting them: *The liturgy is where we rehearse the hypothesis of the world.* Two words need definition in that proposition.

First, "hypothesis." *Hypo* means "under" (think: hypodermic), and *thesis* means "a principle or theory or premise." A hypo-thesis means the thesis standing under something. In a literary context, it was taken to mean the plot or outline of the drama, and Aristotle took it to mean the first principle, which directs the goal of an argument or the intention of a decision. The goal of health is the hypothesis for a doctor, and this underlying starting point determines what kind of medicine he prescribes. He would prescribe a different medicine if he had a different hypothesis. Apply this, now, theologically. You might remember that Irenaeus objected to the Gnostic heresies by saying they had the same Scripture as the Catholics but were led into heresy because their foundational principles were wrong: they had an erroneous hypothesis. Irenaeus used the illustration of having the same mosaic tiles (i.e., the same collection of Scripture verses) but making out of them a picture of a fox instead of a king. Both heretic and Catholic begin with the same pile of LEGO bricks, but one builds a castle and one builds a ship according to the hypothesis by which they piece the bricks together.

The accumulation of Scripture verses did not save the heretics from making a false picture because they didn't know how to organize—hypothesize—the collection of Bible verses. We may apply the same thought to our lives being composed by an accumulation of experiences, but these experiences do not, by themselves, guarantee a true picture of a human being. Heretics (who are still around) can be misled by the pressure of the world's forces into a false hypothesis about the world, about ourselves, and about God's design for us. The collection of our life experiences should reveal the image of a royal priest—the very *imago Dei* that God had stamped upon the soul. That is our human base, our foundation, our principal identity. Man and woman are royal priests of a cosmic liturgy, and the liturgical hypothesis is the first principle that prescribes the kind of life we should live.

The second term to define is "rehearse." The etymology of the word has several registers of meaning. First, *rehersen* means to repeat, to go over again, which is probably how we come to our narrow, modern use of the word for actors narrating the same story in preparation for a play or musicians practicing the same music in preparation for a concert. The practice exercise is a trial, a test. But behind *rehersen* stands *rehercier*, which literally means to rake over, turn over (soil, ground), from *re-* "again" + *hercier* "to drag, trail on the ground." It means to harrow. Christians have a story to tell; they received it from Jesus, and they must repeat it accurately. When they tell it to others, it's called evangelization; when they repeat it for themselves, it's called catechesis (which means "resounding in the ear"). Our liturgical rehearsal for heaven involves giving a regular, repetitive account of salvation history until the Paschal mystery harrows our hearts. This rehearsal should turn over the soil to prepare it for new life.

I mentioned in an essay that Aidan Kavanagh used to say that "liturgy is doing the world the way the world was meant to be done." I can now translate this as: *doing the world with the correct hypothesis.* That hypothesis must be revealed by God. It is recorded in Scripture; it is explicated in doctrine; but, most importantly, it is rehearsed in the little liturgy so we can apply the hypothesis to the great liturgy of our lives. That's why it's important for the liturgy inside to be orthodox (I mean, to get it right, so its smallest movements are faithfully done) and for the liturgy outside to be catholic (I mean, to be expansive, so it stretches to the furthest limits of our lives). The little liturgy rehearses piety for daily exercise in the great liturgy. Thomas defined piety as "a habitual disposition which the Holy

Conclusion

Spirit infuses into the soul to excite in us a filial affection toward God."[1] In the liturgy we rehearse "Our Father, who art in heaven" so that this hypothesis turns into a daily lived filial affection. A fundamental dogma of the Christian religion is that, through the Holy Spirit, God the Father has adopted us in his Son Jesus Christ. This changes everything. We *celebrate* liturgy and *live* liturgy so the Paschal Mystery can work its miracle and harrow otherwise dying hearts. The collect for the fifth Sunday of Easter entreats God to "constantly accomplish the paschal mystery within us." We do not come to the little liturgy to simply remember a historical miracle; we come to the little liturgy to beg God to constantly accomplish that very same miracle within the great liturgy of our lives.

---

[1] Thomas Aquinas, *Summa Theologica* II-II, q. 121.